In Quest of the White God

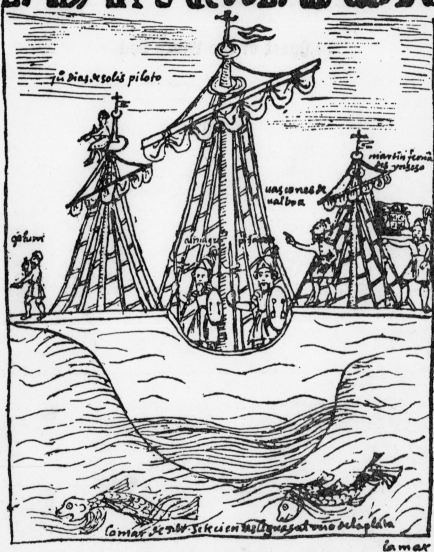

How the Indians saw the arrival of the White Gods. Drawing by
Guaman Poma from an Inca chronicle

PIERRE HONORÉ

In Quest of the White God

The Mysterious Heritage of South American Civilization

Translated from the German by
OLIVER COBURN AND URSULA LEHRBURGER

HUTCHINSON OF LONDON

HUTCHINSON & CO. *(Publishers)* LTD
178–202 Great Portland Street, London, W.1

London Melbourne Sydney
Auckland Bombay Toronto
Johannesburg New York

★

First published in Great Britain 1963
First published by Verlag Heinrich Scheffler under the title
ICH FAND DEN WEISSEN GOTT
in a slightly different form

© Verlag Heinrich Scheffler, Frankfurt a. M. 1961

English translation © Hutchinson & Co. *(Publishers)* Ltd., London, 1963

This book has been set in Fournier type face. It has
been printed in Great Britain by The Anchor Press
Ltd., in Tiptree, Essex, on Antique Wove paper.

Contents

PART FOUR

TOWARDS A SOLUTION

Photographs

PHOTOGRAPHS

PHOTOGRAPHS

Line Drawings

Maps

PART ONE

The Mystery

1

The Legend of the White God

'My messengers report that after a march of twelve miles they found a village with perhaps about a thousand inhabitants. The natives, they say, received them with great ceremony, lodged them in the most beautiful houses, carried them around on their arms, kissed their hands and feet, and, in short, tried to make clear to them in every possible way that it was known the white men came from the gods. About fifty men and women asked my messengers to be allowed to travel back with them to the Heaven of the eternal gods.'

COLUMBUS, November 6th, 1492

'They could do practically anything, nothing seemed too difficult for them; they cut the greenstone, they melted gold, and all this came from Quetzalcoatl—arts and knowledge.'

FRAY BERNANDINO SAHAGUN

ANCIENT Indian legends tell us that at some point in the mists of pre-history white men with beards landed on the shores of the New World. They brought the Indians all their science, knowledge of engineering, laws, and their higher level of civilization. These men became the White Gods of the Indian countries.

They arrived in huge foreign ships with swan wings, hulls gleaming so brightly that it looked as if gigantic serpents were gliding over the water. When they reached the shore strange men emerged from the ships—fair-skinned and blue-eyed, wearing gowns of a coarse black material with a circular opening at the neck and short wide sleeves. The strangers wore ornaments round their foreheads that had the shape of a snake.

The legend of a particular White God has survived to our day from all the ancient civilizations of Central and South America. The Toltecs and Aztecs of Mexico called him Quetzalcoatl, the Incas called

15

him Viracocha. To the Maya he was Kukulcan, who brought them all their laws, also their script, and was worshipped like a god by the entire people. To the Chibchas he was Bochica, the 'white mantle of light'. To the Aymara of Peru he was Hyustus, and to this day they will tell you that he was fair and had blue eyes.

Quetzalcoatl (plumed serpent) was in fact the fifth king of the Toltecs (A.D. 977 to 999). He came from a land of the rising sun and wore a long gown. He reigned in the city of Tollan, and his houses were crammed with gold, jewellery, precious stones, and feathers. He taught his people science and morality, gave them wise laws, and showed them how to till their land. He forbade human sacrifice and preached peace. Men were no longer to kill animals, even for their food; they were to live on fruit and vegetables.

This golden age did not last long, for (say the legends) a demon plunged Quetzalcoatl into sin, made him succumb to vanity, drink, and the lowest forms of debauchery, so that he neglected his religious duties. But he was full of grief and shame for his misdeeds and he left the country with his followers after burying his treasures. Before he went he made the tropical birds fly away and changed the trees into thorny acacias. He left his people for the southern coast of the Gulf of Mexico.

Some legends have it that he stayed twenty years in Cholula, where a great pyramid was built in his honour, and at the end of the twenty years passed on to the coast. After speaking to the people once more, he went down to the sea and burned himself. His heart became the morning star, which the Aztecs called Ce-acatl after him. According to other legends, he boarded a ship on the shore, which sailed back with him to the land he had once come from. But before his departure he promised to return.

So much for Mexico. As for South America, one of the Spanish chroniclers, Cieza de Leon, records the appearance of a white man with a beard by Lake Titicaca long before the time of the Incas. He was a mighty man who taught the people everything to do with law and civilization. He was creator of all things and commanded men to be good to one another and live without violence. His name was Tiki-Viracocha; and he was also called Tuapaca and Arunau.

This White God with a beard built a great city with temples which contained many statues of himself, as did all the other temples in the country. But later on he left his people, admonishing them once more before his departure to follow his teachings. Legends made him the god who created sun and stars, for before him darkness had reigned upon the earth. Then he turned big stones into human beings and animals, men and women, and gave mankind a king.

According to two other chroniclers, white men with beards turned up on the shores of Lake Titicaca, built a great city, and taught the inhabitants a more civilized way of life. The Indians said that White Gods had built this city 2,000 years before the time of the Incas.

Afterwards the White God went to war with the chieftain Cari of Coquimba, who conquered him and killed all his men. His city was destroyed, and only the women and children escaped with their lives. Viracocha himself also managed to flee with a few of his followers; he reached the sea, and, after promising that he would come back, made off on a magic carpet carried by the waves. The literal translation of Viracocha is foam of the sea, and he is still the God of Wind for the Colla of Bolivia. When a storm whips up Lake Titicaca, putting white crests on the waves, old people will say: 'It's Viracocha coming.'

Everywhere in the Indian states of Central and South America the legend of the White God is known, and it always ends in the same way: the White God left his people with a solemn promise that he would one day come back. The legend, however, was one of the main reasons for the quick downfall of these Indian states. The people had the image of the White God so firmly fixed in their minds that they immediately accepted the Spaniards as the White Gods who had returned.

The Aztec priests in Mexico had worked out that their White God, who had left them in the year Ce-acatl (1 Reed), would also return one day in the year Ce-acatl. In the Aztec calendar this year Ce-acatl recurs every fifty-two years. Before every such recurrence the stars and other portents were carefully observed, and each time the priests predicted whether the White God would return on the first day of the new cycle.

By a strange coincidence it was just before a new cycle started that word got round among the Aztecs of 'water houses with swan wings' cruising off their shores. Soon after the new year '1 Reed' began Cortés landed on the coast of Mexico. Even the date, the day of the White God's return, tallied exactly with the one the priests had worked out from their ancient records: the White God would return in the year 1 Reed on the day '9 Wind'. The date by our reckoning was April 22nd, 1519, Maundy Thursday of that year.

The White God who had come to the Indians so long ago had worn a black beret and a black gown. Cortés wore both these, and he landed at almost exactly the spot where the White God had once bidden his people farewell, promising to come back. How could the Indians doubt that he was the god, returning to take possession of his former realm?

But the white men with beards were a motley crowd of mercenaries and adventurers, to whom life was cheap; they came with fire and

B

the sword. The credulous Indians took their sufferings at the Spaniards' hands as a judgment from the White God, and this allowed a handful of adventurers to destroy the high civilization of an entire continent.

Their languages survived the disaster. Over two million Indians still speak Maya, more than half a million speak Aztec, and nearly a million speak the language of the Otomies and Zapotecs, the Mixtecs and the Tarascans. Several million speak Aymara, Quechua, and Mochica. A Peruvian census in 1940 showed that 40 per cent of schoolchildren still spoke Quechua, the oldest Inca language, or Aymara; and over a third did not understand Spanish.

The people who live in the Peruvian highlands still have features very like the old statues and head-shaped jugs—it is almost as if those statues had sprung to life. And, as of old, the Indians' salute to a stranger whom they trust is still 'Viracocha'; that is, 'White God'.

Enter an Indian hut in the Yucatan jungle; join the elders round their fires on the icy Bolivian plateau; talk to Indians in the jungle on the banks of the Amazon: wherever you go you will hear the legend of the white men with beards who came to the Indians in the dim past and became gods of the New World.

2

White Men before Columbus

EVERY history book calls Columbus the discoverer of America, as if he and the Spaniards after him had been the first white men in the New World.

The Spaniards themselves provide evidence against this belief. For one thing, they heard from the Indians the legend of the White God; but, more than that, some Spaniards met white men and spoke to them—men entirely different from the Indians, looking almost like their own fellow-countrymen in Spain or even like north Europeans.

The reports of white Indians are as old as the New World itself. Columbus mentions that he was greeted as a god and the 'son of heaven' by primitive Indians of Guanahani, later San Salvador, and that he had often seen Indians who were 'nearly as white as Spaniards'.

The Incas of Peru show a particularly strong 'European' influence. Pedro Pizarro wrote of them:

'The ruling class in the kingdom of Peru was fair-skinned with fair hair about the colour of ripe wheat. Most of the great lords and ladies looked white like Spaniards. In that country I met an Indian woman with her child, both so fair-skinned that they were hardly distinguishable from fair, white men. Their fellow-countrymen called them "children of the gods".'

The ruling Incas were one large family, which supplied all the country's governors, generals, and dignitaries, and reigned over an immense territory inhabited by native Indians. These aristocrats shunned all intermarriage with the Indians. They were nearly white and had fair hair. They spoke a language of their own and were better educated than their subjects. There were 500 members of this 'royal family' when the Spaniards arrived.

Later travellers' accounts refer often to white men among the

Indians of the Amazon; so do the old chroniclers. One of the latter, for instance, says that the eighth ruler of the Inca dynasty, Virococha Inca, was white and bearded, and that his wife was 'as white as an egg'.

Another of the chroniclers, Garcilaso de la Vega, son of an Inca princess, has an impressive description of how, as a boy, he was taken by Polo de Ondegardo (later to become a chronicler himself) to see something he was to remember all his life. Ondegardo led the boy into a room of his house in Cuzco and showed him several mummies lining a wall; Ondegardo said they were of former Inca emperors, and he had saved them from destruction. So young Garcilaso was looking at his own ancestors.

Quite unconsciously he stopped before one of them which had hair 'as white as snow', in contrast to all the other mummies. Ondegardo told him it was the mummy of the White Inca, eighth ruler of the Sun. As the White Inca is supposed to have died fairly young, this cannot have been the whiteness of old age. It must mean that his hair was not black to start with, and got even lighter in the course of the centuries; whereas the other mummies originally had black hair, which did not fade to such a light colour.

So clearly the Indians knew white men long before the Spaniards' arrival, but it was natural that Columbus and his successors should believe they were the first men of any degree of civilization to come to the New World—and 'white men' became equated in their minds with 'civilization'. On the islands where he first landed Columbus saw only naked Indians who were still living in stone-age conditions. When he landed on the island he called Santa Maria de Guadalupe, he found cannibalism. The Indians there had castrated captured Arawak boys and kept them in cages, fattening them like pigs. Columbus saw young women held captive for the sole purpose of bearing children to be eaten. A new-born baby was considered a delicacy.

When he returned to Spain with his parrots, strange animals and plants, utensils of the savage tribes and six Indians, he was given a triumphal welcome. On his pilgrimage to Our Lady of Guadalupe in Spain, he received immense honours from the court and people. His diaries, however, disappeared into the national archives, and the few people who read them felt so superior to the wild Indians that it seemed a matter of course their representatives should have been received in the New World as White Gods. Yet, besides meeting white men in the New World, the later Spanish conquerors had other experiences which should have made them wonder.

For centuries the court painters of Europe have been painting portraits of their emperors, kings, and princes, their bishops and

nobility, and these portraits invariably portray their subjects with certain recognized insignia. Kings and emperors are shown riding through the countryside on horses which usually seem to be rearing. They carry a sceptre in one hand, and a cloak, always in a shade of purple, flows down from the royal shoulders. There is usually a heraldic device painted into a corner of the picture.

Sometimes the rulers sit on a huge throne draped in precious cloths and decked out with golden ornaments; or else they recline in an easy chair, often with a canopy over them. The chair is carried on poles by noblemen, who apparently never tire of trotting around with their royal burden. Throne and litter, sceptre and crown, flowing drapery, purple, heraldic beasts: such are the insignia in Old World civilizations.

The oldest litter in Europe was found by Evans in the palace of Knossos in the shape of a little clay model. The litter can be traced in all civilizations of the Old World, as can the crown and the sceptre. The oldest European sceptre was found on a soapstone chalice from Hagia Triada in Crete. The chalice is from 1650 B.C., and shows a Cretan ruler holding a sceptre.

Rulers have sat on thrones from time immemorial, and the shape of the throne in the Old World has always been taken from animals; its legs were lion's paws or gryphon's claws in Mesopotamia, Egypt, Greece, and Rome. The throne of Minos of Crete was different, however: it was a hewn stone covered with relief work in such a way that it appeared to be made of wood. Again, rulers have always had a heraldic device. One colour, purple, has been reserved for them in all the Old World's civilizations. All these symbols of reigning power have been taken over by one people from another, and have thus been passing from country to country since the earliest times of human history.

The Spaniards found these symbols in the New World as well. They have no 'functional' use, so it is hard to believe that they were invented independently in parts of the world so remote from one another. Clearly the Indians had been familiar with the symbols, and with white men, long before the Spaniards came.

For instance, the Indians knew the head-dress of feathers as the White God's crown. This was Montezuma's greatest treasure, and at one point he sent it to the Spanish camp, together with a mask of the White God—a gesture meant to show Cortés that he was giving the crown to its rightful possessor. When boys today use this head-dress in a Red Indian get-up they do not realize that it is something European in origin, dating back to the civilization of ancient Crete. This civilization was, of course, completely unknown to the Spaniards, and when they caught sight of the head-dress they thought it was something peculiar to the Indians. Sending Montezuma's presents to the Spanish court, Cortés said he was sending the crown only to show what odd things these Indians had.

A coloured six-foot frieze of stucco in the palace of Knossos has a Cretan prince wearing a crown of lilies with a plume of peacock feathers; men wearing the plumed crown are also shown on the Hagia Triada sarcophagus. The Indian emperors' crowns are adorned with long tail-feathers of exotic birds: gold crowns have been found with imitations of these feathers in very thin gold-foil. But while no plumed crowns have come down to us from Crete apart from pictorial representations, the plumed crown worn by the White God of the Indians is still with us in the Vienna Ethnological Museum, where it is preserved and shown as a great treasure. It is shaped like a bird diving with spread tail. The Quetzal birds have only from two to four green tail-feathers each, whereas the Vienna crown is unique in having 459 such feathers. Its centre-piece shows four concentric bands made from the feathers of the Cotinga bird, inlaid with 193 pieces of gold-leaf.

There was an interesting little incident when Montezuma sent one of his nobles called Teuhtlile to the Spanish camp. Teuhtlile brought a wicker basket filled with ornaments of wrought gold, gifts from his emperor. As he set them out before Cortés, and the soldiers pressed closer to see the golden splendour, Teuhtlile spied among them a man whose helmet had a thin gold plating. He was fascinated by this, and when Cortés handed him the return presents for Montezuma, Teuhtlile declined them, asking only for the helmet. 'I must show it to the Emperor, for this helmet looks exactly like the one that was once worn by the White God.'

'Cortés expressed his willingness that the helmet should be sent to the Emperor, intimating a hope that it would be returned filled with the gold dust of the country, that he might be able to compare its quality with that in his own. He further told the governor that the Spaniards were troubled with a disease of the heart, for which gold was a specific remedy.' (Las Casas)

The first litter the Spaniards saw belonged to Montezuma's nephew, Cacama, the lord of Tezcoco. He came to meet them on it when they were approaching the Aztec capital, Tenochtitlán, after their march of several days. The litter was richly decorated with plates of gold and precious stones; it was carried by nobles and preceded by officers who swept the ground before the ruler after he had descended.

At the outskirts of Tenochtitlán Cortés was received by Montezuma himself, also in a litter; this was the first meeting between the Spanish leader and the Aztec emperor. A contemporary account says:

'Amidst a crowd of Indian nobles preceded by three officers of state bearing golden wands, they [the Spaniards] saw the royal palanquin blazing with burnished gold; and over it a canopy of gaudy featherwork, powdered with jewels and fringed with silver, was supported by four attendants of the same rank.'

Montezuma descended from his litter and advanced towards Cortés, leaning on two of his nobles. Thereupon Cortés dismounted and went to meet the Emperor, also escorted by two of his officers.

1. The Inca in his litter. Drawing by
Guaman Poma from an Inca chronicle

Montezuma was wearing a cloak with a girdle, sandals with gold soles and fastened by gilt straps. His cloak and sandals were embroidered with pearls and precious stones. The Emperor was tall, slim, and about forty years old. He had black, straight hair, a thin beard, and his skin was paler than that of the other Indians.

The later Spanish conquerors were to see another litter, in the kingdom of the Incas of Peru. The Inca ruler always used it on his travels, and we still have a picture of it. He also wore purple, as did the Aztec emperor. For solemn occasions the Inca held a golden sceptre as large as a halberd. His big leather shield was adorned with a heraldic bird, a falcon. We know both throne and sceptre as emblems of royal dignity not only from the Aztec and Inca empires but also from drawings on ancient Mayan vases and the painted friezes of Bonampak.

On their heads the Inca priests wore something like a tiara, decorated with a golden sun. The Incas therefore immediately recognized the Spanish bishops with their mitres as the high priests of the new religion. Similarly, William Prescott—the great nineteenth-century historian of the *Conquista*—says of Montezuma: 'His brows were covered by the *copilli* or Mexican diadem, resembling in form the pontifical tiara.' And in Montezuma's palace at Tenochtitlán the Spaniards also found a device known to them from the Old World: an eagle with a panther in its talons was carved in stone above the main entrance.

The Spaniards were so impressed by what they found in the Aztecs' country that Bernal Diaz del Castille, who accompanied Cortés on all his expeditions, wrote: 'The Mexicans are here what the Romans were to the Old World.' And in a letter to the Emperor Charles V, Cortés wrote: 'Montezuma's town palace is of such great and wondrous beauty that I hardly find words to describe it. I confine myself to the large statement that we have nothing to match it in Spain.'

Montezuma's palace was not even the biggest the Spaniards saw. The King of Tezcoco's contained over 300 rooms, and measured 2,600 by 3,300 feet. It was surrounded by a vast park. One of the letters sent home by the Spaniards says:

'Those gardens also had numerous mazes, from which, once you had lost your bearings in them, it was impossible to find your way out. The water for the fountains, basins and trenches for the irrigation of the flowers and trees in the park came straight from a spring. To get it there from an incredible distance, over hills and valleys, an aqueduct had to be built on tall, thick concrete walls, reaching the highest spot of the park.' (Prince Ixtlilxochitl)

When Cortés and his men entered Montezuma's palace for the first time they had to cross several inner yards with fountains squirting crystal-clear water into the air. Their way led them through great chambers with ceilings panelled in aromatic woods and beautifully carved. Incense-burners spread a pleasing and pervasive scent.

In the antechamber to the Emperor's hall the Spaniards were greeted by members of the nobility, who took off their shoes, hid their robes under a cloak of the coarsest cloth, and then, barefoot and with downcast eyes, stepped humbly into their emperor's presence. A murmur of amazement rose from the ranks of the Spaniards as they finally stood before Montezuma: the Emperor was sitting on a throne, just as their own rulers did—and the courtiers paid their respects before the throne in the same way as the Spaniards would have done at home.

At this meeting Montezuma spoke about his people. He said that a great white man had led them to this land in the dim past, and had given them their laws. One day he had left them, had gone east, in the direction the Spanish white men had now come from, and had promised the people that he would eventually come back to them. Montezuma even said that he and his people believed the white men who had now come to them must be the White Gods returned. So the Spaniards heard from the Emperor's mouth the legend they had already been told so often in his country.

Another 'European' thing they saw was the commanders' stand-dard; it was this emblem, in fact, which saved the remnant of their force after the *noche triste* of the exodus from Tenochtitlán, when Quauhtemoc, the last Aztec emperor, tried to block their retreat with an army of 20,000 men. The outcome seemed a foregone conclusion, for the Spaniards were only a few hundreds. Dozens were killed, and the rest were encircled. But then Cortés recognized the Indian com-mander by his standard on a nearby hill. He jumped on his horse, called his horsemen to follow; with drawn swords they stormed against the phalanx of Indians, who retreated before the horses, clear-ing a narrow lane for the attackers. Cortés galloped up the hill, felling the Aztec commander at his first charge, seized the standard, and waved it above his horse. So 20,000 Indians turned tail in panic fear of the White God returned.

The Spaniards' records are much concerned with a particular marvel of the New World: the pyramids.

It took 100,000 men twenty years to build the pyramid of Cheops in Egypt. They piled over two million blocks of limestone on top of one another, each measuring more than thirty-five cubic feet. For twenty years 100,000 men were driven by the slave-drivers' whips as they pulled the sledges rolling on cylinders, loaded with the heavy blocks, from the Nile to the building site. For twenty years 'Echet Chufu' was growing, with its toll of blood, sweat, and tears, and the death of thousands: a single pyramid, the largest in the Old World, covering thirteen acres of ground, with each side of its base measuring 165 feet. It was created by one man's will and *for* that man—Cheops, the god-king, whose tomb it was to be. In all civilizations of the past, in Mesopotamia as well as on the Nile, the rulers showed their fanatical, barbaric determination to assert their divinity by building such vast tombs, temples and statues.

It was the same in the New World; and the pryamid at Cholula is the largest in the world. It is only half as tall as the pyramid of Cheops, but almost twice as long, its sides measuring 1,200 feet. Tens of thousands worked on this one building in honour of the White God.

When Cortés reached Cholula with his army he praised the splendour of its 400 temples, its ample water supply, and the lushness of its pastures. But, learning of a conspiracy against the Spaniards, he had 3,000 Indians mown down by bullets in a palace courtyard, and a large part of the thriving city went up in flames.

'The Indians made use of a desperate measure. According to an old legend, water would rush out and flood the town if certain stones were broken from the pyramid. They tore out the stones, but not a drop of water came out. What else could they do? The fire was already destroying the temples. An Indian who had stayed in the main temple surrendered to the Spaniards, the others succumbed to fire and sword. Since they saw themselves abandoned by their gods, many preferred to plunge to their deaths from the pyramid.' (Fernando Benitez)

The pyramid formed four huge steps; an outside staircase of 120 steps led up to the platform. This was the site of the temple which housed the White God's statue. Passing through Cholula on his way to Tenochtitlán, Cortés may have climbed these steps, because he left a description of a statue 'with sombre features and a plumed crown on its head. It had a gold band round the neck and turquoise earrings. It held a sceptre inlaid with precious stones in one hand, a painted shield in the other.'

Thousands of pilgrims from all over the country flocked to this statue of their highest god. The pyramid was their Mecca, crowds of believers and beggars camped at its base. When Cortés learned of the 6,000 people sacrificed to the god every year, he became convinced that this White God was merely one of the Indians' many idols. He must have been quite certain after visiting the great Teocalli Pyramid.

This stood in a walled square, big enough, Cortés declared, for 500 houses to be built in it. The outside wall was decorated with snakes in relief work. Four gates led into the town, facing north, west, south, and east, with a big building based on each gate—the arsenals for the army.

Montezuma had hesitated for a long time before acceding to the Spaniard's request to let him see the pyramid. Cortés crossed the yard paved with slabs of stone polished smooth as a mirror. He mounted the steps to the pyramid, while the Emperor had himself carried up. When Cortés reached the platform the first thing to catch his attention was a large block of jasper. Its peculiar shape indicated that it was the block the hapless victims had to lie down on to be sacrificed.

'On the far end of the platform', Cortés wrote, 'stood two towers, each consisting of three storeys, the lowest built of stone and stucco, the two top ones of carefully carved wood. In the lowest part were the idols of their gods. In front of each of these holy places there was an altar with that eternal flame the extinction of which spelt so much misfortune for the country—as with the vestal fire of Rome. . . . Since the temple on which we stood rose so high above all the capital's other buildings, it afforded a magnificent and extensive view. The town was spread out below it like a map.'

The Spaniards entered one of the temples.

'Before the altar in this sanctuary stood the colossal image of Huitzilopochtli, the tutelary deity and war-god of the Aztecs. His countenance was distorted into hideous lineaments of symbolic import. . . . The huge folds of a serpent, consisting of pearls and precious stones, were coiled round his waist, and the same rich materials were profusely sprinkled over his person. . . . The most conspicuous ornament was a chain of gold and silver hearts alternate, suspended round his neck. . . .' (Prescott)

Above the statue hung a canopy of gold and on the altar lay the human hearts that had just been sacrificed. The stucco walls were covered with clotted human blood.

'The stench was more intolerable than that of the slaughter-houses in Castile. . . . There were several other Teocallis, built generally on the model of the great one . . . the altars crowned with perpetual flames, which, with those of the numerous temples in other quarters of the capital, shed a brilliant illumination over its streets through the long nights. Among the Teocallis in the enclosure was one consecrated to Quetzalcoatl, circular in its form, and having an entrance in imitation of a dragon's mouth, bristling with sharp fangs, and dripping with blood.'

Utensils dripping with blood were lying on the altars here too, and the priests' vestments were stiff with clotted blood. The Spaniards referred to the temple of Quetzalcoatl simply as 'the hell'. But this was not the worst. On their return from the city they came upon a mud platform with scaffolding on top, and saw something gleaming a ghastly white. Going nearer, they found a large rack covered with thousands of human skulls—the skulls of the victims, mostly prisoners of war, who had been sacrificed to the god. It was these remains of people massacred and sacrificed to the god which made the Spaniards feel morally justified in destroying such a barbarous society. Also it must have banished from their minds any suspicion that white men from Europe could possibly have come to the New World before.

They saw nothing incongruous in the existence of pyramids here, for probably they did not even know about the pyramids in the Old World. It was not till centuries later, when Napoleon invaded Egypt, that Europe came to hear about these. Today we can assert that the White God was building on an even vaster and more impressive scale than the god-kings of Egypt, but using the same methods as were used on the Nile.

When the Spaniards entered Tenochtitlán they strode along wide streets with huge mansions built of a red porous stone, nearly all

2. Tenochtitlán on the Spaniards' arrival. Attempted reconstruction

having roof-gardens full of luxuriant plants. They went by the huts of the common people, which were built of mud and rushes, they crossed large squares bordered by rows of stone or stucco pillars, and passed hundreds of pyramids with fires smoking on their platforms.

It was not only the strangeness of everything which made them marvel as they marched into the heart of the Aztec capital. Between the lines of their accounts you can also read amazement at finding here in the Indians' country so much that was familiar to them or was very like things they knew in Spain. The extensive Aztec buildings with their halls, pillars, and arcades are often compared to Spanish ones in

these reports, which say: 'Like at Salamanca ... like at Barcelona ...
like at home in Seville.'

In the *Historia verdadeira de la Conquista* Bernal Diaz wrote:

'And when we saw so many towns and villages on the surface of
the water and many more still on the mainland, we were seized with
wonder, and we said, it must be magic ... for everywhere great
towers, temples and pyramids rose out of the water; many a soldier
thought he must be dreaming.'

And Cortés himself recorded in surprise:

'You find houses like those kept up by apothecaries, where you can
buy medicinal potions ready for drinking, ointments and plaster. You
see barbers' saloons where you can take a bath or have your hair cut.
You come across houses where you can eat or drink against money.'

The conquerors' column halted in front of the largest temple in
the city, with its pyramid towering over the others. Opposite was a
big complex of buildings, the palace of Axayacatl, the Emperor's
father, where Cortés and his retinue were to stay. It was here the next
meeting took place between Cortés and the Emperor, who was at the
entrance waiting to receive his guests. In greeting Cortés, he put a
necklace round his neck; it consisted of shells of small crabs set in gold
and joined together by gold rings, with gold ornaments hanging from
this chain.

Now, the King wore a heavy gold necklace in Spain as well. Moreover (although the Spaniards could not know this), the gold necklace
as a symbol of power and royal office can be traced back to the oldest
civilizations: for instance, the rulers of Mycenae wore such necklaces,
with links showing double eagles.

Tenochtitlán had about 60,000 houses and 300,000 inhabitants.
The Spaniards found the streets swept clean and well washed. Strong
pipes carried fresh drinking water from the mountain of Chapultepec
right into the middle of the town. At the height of its prosperity,
it was then a lively, teeming city, with arsenals, granaries, an aviary,
an enclosure for wild animals looked after by keepers (just as in the
zoos of our day), many fountains and fish-ponds, large reservoirs set
in chequered marble. There were residences for state visitors, schools,
special blocks for priests' living quarters, and other large buildings,
and a wonderful market. Bernal Diaz wrote: 'When we reached the
square called Tlatelolco we stared in amazement. Not only at the mass
of people and the profusion of goods but also at the orderliness that
reigned in everything, because we had never seen the like of it before.'

Cortés himself was so struck by the market that he wrote: 'There
is ... still another market, twice as large as Salamanca's and entirely

surrounded by arcades. Sixty thousand people collect there every day to buy and sell.' It also reminded him of the silk market at Granada.

The Spaniards could not say enough about the fantastic spectacle, the tens of thousands who went there daily. The men wore cloaks slung over one shoulder and tied round the neck; their robes were adorned with wide belts, fringes, tassels, and all sorts of jewellery. The women wore several skirts, one on top of another, with very ornate ribbons and beautiful embroideries. Many had their faces covered with thin veils made from aloe fibres or rabbit wool. All the women wore long plaits.

Everything the New World produced was to be had in this market of Tenochtitlán. There were special stands for Cholula's jewellers and potters, Azcapotzalco's goldsmiths, Tezcoco's painters, Tenayuca's stone-cutters, Xilotepec's hunters, Cuitlahuac's fishermen, Quauh-titlan's basket- and chair-weavers, Xochimilco's florists. There were medicinal herbs and apothecaries' goods and even barbers (the barbers were kept very busy, because the Indians, although they did not wear beards, used to have their heads shaved).

There were a great variety of curios you could buy there: golden fishes with little scales of gold, golden birds with golden feathers and movable heads, vessels made from all kinds of wood, varnished or even gilt, bronze axes, warriors' helmets with crests of animals' heads, quilted cotton waistcoats for the warriors, feather armours, Mexican swords with obsidian blades, razors and mirrors from cut stone, hides and leather goods of all sorts, fans made of hides or cotton or agave fibres, tame and wild animals—and also slaves.

At the food-stalls mountains of poultry, fish, and game were being offered, a luxuriant array of vegetables, maize, baker's wares, bread, cocoa, and *Pulque,* an intoxicating drink. There was also a profusion of flowers, making a blaze of brilliant colour beyond anything the Spaniards had seen. For when they came this was the country of flowers. There was no country in the world which cherished and revelled in flowers more than Mexico, said to be a land of savages.

Altogether the Spaniards were fascinated by their visit to the market of Tenochtitlán with its cheerful bustle and hubbub. The fairs of ancient Crete and Egypt must have been rather similar; as for clothing, what the noble Indians wore was very like the attire of the ancient Greeks; we know about it from the chroniclers' descriptions and in particular from the drawings in an old manuscript to be found in the Madrid Museum.

Plates, spoons and forks did not come into general use in Europe till the late sixteenth century. Till then people simply ate with their

fingers off the table or from a communal dish. In the Indian civilizations, however, these requisites had been in use for at least 1,000 years
before the Spaniards discovered the New World.

According to the Spaniards—who watched Montezuma when he
was their prisoner—the Emperor used to eat alone. Hundreds of
dishes had been prepared for him in earthenware, gold and silver
bowls. His favourite dishes were kept hot for him in special vessels.
He sat on a big cushion on the floor, with a low table in front of him.
Plates and cups were made of pottery. After he had used them once
he would give them away to his attendants. He also owned a golden
set, which was used only on holy days. Torches of resinous wood lit
the large room where the Emperor took his meal. Five or six of his
intimate councillors stood in silence at the far end of the hall during the
meal. The dishes were served to him by young girls.

After the main course there was bread, cakes and pastries of all
kinds, which were baked by the girls in the halls itself; for instance,
rolls and 'waffles'. Then the Emperor would drink his 'chocolate',
viscous like honey, from a gold mug, and use a gold spoon for it.
After dipping his hands in the water, which was brought him in a
silver bowl, he smoked his pipe and let himself be entertained by
conjurers, jugglers and clowns. Then he had a siesta, which was
followed by receptions for dignitaries and emissaries. They would
appear before him with lowered eyes, wearing a hirsute gown, bare-
footed, and walk backwards when they left his presence.

The procedure was similar at the table of the Incas of Peru,
where there were also spoons, and plates and cups made of pure gold.
So here were these requisites being used before they had come into
use in Europe. But, even more surprising, they were quite current in
the ancient civilizations of Egypt and Crete. The Egyptians had spoons
3,000 years before the birth of Christ. Assuming, therefore, that these
utensils were at one time brought into the New World from the Old,
they could only have come out of one of the very ancient civilizations.

In the seventh chapter of Genesis it says: 'On the same day were
all the fountains of the great deep broken up, and the windows of
heaven were opened. And the rain was upon the earth forty days
and forty nights. . . . And the waters prevailed upon the earth an
hundred and fifty days. . . .'

Before Cortés the Spaniards mostly had very friendly relations
with the Indians. On earlier Spanish expeditions some of their country-
men had been taken prisoner and kept for years on off-shore islands,
where they had picked up the language of the Maya. With these
men as interpreters, Cortés's men could talk to the Indians; and in a

Head of an Aztec noble warrior. Rodin said he could never have produced such a masterpiece

The plumed crown of the White God Quetzalcoatl was preserved by the Aztecs over centuries and later presented to Cortés. With the Hapsburgs it came to Vienna and is kept in the Museum of Ethnology there, the Museum's greatest treasure

Bearded priest of the Maya

conversation with educated Indians which has come down to us, one of them recounted a legend strikingly similar to the Old Testament story of the Flood, even including the dove.

In ancient times—so the legend ran—there was a god-fearing man called Tapi living with his wife in the Valley of Mexico, to whom one day the god revealed himself and gave a very strange commandment. The man should set himself immediately to build a ship, and should take on to it his wife and all his possessions and two of every kind of beast. Tapi carried out his god's orders, ignoring the taunts of his neighbours, who thought he had gone mad.

He had scarcely built his ship and taken on board his wife, his possessions, and all the beasts, when it started raining as it had never rained before in Mexico. It rained for days and nights without ceasing, and the water in the rivers rose and rose, soon flooding the banks. The rain fell and fell in the Valley of Mexico and the ship floated on the water. The huts of the people living on the banks were flooded, and men and beasts tried to escape into the mountains. But the waters rose so high that even the mountains were flooded, and in the end the whole land had become a vast ocean, and of all living things only the occupants of the ship survived.

At last the rain stopped in the Valley of Mexico, and the sun shone again, and the waters dropped; before the people on the ship could see any dry land Tapi sent out a dove. It flew off, but did not return, for it had found land. That was where Tapi steered his ship, and he found the dry shore. He let out all his beasts and became the father of mankind.

When the old chronicle with this story was found, the only possible explanation people could think of was that the Indians knew our Bible; some even suggested that one of the apostles must have found his way into the New World. Critics pointed out that by the time the chronicle was written—presumably some time after the Spanish conquest—the Indians would have become familiar with the Old Testament story of the Flood through the church and convent schools. But even if it was written down later, the legend may still have been known before the *Conquista*.

There were other strange things the Indians told the Spaniards. There was a story about one of their ancient kingdoms where the people had started to build an immense tower, so high that its spire touched the sky. But then the gods came and destroyed this presumptuous work and wiped out the whole kingdom so that not a trace of it remained.

The Spanish chroniclers also recorded some odd customs which they found among the Indians. They described a 'baptism' in one of the temples of Tenochtitlán, when a child was sprinkled with water

C

and given a name, just as in the churches of the Old World. The priest said: 'Take and receive, for on this earth you will live on water, water makes you grow and flourish, water gives us what we need for our life—receive this water.' The Aztecs also used incense (so did the Incas). They received large quantities of resin for incense, as can be seen from their tribute lists.

The Spaniards saw the Aztec priests 'forgive sins'. At this ceremony small pieces of bread were distributed among the faithful in the temple. They ate the bread in a very devout manner, thereby propitiating the gods—so one of the Indians explained the ceremony. In the time of the first Spaniards a form of 'confession' was still going on in the Indian temples; they watched the priests blessing a marriage, saw the sacred crosses in the temples, and heard of the White God of the Indians, said to be born of a virgin by immaculate conception.

When Spaniards eventually settled—as priests, 'civil servants', or judges—they became more familiar with Mayan customs, and made some new and astonishing discoveries. The Maya were still celebrating their age-old festivals in the same way as they had done for centuries; these were strangely like the festivals of the Catholic world, and even fell on almost the same days. The 16th of May, for instance, was for the Maya the day when the waters were blessed; in Europe it was the day of St. John Nepomucen (patron saint of Bohemia), saint of the water. The 8th of September for the Maya was the birthday of the White God's mother—in Catholic countries it is the day of the Blessed Virgin's birth; and the White God's birthday was celebrated on the 25th of December. On the 2nd of November, when Catholics even today visit the cemeteries to put flowers on the graves of their dear ones, the Maya used to go to the graves of their dead and decorate them with flowers.

Of course the Maya may have introduced or 'fitted in' these holy days later on, when the Spaniards were already in their country. But it seems possible, none the less, that they did know the Bible. The parallels are too numerous and striking for mere coincidence.

About 100 chemical elements are known today. Before chemistry became a science there were only four, the elements of the ancient Greek philosophers: earth, water, fire, and air. The Hindus, in their old sacred books, particularly the *Bhágavata Purâna*, described four ages of the world and how these passed away. The ages correspond to the four points of the compass, and were the ages of earth, water, fire, and air. The Maya also had these four ages, each divided into five periods, each of the periods ruled by a god. There are thus twenty gods involved, the twenty gods of the Mayan myths. They are symbolized in the Mayan twenty glyphs, and they give names for the twenty days of the Mayan months.

The Maya knew Heaven and Hell. They distinguished between thirteen heavens, each ruled by a god; the lowest was the earth. Below the earth there were nine underworlds with nine head gods, and the ninth or lowest of these underworlds was the realm of Ahpuk, god of death.

The Maya also had the four points of the compass; and the four giants who carried the celestial roof from the four directions, just as in the Old World myth the giant Atlas is condemned to carry the roof of Heaven. These giants are found in all Mayan chronicles and myths, and in the legends of the Indian civilizations. They are the same family as the giants and titans who fought the gods, the builders of the walls of Cyclops, and of the Nordic Valhalla.

Altogether some of the Indians' ideas and customs, in the religious field alone, are amazingly like those of the Old World—and of the Far East. When archaeologists compared the elements of mythology, ritual and iconography in Indian art with those in the art of South-East Asia, they found very similar forms on both sides of the Pacific. The central idea in both was the dualism between light and darkness, life and death. In both Central America and China darkness was portrayed in the shape of either a snake or a dragon.

The parallels sometimes extend even to the details of acts of worship: with the Maya, as well as on the other side of the Pacific, boys were baptized and given a name on the fifth day after their birth. When they were between three and four months old they were circumcised in a solemn ceremony.

To sum up: crowns, thrones, litters, heraldic devices, standards; cups, plates, spoons and forks; the Bread of Heaven, baptism, confession, the blessing of the waters; the stories of the Flood and the Tower of Babel: it seems incredible that all these things were discovered and 'invented' by the Indians. So they must have been brought in from the Old World by people who came to American shores very much earlier.

This conclusion is confirmed by the study of one piece of evidence which does not disappear even after 3,000 years: the script.

3

The White God wrote Cretan Script

WHEN the Spaniards came to Mexico, the Aztecs' script had not yet got beyond the primitive stage of phonetic hieroglyphs. Now, if men from another continent did at one time find the New World, they would surely have taught the Indians their own script. However, any script from the Old World was much further developed than the Aztec hieroglyphs; this has often been used as evidence against the theory of a transfer of civilization. But suppose there was a highly developed script in earlier Indian civilizations, which afterwards perished? It may sound unlikely, but the Maya did in fact have such a script, and an extremely complicated one.

The development of a complicated script is usually a gradual process and does not go with the beginning of a civilization. Yet while the buildings, stelae and statues at Uaxactun, the oldest Mayan city (about A.D. 300), are still clumsy and ill-proportioned, the script was already complete then, nor is there any indication of an 'embryo' script among the primitive nomadic tribes before that time. Scholars have tried to explain the sudden creation of the Mayan script as being the work of a single unknown genius, the 'Mayan Hipparchus'. But the Maya themselves said it was their White God Kukulcan who once brought them their script.

Among the most frequent symbols in Mayan script are those for their days and months. Chuen, Eb, Akbal, Ben, Manik, Caban, Eznab—such are some of the names—sound distinctly Semitic. They are indeed very like the names of the ancient Phoenician and Greek letters; some, in fact, are almost identical. Here are a few instances—giving the letters in Greek, Phoenician, and Mayan in that order:

36

Alpha, aleph, ahau   Iota, iud, ik
Beta, bejt, baaz   Kappa, koph, queh
Gamma, gimel, ghanan   Lamda, lamed, lamat
Epsilon, eh, eb   Tau, tav, tihax

In many cases the Phoenicians and the Maya have very similar 'characters' for the same letters, and also similar meanings for the characters.

Now, the Maya cannot possibly have hit upon not only the names but also the order of the names by mere chance—the very same names and order as in the Phoenician alphabet. So at first sight it looks as if the Mayan script had come from the Phoenicians. But the Phoenician characters are very simple, in contrast to the complicated day-symbols of the Maya. It therefore seems probable that both scripts have a common root, older than the Phoenician script, from which they both developed.

This old script must have consisted of hieroglyphs—i.e. it must have been pictorial. For the Mayan symbols are much more like hieroglyphs than they are like the Phoenician letters. They can hardly have come from Egypt, for the Egyptian hieroglyphs were based on very different principles, but they are extremely like the symbols of the ancient Cretan script. Both scripts have simple symbols in common, like circle, cross, hand, eye, etc.; but both also contain many symbols so abstract you cannot see what picture they were taken from. Almost identical abstract symbols could not have been invented independently in two different parts of the world.

It would be highly significant if the same phonetic values could be proved for both symbols, but this is where research still disappoints us. While such values for Cretan 'Linear B' have largely been worked out, we do not know them for the older script form of 'Linear A', or for the Mayan symbols. In the few cases, however, where we know the phonetic values of both Cretan and Mayan symbols (e.g. the glottal 'p' and the 't'), they tally.

We may therefore safely say that the Mayan legends were right: Kukulcan, their White God, taught his people the script he had brought with them. And this script was Cretan.

When the Spaniards conquered the New World, they brought their own language in Roman letters. Roman script was originally invented only for the Latin language, but today we use it for writing all languages. When the Maya write their own language (there are still a few million Maya in existence) they also use Roman letters.

It was the same with the Cretan script; in theory other languages could be written in Cretan characters. This raises the question whether

the glyph texts of the Maya with their Cretan characters were really
written in the Mayan language—whether indeed the language can be
written at all. It is impossible to reproduce the language's clicking, hissing
and explosive sounds by the phonetic values of our (Roman) letters.

Might this have been easier with the Cretan syllabic signs? On the
contrary, it must have been much harder, since they had been invented
for a language rich in vowels, while in the Mayan language consonants
were uppermost. So Mayan language was singularly difficult to render
by Cretan symbols, and if it is reproduced correctly by Mayan symbols, then the phonetic value of the original Cretan symbols must have
been a good deal altered in adaptation to it.

Of course the Mayan glyph texts may reproduce the Cretan
language—if kings and priests passed it on to their descendants and
successors, guarding the secret of a language of the gods which the
people could not understand. In this case the language would not
have remained purely Cretan, for Mayan glyphs originated over
1,500 years after the symbols had come from Crete. Many generations
of Indian kings and priests would have had to pass on the tradition in
a more or less garbled form. Could a language have survived so long
in these circumstances?

According to the Spanish conquerors, the large family of the Incas
of Peru, which included all the country's notables, spoke their own
language, which neither the people nor the interpreters could understand. Perhaps this was the ancient Cretan language.

Cretan script developed at first as a purely pictorial script. About
1700 B.C., it changed into simpler symbols, which were even further
simplified around 1450 B.C. Three different scripts, succeeding one
another in time, have been found in Crete. The oldest is the pictorial
one which cannot be deciphered. The next has smaller symbols and is
known as Linear A. It is unintelligible, but half of its characters are
found again in the youngest Cretan script, called Linear B, which
consists of simple symbols developed from the original hieroglyphs.
Today we can read sixty-five out of its eighty symbols.

Those who deciphered it discovered to their surprise that they
were dealing with a script of the Greek language. Probably the Linear
A was changed into the Linear B to make it possible to write Greek
words. For the destruction of the palace of Knossos, which may be
ascribed to Greek conquerors, falls around the time of the change
(1425 B.C.). Linear B is a syllabic script. Its name for gold is 'kuru-so'
(krusos in Greek); king is 'va-na-ka' (anax in Greek); 'a-ta-na-po-ti-
ni-ya' (Athena Potnia in Greek) is Mistress Athene; 'po-se-da-o is
Poseidon, and 'Di-vo-nu-si-yo' Dionusos.

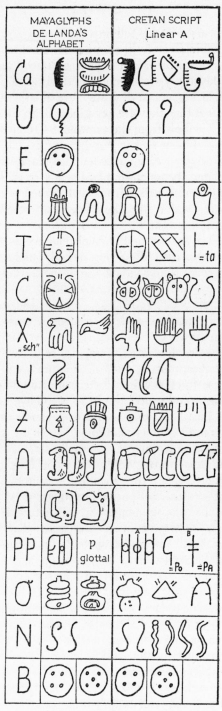

3. De Landa's glyphs and the ancient
Cretan script

The two Linears A and B fell into disuse in Crete about 1400 B.C. Linear B persisted in Greece till about 1100 B.C. Then it too was forgotten. The Greek script proper cannot be traced farther back than 800 B.C. If the Mayan glyphs are compared with the Cretan symbols a very remarkable fact emerges: they are more like the old Cretan hieroglyphs and Linear A than they are like Linear B. So the Maya must have taken over their symbols from the two older Cretan scripts, not from the youngest one. This makes it possible to fix a date so far missing: the Cretan hieroglyphs which reached the Maya were transformed around 1700 B.C. into the much simpler linear scripts. The later, simplified Cretan characters are strikingly similar to the Phoenician ones, and we may therefore assume that the Phoenician script too developed from the Cretan symbols and took over their names. This would also explain why the Mayan and the Phoenician letters resemble each other.

So the transfer of the old Cretan hieroglyphs to the New World must have taken place round the middle of the second millennium B.C.

When the first White Gods came to the Indians they brought along things and concepts—and, of course, names for them—which till then were unknown to the Indians, such as: king, copper, gold, bronze, lead, pewter, alloy, cast, wire, tin, soldering—as well as the name for jade, amber, mortar, pyramid, mummy, and many more.

Just as we use foreign words for certain things introduced to us from abroad, one would expect the Indians to have taken over names and words from the old languages of Europe; and so they did. All the important things the White Gods brought them are known by words with roots from those languages, especially Crete. For instance, the Incas called gold 'kuri'—compare 'ku-ru-so' in Linear B; and perhaps the name Pota Kauri, one of the kings of the Chimu, had more than an accidental likeness to that of 'potnia', mistress.

Apart from the Semitic names there is a further mystery about the Mayan script. It always contains the twenty Tzolkin, the signs of the Mayan days. But these signs were also numbers for days. So a combination of characters in the Mayan script may be either a word or a number, and a Mayan inscription tells something and counts at the same time. The words for telling and counting are similar or identical in many languages today: cf. tellers and tally in English; (ra)conter, compter in French; erzählen, zählen in German; at taelle, at fortaelle in Danish; contar, contar in Portuguese.

With the Mayan script this dual function shows its great age, and is also evidence that it must have developed elsewhere, since originally Hebrew and Greek hieroglyphs both had the same dual function. As late as 100 B.C. the Greeks still used their letters to denote their months.

The Hebrews carried their symbolism of numbers still further: if you added the value in numbers of the single letters in the word 'shanah' you arrived at 365, the number of days in a year—and 'shanah' was the Hebrew word for year.

Clearly, in fact, many cultural influences from the Mediterranean area reached the Indian civilizations very early in history; and one of the most important was the Cretan script.

Now, Mayan civilization started between 300 B.C. and A.D. 300. But the Cretan script had perished as far back as 1400 B.C., and Crete's successors in the Mediterranean area no longer knew about it. So the Maya must have taken over this and other components of their civilization (such as the pyramid, stele, holy arch, use of stucco) centuries afterwards from an even more ancient Indian people, which received such features from the Old World at a time when Crete still existed. If we could find such a people, its civilization would point even more clearly than that of the Maya to its Old World origins.

PART TWO

The Return

4

The Conquest of Mexico

'Gentlemen, let us follow our flag, which is the sign of the
Holy Cross, for with it we shall conquer.'
CORTÉS addressing his soldiers before the battle for Tlaxcala

'Everything lies shattered on the ground and not a thing is
left standing upright.'
BERNAL DIAZ on the destruction of the Aztec cities

'I have come to get money for myself, not to till fields like
a peasant.'
CORTÉS on arrival in the New World

ON OCTOBER 12th, 1492, Columbus landed on a small island in the
Bahamas group, which he called San Salvador (today's Watling
Island). On this day Spaniards and Indians met for the first time. In a
letter addressed to the Spanish court Columbus wrote: 'I saw that
they are people who could be converted to our sacred beliefs by gentle-
ness rather than force, and I gave some of them glass beads and coloured
caps, which pleased them very much and quickly secured us their
friendship. . . .'
Twenty years later others explored the South American coast
down to the Rio de la Plata. Sebastian Cabot came from the north and
got as far as Florida. Balboa crossed the isthmus of Panama and hoisted
the Spanish flag on the Pacific coast. But the most stupendous discovery was yet to come, for the cities and states of Mexico beyond the
wide gulf were still entirely unknown. So far the Spaniards had settled
only on the off-shore islands, where they had established an administra-
tion.
In 1504, when Columbus's great patroness Isabella of Castile died,

there were Spanish settlements on many of the 'West Indian' islands, sending exports to Spain—mainly dyewood, metals, and sugar-cane. The Spanish governor, Velasquez, had his residence in Cuba, and a merchant adventurer who had once been stranded on the mainland told him about its rich Indian cities. In 1518 he dispatched a few ships, which eventually reached the coast of Central America. But the primitive Indians of the islands spoke of a land of gold still farther west, and Velasquez decided to launch an expedition to find it.

On February 18th, 1519, a fleet of eleven ships, with 110 sailors, 553 soldiers, 200 Indians, and sixteen horses on board, ten heavy guns and four light ones, left the island of Cuba to discover the legendary Eldorado. The expeditionary force was commanded by Hernando Cortés, a Spanish nobleman of thirty-three, who had settled in Cuba in 1511 and had since then made a fortune by acquiring land and washing gold.

The *Conquistador* (as Cortés has become known in history) sailed along the coast of Yucatan as far as the mouth of the river Tabasco, where he was met by armed Indian warriors. They joined battle in the plain of Ceutla—not far from the ruins of Palenque, which were to become so famous later on. The Spaniards with their superior arms emerged victorious, and occupied the town of Tabasco. The Indians surrendered, and brought expiatory gifts, among them twenty young Indian women.

One of these became Cortés's interpreter. She was intelligent, faithful, and reliable, accompanied him everywhere, and was also his mistress. She was a chieftain's daughter from the Aztec highlands; after her father's death her stepfather sold her as a slave to Mexico, with her mother's consent, in order to cut her out of her inheritance. The Aztecs called her Malintzin, the Spaniards Doña Marina; and according to the chronicles she must have been a woman of singular attractions and noble character. 'She could bend the Indians entirely to her will,' it was also said, 'and because of this she became of extreme importance to us.' She played a vital part in the adventure which was now starting, one of the most decisive events in human history.

The Aztecs ruled a vast empire with an iron hand. Montezuma, their emperor at the time, had early news of the Spaniards' landing. He sent messengers to Cortés with gifts, but also with the request that the strangers should leave the country again. Cortés, of course, had no intention of complying.

The first big city of the New World the Spaniards set foot in was Cempoalla, the capital of the Totonacs, with about 30,000 inhabitants. The people here differed from the simple near-savages of the islands: they wore richly embroidered clothes and had built themselves houses, temples and palaces from mud and stone. They gaped in awe at Cortés and his men in their shining armour, especially at the horsemen, who seemed to them such an uncanny hybrid of man and beast.

Here Cortés learnt for the first time that the Aztecs were hated masters of brutally subjugated peoples. He heard that they extracted tribute ruthlessly from the country of the Totonacs, with its thirty

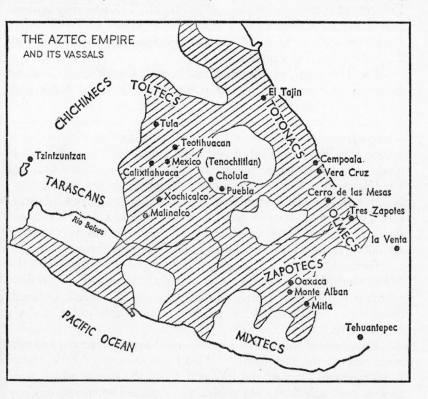

THE AZTEC EMPIRE
AND ITS VASSALS

CHICHIMECS TOLTECS
El Tajin
TOTONACS
Tula
Teotihuacan
Tzintzuntzan
Mexico (Tenochtitlan) Cempoala
Calixtlahuaca Vera Cruz
Cholula
TARASCANS Cerro de las Mesas
Xochicalco Puebla
Malinalco Tres Zapotes
Rio Balsas OLMECS
la Venta

ZAPOTECS
Oaxaca
Monte Alban
Mitla

PACIFIC OCEAN
MIXTECS Tehuantepec

towns and villages, and that if the tribute was not paid on time Aztec warriors would drag off youths and girls to be sacrificed on the altars at Tenochtitlán, the Aztec capital on the Mexican plateau.

From Cempoalla, Cortés returned to the coast, to Vera Cruz. Here he wrote a letter to his sovereign, Charles V, and painted in glowing colours the chances of winning an empire. But before the ship which was to take the letter to Spain set sail, he uncovered a plot against himself initiated by Velasquez. He put to death the leaders of the conspiracy, then had his ships destroyed to sever all ties with the outside world and stop any of his soldiers trying to return home.

Their boats thus burnt, his small force marched west from the coast, through a mountain wilderness, and after several days reached the country of the Tlaxcatecs, where they had a hostile reception. Skirmishes were followed by a pitched battle, ending in such high losses to the Indians that they sued for peace and surrendered to the Spaniards.

Here in the city of Tlaxcala, so beautiful and splendidly designed that it reminded Cortés of Granada, messengers again arrived from the Emperor Montezuma with new and lavish gifts. This time they brought permission for Cortés to visit him at his residence in Tenochtitlán; the only condition he made was that the Spaniards should come by way of the town of Cholula.

The Tlaxcatecs, who by now had become Cortés's allies, warned him urgently against taking this route, which they said was a trap, an ambush for him and his men. He hesitated, but when the town of Cholula sent him an invitation he decided to go that way after all.

It *was* a trap. Waiting at Cholula for the foreign invaders were 20,000 men. But Cortés's horsemen and guns, together with his new allies, were too strong for even this vast army. The Indians fled, and Cholula's end was marked by toppling houses, burning beams, blazing fires, by horror and murder. The priests who had barricaded themselves in the great temples plunged to their death from the roofs as they saw that the battle was lost. When the battle was over most of Cholula was destroyed. Six thousand dead lay in the streets.

To the Indians this disastrous defeat spelled the judgment of the White Gods. Many towns in the vicinity sent messengers to offer their submission and now Cortés pushed on over the Sierra Oriental, marching along the snowline to the capital, Tenochtitlán, today's Mexico City.

The city was built on an island in the Lake of Tezcoco, and was connected to the mainland by three large causeways; little Indian boats swarmed all over the lake and down the canals, which were used as road substitutes like a Mexican Venice. The crowning glory was the royal mountain of Chapultepec, rising out of the western bank of the lake, with the Emperor's castle built on a high rock, giving a view of fantastic beauty down on to the valley of Mexico. Today the royal mountain is covered with thick undergrowth, and giant cypress trees, already hundreds of years old when the Spaniards arrived, mark the spot where the fairy-tale castle once stood.

Inside the castle there was gloom and despondency, for all the omens showed that the Emperor's power was nearing its end. His messengers brought Cortés four loads of gold and offered annual tribute if only the Spaniards would leave again. His brother had wanted to draft an army at once which would destroy the strangers, but Montezuma decided to receive them peacefully, asking in despair:

Fresco of the Prince of Knossos

The plumed crown comes from Crete

An Indian ruler from Palenque, Yucatan (from Lord Kingsborough)

Aztec step pyramid of Teopanzolco, near Cuernavaca, Mexico

'Of what avail is resistance if the gods have declared themselves against us?'

On November 8th, 1519, Cortés entered Tenochtitlán with 400 Spanish soldiers, a dozen horsemen, and a few guns. The small army made their entry along one of the causeways, and lodged at the palace of Montezuma's father, a fast vortified building in the middle of the city. The Emperor received them lavishly, and they were given everything they desired. But the teeming city cramped their movements, particularly affecting the horses, which had played such a decisive part in all their battles.

The Spaniards soon began to behave with great arrogance. Goaded on by their new allies, the auxiliaries from peoples enslaved by the Aztecs, they asked too many questions about the extent of the human sacrifices. It was evident that if there were open hostilities, the bold adventurers would be captives in the middle of a lake on an island difficult to defend. Their superiority in arms had become irrelevant.

Cortés tried a daring coup. Making some trifling charges against Montezuma, he took the Emperor prisoner in his palace, gaining a hostage to be skilfully exploited. Meanwhile the Aztec noblemen, the Emperor's suite and courtiers, watched the course of events with dismay, their first secret admiration for the White Gods transformed now to bitter hatred. They began making plans for liberating their Emperor.

Cortés had been hoping for reinforcements from Spain. Instead a fleet of eighteen ships sent by Velasquez landed at Vera Cruz with 900 soldiers, eighty-five horsemen, and twelve guns, under the command of Pánfilo de Narvaez, who was to take the rebel Cortés to Cuba in chains, and continue with the conquest in his place.

Cortés left 140 men in the capital to guard the Emperor, and marched with the rest of his troops to meet the adversary from his own country. He was joined by the garrison of Vera Cruz, and even some of Narvaez's Spanish mercenaries went over to him. He attacked Narvaez and captured him after a brief battle near Cempoalla.

The tide had turned once more. The miserable band of soldiers, badly reduced by earlier battles, was transformed into a large army with an impressive detachment of heavily armed cavalry. Cortés and his men immediately set out on the march back to the capital, to find his cause there gravely in jeopardy. His deputy had executed some Aztec nobles and had produced a faction of embittered opponents. The relieving army had scarcely reached the city when fighting broke out. A vast force besieged the palace, and whenever the Spaniards emerged from their fortress they were met by a hail of arrows and other missiles.

Montezuma offered to speak to his people. The proud Emperor, a

D

fierce war-lord who had won many brilliant campaigns, was now bowing to a superior enemy and humbling himself before his own subjects. But they had ceased to regard him as their ruler. As he stepped on to the battlements to address them he was greeted with abuse; and soon a stone hit his temple. He refused all medical treatment from the Spaniards and would not eat; a few weeks afterwards he died.

Cortés's position was now desperate, and on the night of June 30th, 1520, he started out on the dangerous retreat along one of the causeways across the lake. It cost him all his guns and powder, nearly all his horses, and most of the vast treasure he and his men had amassed. He reached the mainland with less than half his men. This was the *noche triste*, the sorrowful night, in which he and they counted themselves lucky to escape with their lives. Looking back, they could see the sacrificial fires of Tenochtitlán and hear the cries of their comrades-in-arms who were now being massacred. Even on the mainland they found all retreat routes blocked; the Aztec people had risen to a man. Pursued by far superior forces, Cortés marched along the lake's shores. Hardly a soldier was unscathed, and he himself was wounded in several places. The army of Quauhtemoc, the new Emperor, grew from day to day, and Quauhtemoc was throwing in all his reserves.

Finally a decisive battle took place on July 8th, near the village of Otumba. The Spaniards seemed to be beaten, when at the last moment Cortés called for a desperate effort, attacking with his few horsemen. Once again the Indians were beaten by their superstitious fear of the dual creature, horse and rider; they fled in dismay, and Cortés's own Indian auxiliaries saw to the rest.

A few weeks later the Conquistador advanced once more on the capital. The Aztecs under Quauhtemoc put up a brave resistance, but this time there were nearly a thousand Spaniards, and their guns were too much for the Aztecs in the end. Far more than a 100,000 dead were left in the streets, and the great city itself was a shambles of smoking ruins, shattered palaces and temples.

The Aztecs, formerly masters of an immense empire, became slaves; and they had to raze their own capital to the ground.

5

Pizarro and the Incas

AFTER subjugating the Aztecs, and taking over their empire, the Spaniards had still not discovered the legendary Eldorado talked of by the Indians. Vasco Nuñez de Balboa was one of the first to drive south from Panama, hoping to find it. In 1513 he made his first journey across the Isthmus of Panama and discovered the 'other ocean', the Pacific. But he failed to reach Peru, and for eighteen years attempts to do so by other explorers were equally unsuccessful.

Among de Balboa's mercenaries on his journey to the Pacific was Francisco Pizarro, born in Spain about 1478. The son of a captain and a servant-girl, he was a swineherd in early youth and remained illiterate. He went to Italy as a soldier, then tried his luck in the New World, meeting Balboa and also Cortés in Panama. The former swineherd had become an ambitious adventurer, brave, daring and resourceful, hard on himself and others, completely ruthless in his conquering course.

At the end of 1524 Pizarro sailed south from Panama for the first time, but the expedition failed because of the shortages and hardships, which were too much for his men. A year later he started out again with two ships, and with the utmost difficulty reached the coast of Peru. But he found it so densely populated that he dared not invade it. He sailed for home with only half his men left; the rest had died of hunger, exposure, or the Indians' poisoned arrows. He had, however, amassed a small hoard of gold and silver, partly by pillaging and partly in exchange for worthless rubbish.

In 1528 he returned to Spain, where he gave Charles V such a vivid description of the dangers he had overcome, and of the riches of Peru, that the Emperor made him its governor—at the time an empty title, which it was cheap enough for Charles to bestow. Pizarro was

51

empowered to select his own officers and 'civil servants', but had to promise to bear the cost of his expeditions himself. In July 1529 he received official permission to conquer Peru and rule there for life as captain-general.

In 1531, five years after his second expedition, he started out from Panama for the third time, with three small ships and 180 men. He landed on the off-shore island of Tumbez, and his first haul of gold was so extensive that news of it induced many adventurers from Panama to join him. But in spite of these reinforcements Pizarro could never have conquered the vast and populous country had it not been racked by internal conflict.

Shortly before the Spaniards arrived, the eleventh Inca, Huayna Capac, had died. He had conquered the adjoining kingdom of Quito and married a daughter of its king. He had a younger son from this marriage, Atahualpa, and an elder son, Huascar, by his first wife. He wanted the two sons to share the kingdom between them after his death, but this division of rule was against Inca traditions—Huascar did not recognize it, and civil war broke out. Atahualpa, supported by his father's army, took his half-brother prisoner, and had all other possible claimants put to death. With the country thus in turmoil Pizarro could penetrate farther into it without meeting serious resistance. He set out for Cajamarca, where Atahualpa was then resident.

The Spaniards marched through forests and up steep slopes, crossed torrents and skirted dizzying precipices, then climbed narrow rocky paths to the ridge of the Cordillera plateau, where the air was bitingly cold. The descent from the mountains on the eastern side took them two days, and as the green valley of Cajamarca unfolded before them, the sight which met their eyes was enough to send shivers down the backs of even the bravest. 'Along the slope there appeared a white cloud of tents, covering the ground like snow-flakes.' It was the Inca's army, thousands of seasoned warriors, and the Spaniards were a mere 106 infantry-men and sixty-two horses.

In the evening of 15th November, 1532 the Spaniards entered Cajamarca, 'a place of considerable size, containing about 10,000 inhabitants. . . . The houses for the most part were built of clay, hardened in the sun; the roofs thatched or of timber. Some of the more ambitious dwellings were of hewn stone.' (Prescott)

In the Inca's army many who had not quite believed in the White Gods' existence must now have shed their doubts. For this strange crowd now approaching must indeed be gods—with their uncanny snorting creatures and the mysterious apparatus which was reported to produce thunder and lightning. The late Inca had heard about them from his scouts and had warned his people not to resist them when

Despite vandalism, civil war and earthquakes the Inca walls of the street of Hatuncolla are still standing today in Cuzco, Peru, so perfect was this people's building technique

The trapeze shape is found in both Old World and New

A doorway in the Inca city of Vitcos (Machu Picchu), Peru

Door to Agamemnon's tomb

Lord Kingsborough's *Antiquities of Mexico* contains pictures of buildings many of which are today no longer extant. Step pyramid near Tepexe

they arrived. As the strangers were gods, they must be aware of this warning: the Indian warriors and noblemen could think of no other explanation for the audacity of the little Spanish force marching right through the huge Indian kingdom.

As soon as the Spaniards entered the town, Pizarro sent his brother Hernando with his riders and horses to the Inca's camp. Hernando found the Inca surrounded by his followers and wrote: 'It was not difficult to distinguish him. He wore on his head the crimson borla or fringe, which, surrounding his forehead, hung down as low as the eyebrow.' He had assumed this badge of Peruvian sovereignty only since the defeat of his brother Huascar.

The Inca's attire gave the Spaniards a foretaste of the riches they could expect in his empire. His tiara was made of feathers, silver and gold, inlaid with diamonds, turquoises, amethysts, rubies and emeralds, and he wore a necklace of emeralds as big as pigeons' eggs and topazes the size of large drops of water.

Hernando Pizarro and another officer rode up close to the Inca, saluting him with a slight bow. They had an interpreter with them, an Indian called Felipillo, whom Pizarro had taken back with him from his second expedition and who had in the meantime learnt Spanish. With Felipillo's help they tried to explain to the Inca that they were emissaries of a great and powerful king beyond the seas. The news of the Inca's great victories, they said, had induced them to come here to offer him their services and to bring him the teachings of the true faith. They invited him to visit their camp.

'To all this the Inca answered not a word, nor did he make even a sign of acknowledgement that he comprehended it. He remained silent, with his eyes fastened on the ground; but one of the nobles, standing by his side, answered: "It is well." This was an embarrassing situation for the Spaniards, who seemed to be as far from ascertaining the real disposition of the Peruvian monarch towards themselves, as when the mountains were between them.

'In a courteous and respectful manner, Hernando Pizarro again broke the silence by requesting the Inca to speak to them himself, and to inform them what was his pleasure. To this Atahualpa condescended to reply, while a faint smile passed over his features, "Tell your captain that I am keeping a fast, which will end tomorrow morning. I will then visit him with my chieftains. In the meantime, let him occupy the public buildings on the square and no other, till I come, when I will order what shall be done."

'De Soto was the best mounted and perhaps the best rider in Pizarro's troop. Observing that Atahualpa looked with some interest on the fiery steed that stood before him, champing the bit and pawing the ground with the natural impatience of a war-horse, the Spaniard gave him the rein, and, striking his iron heel into his side, dashed furiously over the plain; then, wheeling him round and round, displayed all the beautiful movements of his charger, and his own excellent horsemanship. Suddenly, checking him in full career, he brought the animal almost on his haunches, so near the person of the Inca, that some of the foam that flecked his horse's sides was thrown on the royal garments. But Atapualpa maintained the same marble composure as before, though several of his soldiers, whom De Soto passed in his course, were so much disconcerted by it that they withdrew in manifest terror; an act of timidity for which they paid dearly, if, as the Spaniards assert, Atahualpa caused them to be put to death that same evening for betraying such unworthy weakness to the strangers.' (Prescott)

A small troop of men facing an army of many thousands, the Spaniards realized they were at the Inca's mercy, and Pizarro knew that some daring and unexpected move was their only chance of escaping unscathed. He decided on exactly the same course as Cortés had taken in Mexico: he must get the Indian ruler into his power. This was why he had invited Atahualpa to visit the Spanish camp.

On a litter sparkling with gold and silver, borne on the shoulders of his principal nobles, the Inca entered the strangers' camp. Pizarro's chaplain, a Dominican friar, Fray Vicente de Valverde, stepped up to him, opened a Bible in front of him, and began expounding the Christian gospel. But when he talked of submission to the true belief, and the Spanish king's sovereignty, the Inca seized the book from the friar's hands, turned over the pages a moment, then threw it indignantly on the ground. 'Tell your comrades that they shall give me an account of their doings in my land. I will not go from here till they have made me full satisfaction for the wrongs they have done.' The friar, much scandalized, picked up the book and reported to Pizarro, and Pizarro gave the prearranged signal. The Spaniards' hidden guns fired into the crowd, the Spanish mercenaries came out of concealment, the horsemen rode down all who barred their way. The Peruvian warriors dashed off in panic and fear, leaving behind several thousand dead. Atahualpa himself, the last of the Incas, was now the Spaniards' prisoner. They allotted him living quarters in the palace, allowed him to have his wives, and to receive visits from his 'subjects'. But the ruler of the country was now Pizarro.

It did not take the Inca long to discover the invaders' strange lust for gold, and he offered a vast store of it in exchange for a promise of release. Pizarro agreed to this bargain, and the Inca had a great store of gold brought in from all over the country. But Pizarro knew what he and his men could expect if the Inca regained his freedom, and continued to keep him prisoner. Some time later 'he was arraigned before a mock tribunal, and, under pretences equally false and frivolous, was condemned to an excruciating death' (Prescott). In August 1533 the ruler of the Inca empire was garroted like a common criminal—though the next day 'his funeral obsequies were performed with great solemnity. Pizarro and his principal cavaliers went into mourning, and the troops listened with devout attention to the service of the dead from the lips of Father Valverde'—for just before his death the Inca had agreed to have the friar baptize him.

'Atahualpa's remains . . . were laid in the cemetery of San Francisco. But from thence, as is reported, after the Spaniards left Cajamarca, they were secretly removed, and carried, as he had desired, to Quito. The colonists of a later time supposed that some treasure might have been buried with the body. But, on excavating the ground, neither treasure nor remains were to be discovered.'

After Atahualpa's death the Spaniards saw a clear road to Cuzco, the capital. They reached it a year after their entry into Cajamarca. At Cuzco they found what they had been looking for, the gold which had brought them to this country and induced them to bear terrible hardships for so many months. The Inca people grasped too late that the strangers who had come across the sea were no White Gods but thieves and murderers.

A new Inca, a puppet of Pizarro's, soon died, probably a natural death. Then Manco, a brother of Huascar, came to Pizarro as claimant to the throne; Pizarro 'received the young man . . . with great cordiality, and did not hesitate to assure him that he [Pizarro] had been sent into the country by his master, the Castilian sovereign, in order to vindicate the claims of Huascar to the throne, and to punish the usurpation of his rival'.

So in 1534 Manco 'received the fringed diadem of Peru, not from the hand of the high-priest of his nation, but from his conqueror, Pizarro'. But Manco did not remain a willing puppet; he was twice arrested by the Spaniards, but escaped from Cuzco to the Cordillera, and to the mountain 'City of Faith', Vitcos. From here he organized resistance against the Spaniards. Many thousands joined his army, and they occupied mountain passes before marching on Cuzco itself. In the beginning of 1536 the capital was besieged by a large force.

The siege lasted for over five months, with the fortunes of war continually changing. The Spaniards suffered great losses, but in the end the young Inca's revolt collapsed and he had to flee back into the mountains to Vitcos. For years the Spaniards hunted in vain for this secret refuge in the Andes.

Pizarro later founded a new Peruvian capital, which is now Lima. Five years after the battle for Cuzco he was murdered by followers of his former comrade-in-arms Almagro, whom he had put to death for plotting against him. He never saw the 'City of Faith', nor did the many generations of Spanish immigrants who came into the country after the conquerors, nor the tourists visiting the remains of the ancient Inca civilization. Vitcos was buried in the jungle for nearly four centuries, almost up to our own day.

After Manco's defeat and flight, however, there was no further serious challenge to the Spaniards' supremacy: they had destroyed another empire.

The empire was geographically divided into parts, one being the Sierra, the plateau on the Andes between the two Cordilleras, reaching from Argentina over Peru and Bolivia up to Ecuador in the north. The Sierra's height is between 10,000 and 16,000 feet, and it has many mountain ranges dividing it into separate high valleys. The other part of the Inca country, the coastal plain, runs parallel to the Sierra from north to south, a narrow strip of desert bordered by the Andes on the one side and the Pacific on the other.

Despite these natural divisions, and although extending over thousands of miles, the empire was held together by a remarkable network of roads—much of which still survives today. They threaded in and out over the Andes, along precipitous heights and dark gorges, across mountain torrents, and through the plains right to the Pacific. For as soon as the Incas conquered another country, they built new stone roads to connect it with Cuzco, thus welding it to the empire.

When the Spaniards marched towards Cuzco on these Inca roads, they were surprised to find engineering on such a vast scale in the New World. All the Spanish chroniclers stated that the roads were better than those of ancient Rome, nor had they met such magnificent roads in any European country. Now and then the roads were intersected by steps, which apparently the Spanish horses found very troublesome.

Some of the roads were supported by walls up to fifteen feet high, and several led through mountain tunnels. In 'built-up areas' they were bordered with pillars, posts, or low walls; and on marshy ground embankments had been built for them to run on. In the plain they were wide enough for six horsemen to ride abreast, but in the gorges and on the mountains they were only three feet wide. One of the main 'arteries' ran along the plateau of the Andes, the other parallel to it, also from north to south, close to the coast. The two were connected by linking roads.

Yet these feats of engineering were almost dwarfed by the architectural achievements in the capital itself.

Eight hundred years ago the Arab Abdul Latif, visiting the Pyramids of Giza, noted about the great hall of the Cheops Pyramid that the huge stone blocks fitted together so exactly that 'neither a hair nor a pin' would go into the joins between them.' And in 1880 Sir Flanders Petrie, creeping about the passages in the pyramids naked night after night, making sketches of transverse and longitudinal sections, of building angles and planes, found that in spite of the terrific scale of the building work the faults in the measurements and angles were small enough to be 'covered by a thumb'.

The Spaniards saw this degree of architectural precision and accomplishment in Cuzco. Their accounts describe the Inca palaces with their severe façades, which are still standing today despite wars and destruction by fire, earthquake, or vandalism. The walls were formed of polygonal or rectangular stone blocks, exactly cut and showing no joins, often wider at the bottom than at the top; narrow trapezoid openings, usually with a monolith lintel, provided windows and doors. Compared with these walls, a modern traveller comments, 'Roman walls are shoddy constructions'; and Fergusson wrote of Cuzco's architecture that it was beyond anything achieved by the Greeks or Romans or in the Middle Ages. Velarde called it 'crystallized earth shaped into geometrical forms'.

Even more imposing than Cuzco's buildings were the old Inca fortresses from which the Indians organized their resistance to the Spaniards: for instance, the huge fortress of Sacsahuaman, just outside the gates of the capital, and Ollontaytambo, equally gigantic, deep in the jungle of the Andes, the ruins of which have survived. We have to go back to the earliest civilizations of Europe, to Tiryns and Mycenae, to find anything comparable to these Inca buildings.

Pizarro's men found treasures in Peru very like those which Cortés's men had seen and admired in Mexico. But the Incas had something which even the Aztecs did not have: scales of balance. Measurements are the foundations of all science. The Incas had their measures, and used beam scales, like those of the ancient Romans. There was another similarity with the ancient Romans: the division of the Inca army into units of ten, hundreds, and thousands, just like the legions of Rome. The Incas also used the decimal system.

European women of today still buy their eggs by the dozen or half-dozen, counting them by sixes, twelves, or sixties; and our clocks and watches, of course, deal in twelves and sixties. This mathematical system we still use in our everyday life is the old Sumerian sexagesimal system of Babylonian mathematics, which the Semites afterwards combined with the decimal system.

The decimal system is over 4,000 years old. It was already known in Egypt as far back as that, and later, around 1700 B.C., in Crete. The Greeks adopted it from there, the Romans from the Greeks, and it was introduced all over Europe by the Roman legions marching in divisions of hundreds and thousands. But it was not generally adopted in Europe till centuries later, with the blossoming of the natural sciences.

In the Inca empire people were classified by age in ten categories, starting with newly born babies and ending with centenarians. The whole social organization was ruled by the decimal system. The Incas had taken it from the ancient people of the Chimu, who had long been subjected to them; the Chimu had been familiar with the decimal system centuries before the Incas appeared.

It was probably invented by the Hindus, who also invented the figure zero, the most abstract of all concepts—nothing. The concept came to Arabia and Egypt, later to the Moors, who took it to Spain; but it was not generally known in Europe till the fifteenth century. The old Indian peoples not only knew the zero when the Spaniards arrived; they had known it for centuries, roughly since the beginning of our era.

On entering Cuzco, the Spaniards saw another thing which was fairly familiar to them: nearly all the Indian dignitaries had turbans. It was believed in the Old World that only the Arabs wore turbans, but in fact this headgear is much older than Islam. People are shown wearing turbans in paintings and statues of the Hittites, the Babylonians, the Egyptians.

Some of the Spaniards had an odd experience in Cuzco.

Everywhere in the Inca empire they were greeted and addressed as 'Viracocha'. Hearing the word again and again, they at first took it for a form of salute and had no idea of its meaning. In Cuzco they learned that it was the name of the great White God who had come to the Indians in the dim past and brought them all their knowledge.

Then the conquerors heard about the temple which had been erected outside the town to the god who was greater than all other gods. A party of them hurried off there, hoping to find an immense store of gold. They came to the temple of Viracocha, a one-storeyed building about 125 feet by 100. They went in and entered a maze of passages: there were twelve narrow passages going round the building. They made their way from one into another, and finally penetrated to the sanctuary, a small room paved with black slabs.

On a little dais on the far wall there was the figure of a man. When they stood before it even the wildest, roughest and most hardened veterans took their caps into their hands and hastily crossed themselves: they knew that figure from all the churches and chapels in Spain. It was an old man with a beard, standing erect, holding a chain in one hand; the chain was round the neck of a fabulous creature which lay before him on the ground. It was a statue of St. Bartholomew.

When they had recovered from their surprise they slowly filed out into the passage again. They found no treasure here; the great temple contained nothing but the statue of the god. But on their return to Cuzco they told the others what they had seen. More and more Spaniards rode out to the old temple which held no treasure, to see the strange bearded saint whom the Indians called the White God.

Then came the siege of Cuzco, when the Incas made repeated assaults on the town, accompanied by trumpet-blasts, drum-rolls, the jingling of bells and the playing of flutes. Even in the heat of the battle the Spaniards must have been surprised to hear these fanfares for the first time: the Indians had the same musical instruments as they had, and used them, too, for celebrating victories in battle or while making charges.

These instruments, of course, go back a very long way in our ancient civilizations: in the Old Testament we have Joshua and his men blowing trumpets outside the walls of Jericho, 'and the walls came tumbling down'. Trumpets were known to the Incas long before the Spaniards came; a trumpet-blower is depicted on the sun-gate of Tiahuanaco. The Incas also had shepherd's flutes which they called Antara—these consisted of twelve to fifteen pipes made of bulrushes, clay, or stone. All the early civilizations of the Mediterranean area knew the pan-pipe, the Greek syrinx; and this was the most popular instrument in the civilization of Peru. Dozens of Chimu vase-drawings show it—exactly like the Greek syrinx.

Musical instruments, turbans, decimal system, scales—in their accounts the Spaniards periodically noted such familiar features, but without paying any special attention to them. And we have to depend on these accounts, the truth of which cannot always be checked; for almost everything the Spaniards saw with their own eyes and recorded has perished. When they conquered the New World not a single town was spared.

6

The Myth Survives

'Fernando de Alva Ixtlilxochitl, who flourished in the
beginning of the sixteenth century, was a native of Tezcoco,
and descended in a direct line from the sovereigns of the
kingdom.'
                    PRESCOTT on the historian Ixtlilxochitl

'The time had arrived when the sons of Quetzalcoatl were
to come from the East to take possession of the land.'
                    PRESCOTT quoting Nezaualpilli, ruler of Tezcoco

'Very soon they realized they were by no means dealing
with gods.'
                    The chronicler BISHOP DE LAS CASAS

ARCHAEOLOGISTS arriving in Central America a few centuries
later had laboriously to fit together fragments of stone in order to get
a picture of an old Mexican city; the *Conquistadores* and their followers
had made the work very hard. The élite of the Indian peoples had
perished almost to a man—'You could not put down your foot without stepping on an Indian's corpse', Cortés wrote after his entry into
conquered Tenochtitlán. On top of that, his men and Pizarro's melted
down irreplaceable works of art by the ton to get the gold.

Nevertheless, a great many temples and other buildings, statues
of the gods, manuscripts, and other evidence of the Indian civilizations
still existed for some decades after the *Conquista*. But the mercenaries
were followed by zealots determined to root out all signs of idolatry.
The Indians' temples, statues, above all the manuscripts, were works
of the devil, and the fanatical believers put up stakes to destroy all they
could. In a letter to the Chapter of the Franciscan Order at Toulouse,
Juan de Zumárraga, first bishop of Mexico, reported in 1531 that he

Lord Kingsborough gave his *magnum opus* magnificent illustrations.
The pyramid near the village of Santiago Guatusco

The testimonies in stone to the perished civilization of the
Aztecs lie directly under the roaring traffic of Mexico City

Hard as they tried, the Spaniards never found Vitcos, the City of Faith. It was not till 1913 that the archaeologist Bingham penetrated into the jungle above the Urubamba Valley and was faced by the mysterious ruins

According to the legends, the Inca royal family came from the House with the Three Windows. Was it here too that the last of the Inca rulers perished?

alone had had 500 temples razed to the ground and 20,000 idols destroyed.

All over New Spain the stakes were burning. Zumárraga had a particularly large stake erected in Tlatelolco market square, on which all the archives of Tezcoco perished. In the town of Mani all the illuminated manuscripts of the Maya were burned in 1562 by the second bishop of Yucatan, Diego de Landa—who later tried to atone for this destruction. Pablo José de Arriaga, born at Biscaya in 1564, arrived in the New World at the age of fifteen, and became head of various schools and Jesuit colleges in Peru. His fanaticism was responsible for the destruction of all state archives, lists of customs and tributes, the royal and imperial archives, the codes of laws, the archives of the temples, and historical records. Manuscripts were consigned to the stake by the bundle, and the soldiers were incited to ransack palaces and public buildings to collect more manuscripts for the fire.

Only a few manuscripts from the Indian countries have come down to us, the last written memorials to the ancient civilizations. They are carefully guarded as great treasures by the libraries of Oxford, New York, Madrid, Mexico, Bologna, Vienna, and Dresden. Apart from a few minor ones, they consist mainly of twenty longer manuscripts, called the pre-Spanish codices, because they were written long before the Spaniards' arrival. Out of these twenty, only four are from the empire of the Aztecs and only three from Mayan territory. Of the Aztec manuscripts, three deal with religious subjects and only one with history.

Even the memory of these high levels of civilization was wiped out. The discovery and conquest of the new lands caused a big migration from Spain, and when the settlers came, erecting their own New Spanish towns on the sites of buildings that had been razed, they found no more temples, no Indian emperors, chiefs, or dignitaries. They saw only the primitive Indians, living in huts, pressed into slave labour for their conquerors, forced to smash the last remnants of their own temples and idols.

After the disaster which had befallen them the Indians were prepared to do anything, and when they had been converted to the Christian faith by the Spanish priests they even ended up by themselves regarding their old gods as figments of the devil. Again and again people spoke of the dreadful human sacrifices, the heaps of skulls on the racks and the human hearts on the altars, which the Spaniards had seen with their own eyes in the country of the Aztecs. Because of such cruel customs the Christians claimed a moral right to destroy everything which reminded them of these cults.

Only a small minority could read and write in those days, so if there were other reports referring to the high Indian civilizations few would have read them. The new immigrants, who had never seen anything of all this, would have been willing to swear that the Indians, their slaves, were barbaric savages and always had been.

Centuries passed, the accounts of the Spanish chroniclers became known, and more and more remains of the Indian empires were discovered on the soil of the New World. For the spade alone cannot reconstruct a civilization without legends and historical knowledge. Would Schliemann ever have started digging in Troy had he not known the contents of the *Iliad*? What would Evans have made of the maze at Crete if he had never heard of the legend of the Minotaur?

Before archaeology became a science, the recorded history of the Old World was over 5,000 years old and widely known. When excavators hit on finds, they could often interpret them at the same time, establishing a connection with history, epic or folklore. But suppose the Indian peoples had invaded the Old World, instead of the other way round; had completely destroyed all its towns and burned all written records. Suppose that, like the Spaniards, they had gained a continent but wiped out its civilization and history: later generations might then have gazed in surprise at the pyramids in Egypt, without knowing there had ever been an Egyptian people. They would have admired the Capitol without knowing what Rome had been, without even having heard the name of Rome.

In due course archaeologists in the New World, particularly in South America, discovered many ruins of ancient buildings, and the huge ruin-cities of the Maya; but they could not have reconstructed Indian civilization from these alone. They had to base their work on the history of the Indian peoples, as filtered through from the old chronicles.

The writers of the chronicles collected—often as a hobby—everything they could find in the way of old Indian songs and myths, legends and fairy-tales, on laws, government, organization, and religion. It was about 200 years before scholars had worked their way through all this material to arrive at an outline of Indian history—which is the basis for all archaeology of the American continent.

The chronicles fill many volumes, enough to stock a whole library. The originals and old editions extant are almost without exception in the libraries and museums of Madrid. They are all written in Spanish. The writers were priests, jurists, civil servants, noblemen, soldiers, and mere adventurers. The priests were the most numerous, and they wrote about anything and everything. Nor did the jurists confine themselves to collecting laws; they too put down anything which interested them, songs and sagas, traditions and legends, even botanical and zoological descriptions.

One group among the chroniclers was inclined to detract from the Indians' achievements. These were the Spanish viceroys' court historians, such as Sarmiento, who still regarded the Indians as barbarians and approved of the new order which the Spaniards had introduced, on the grounds that 'God had willed it so.'

Another group took pride in the ancient civilizations because they had Indian blood in their veins. Many Spanish officers (following Cortés's example) took Indian wives, and the children of these mixed marriages maintained close contacts with Indian families. Some of the chroniclers were thus princes of Indian blood, like Garcilaso Inca de la Vega, whose mother was a princess of the Inca imperial family, and Juan de Betanzos, who married a daughter of the Prince of Quito. These men learned Spanish and wrote their chronicles in Roman letters in that language; but they knew everything about the Indian empires, the kings and princes, wars, victories and defeats, gods, temples, religious tenets, festivals and customs. They even put down things that were discussed in the Inca privy council.

They were naturally inclined to embellish where their ancestors were concerned, wishing to show that the destroyed civilizations were anything but barbaric. They wrote about age-old empires, the traces of which were lost in the mists of history; they recorded the old legends of Tula or Tollan, of the country of Olman; they wrote about the Zapotecs and about the people of Teotihuacan, which means 'the place where the gods were made'.

Extensive and detailed as all these chronicles are, they were a highly inadequate and inaccurate guide to the Indians' ancient history and civilization. Their material was largely legend and fantasy, nor were the writers impartial or at all systematic. Some wrote soberly and to the point, others were long-winded or allowed their imagination full play. Sometimes they reported only one special incident, and mostly they were writing about a small and limited area or subject in which they happened to be interested.

Suppose all our written records had perished, with the greater part of our civilization, and chroniclers after us were trying to reconstruct our distant past from word-of-mouth traditions, legends and fairy-tales, the memories of simple people. Such people might just have heard of ancient Rome, perhaps of Julius Caesar, but they would not be able to give any sort of date. They might tell the chroniclers the legends of figures like Robin Hood or Queen Elizabeth, and there would be one story particularly prevalent, about a man born in the East as a saviour, who preached wisdom and kindness and taught men to be good to one another, but who was then killed by men and ascended to Heaven and promised one day to return. All this the chroniclers would meticulously put down, but they would never be sure which was pure legend, which was history, and which a mixture of the two. It was rather like that when the chroniclers of the New World set out to re-create the past from the survivors' tales.

There was a mass of tangled material, much of highly dubious value, which scholars had to synthesize, edit, and classify, stripping the tales of their imaginative trimmings, trying to glean a clear out-line of the real events. Among these scholars the man whose books attracted most attention was William Prescott. Born at Salem in New England in 1796, he studied law at Harvard. He was nearly blinded in a student prank, but despite this handicap he wrote with extraordinary energy and diligence, examining everything he found among the chronicles, and following up even most trivial notes or allusions. Through him and other such scholars, working away in their studies for years, the story of the *Conquista* and the whole history of the Indian empires was gradually pieced together.

The history of the Incas is the history of a dynasty of twelve Inca kings, starting from the legendary Manco Capac and ending with Atahualpa, who reigned only a few weeks. For in the evening of the day when he defeated and captured his brother Huascar, and put on the purple headband, he was told that white men had landed on the shores of his empire. His successors, being merely Pizarro's nominees, cannot really be called Inca kings.

THE INCA KINGS

Manco Capac	about A.D.	1080
Sinchi Roca	about	1150
Lloque Yupanqui	about	1180
Mayta Capac	between	1200 and 1300
Capac Yupanqui	between	1200 and 1300
Inca Roca	about	1340
Yahuar Huacac	between	1340 and 1400
Viracocha Inca	between	1340 and 1400
Pachacutec	between	1400 and 1500
Tupac Yupanqui	between	1400 and 1500
Huayna Capac		1485–1525
Huascar and Atahualpa		1525–1530

The Inca were a dynasty of warriors, and their history is one of continual new conquests. The little municipal state which the dynasty

The Mayan temple of Tulum. Seen by Jeronimo Aguilar, shipwrecked Spaniard who was made a slave by the Maya, then escaped to Cortés and acted as his interpreter

The oldest Mayan pyramid so far known to us, uncovered from later superstructure at Uaxactun by the American archaeologist Ricketson (from Wilhelm Museeler, *Kunst der Welt*, Safari Verlag, Berlin)

Today there are four miles of tunnel stretching beneath the pyramid of Cholula

The pyramid also hid a secret tomb. During the tunnelling a skeleton was found; there was also a woman's skeleton in the same place

had originally ruled became the centre of a vast empire which conquered and subjugated all the peoples of Peru and the Andes, whose
immense armies could stand comparison with any of the Old World's
armies; the accounts mention 40,000, 80,000, and even 100,000
warriors.

The chronicles speak of strength and power, and also of treason
and fratricidal quarrels, of rebel sons and court intrigues, the hardships
of rigid discipline and slave labour, as well as feasts and festivals and
victory celebrations.

The figure of the eighth king, Viracocha Inca, is of special interest
to us. He ascended the 'throne of the sun' about 1350, the time of the
Black Death in England. His father was the only weakling among the
rulers in the dynasty, for in the face of death he had burst into bloody
tears—so the chronicles have it: his name, Yahuar Huacac, means
'he who weeps bloody tears'. Viracocha's portrait has come down to
us, and we have no reason to doubt the chroniclers' description of him
as white of body and with a trace of beard. According to the legend
reported by Garcilaso, he acceded to the throne in extraordinary
circumstances.

The legend says that as a prince he was so extremely unruly,
breaking the statues of the gods and trying to burn down the temples,
that his father, Yahuar Huacac, banished him from the court. For some
years he was a cowherd near the capital, but then he had an apparition.
He went to the palace and told his father about it. He had been asleep
under a rock when a man appeared to him whose face was 'very
different' from the Indians' faces. The man had a long beard and wore
a coat which came down to his feet, and he was holding an unknown
animal on a leash. He said he was the son of the sun and the brother of
Manco Capac, his name was Viracocha; he ordered the banished
prince to go at once to his father and warn him of an imminent invasion
by tribes from the north which had been arming against Cuzco and
meant to destroy the dynasty.

The father, the man who had once 'wept blood', dismissed his
son scornfully, saying the whole story was nonsense; but the prophecy
proved correct. Two northern tribes rose in rebellion and marched on
the capital with 30,000 men. The 'weeper of blood' was on the point
of surrendering when the young prince appeared again and in a few
days recruited an army of 20,000 men which he led against the enemy.
Before the battle he formed a reserve of 5,000 men and had them lie
in concealment behind a mountain. They emerged in the late afternoon, after the battle had been raging all day, and turned the tide to
win victory for the young prince. Thirty thousand dead lay on the
plain of Yahuar Pampa, 'the plain of blood', when he entered Cuzco

E

in triumph as its new ruler. Later on he expanded his empire to the south, crossing the Andes and advancing as far as the Chilean border.

When he became Inca, he built a temple sixteen miles outside Cuzco in honour of the apparition he had seen under the rock, the man with the beard and the long flowing coat; the temple contained the statue of Viracocha, made from the Inca's description, and it was this statue which Pizarro's soldiers, searching for gold in the temple, took to be St. Bartholomew.

A few years before his death (in 1525) Huayna Capac had news of white men sighted off the coasts of his huge empire. His relay runners sped over the country by day and night, passing on their news by word of mouth to the next messenger. For weeks and months the password they were given echoed through the wide roads, and even travelled back to the palace—the password 'Viracocha'.

The Inca and his intimates were worried when they heard the word, and the people remembered the old tradition, whereby Viracocha, the White God, would return. At night comets flashed over the sky, earthquakes shook the country, more violently than ever before, and fiery rings appeared round the moon in all the colours of the rainbow. During a thunderstorm in Cuzco lightning struck the palace and it went up in flames. But the worst portent was a condor, a bird of the sun, their highest god, which fell dead in the midst of Cuzco's market square, hunted down and torn to pieces by several hawks. Huayna Capac called together the leaders of his country and prophesied to them that the country would be destroyed by white men—thus fulfilling the oracle that the empire would be destroyed after the twelfth Inca. He ordered his counsellors not to resist Heaven's command, but to submit to its envoys.

Cusi Hualpa, the old Inca general, described the assembly to his nephew, the chronicler Garcilaso, who recounted a speech by the Inca:

'Our father, the sun, has revealed to me that after the rule of twelve Incas, his children, men of a kind unknown to us, will come into our country and subjugate our states. Without doubt they belong to the people whose men were sighted off our coast. . . . Let me assure you that these strangers will come into our country and fulfil the oracle.'

Indian princes also described what happened at Montezuma's court when news reached Tenochtitlán of the White Gods' landing; and there are striking similarities between these Aztec accounts and those of the Incas.

One of the chroniclers, a descendant of the Emperor, recorded that when Montezuma was crowned the priests addressed the traditional warning to him: 'Remember that this is not your throne, that it is only

lent to you and will one day be returned to the one to whom it is due.'
When the Spaniards landed, Montezuma was convinced the White
God was returning to reclaim his throne. He summoned his counsellors, and some were in favour of immediate resistance. But the
will of Montezuma and the king of Tezcoco prevailed: they said
resistance was useless.

Montezuma made a speech to his ministers and high dignitaries:

'You know, as I do, that our ancestors did not hail from this
country we live in, but came here from a far distant land, led by a
great prince. This prince then left the country again with only a few
of his followers, but returned a long time afterwards. He saw that our
ancestors, his subjects, had built towns, had chosen wives from the
daughters of the country, and had had children by them; that they had
settled in their new land and would not go back with him, their prince.
Since they no longer wanted him as their ruler, he went away alone,
announcing that he would one day in the remote future he would
either return himself with an immense army or send someone in his
name to take back what was his due.

'You know too that we have always been expecting him. All we
have heard about the foreign commander and his emperor who has
sent him to us across the great sea, from the direction where the sun
rises, the direction in which that great prince of our ancestors once
went back—all that makes me believe this is assuredly the great
master we have ever been expecting. . . .'

According to the chronicles, the people of the Aztecs were the
largest group in the Nahua tribe, and emigrated from North America
to Mexico. In the course of their wanderings they came to Tula or
Tollán, centre of the world, where they acquired all the skills of a
higher civilization, ceased to be nomads, and became town-dwellers.
Tenochtitlán was founded in 1324, and in less than two centuries they
had grown into the ruling people of Central America.

First they were ruled by chiefs, then by kings, the first of whom
was Acamapich (1376). All their kings called themselves successors
of Quetzalcoatl, White God of Tula. The fourth king, Itzcoatzin
(black-stone-snake), destroyed the kingdom of the Tepanecs. The
fifth, Montezuma Ilhuicamina (celestial hunter), concluded a tripartite
pact with the kings of Tezcoco and Tlacopan, and then led his country
on a steep ascent to imperial power. Itzcoatzin's great-grandson,
Montezuma Xocoyotzin, was the Emperor the Spaniards met, and
after his death as a prisoner of Cortés he was succeeded by his brother
Cuitlahuac, who died of the smallpox the Spaniards had brought with
them. Then came Quauhtemoc (diving eagle), who roused the whole
country against the Spaniards, but was finally defeated at Tenochtitlán.

The Aztec empire was merely a number of tributary territories subjugated and exploited. The Aztecs did not add much to the civilization of the high valley of Mexico—in the chronicles they were sometimes called 'gifted upstarts' who took most of their organization from the Toltecs and Mixtecs before them. Their wealth came from war, trade, pirating, and, above all, tribute, ruthlessly exacted from the tribes subjected to them—who were kept in check by strong military garrisons. There were thirty-eight such provinces paying tribute in cocoa, maize, cotton, tobacco, jaguar-skins, feathers, copal wood and india-rubber, gold, silver, and precious stones. The empire, really a federation of three kingdoms, did not have the same inner strength and cohesion as the Inca kingdom had in Peru, and historically it was a fairly short episode in the life of the ancient Indian peoples, lasting from only about 1430 to 1521.

The chronicles speak also of older kingdoms, which had long perished when the Spaniards came: for instance, the Chichemecs, once a tribe of wild hunters, who then became peaceful and civilized under the influence of the Mixtecs, and quite soon turned into an agricultural people. Their story begins with the legendary king Xolotl, who destroyed the Toltecs' kingdom. He conquered Mexico in the twelfth century and Tenayuca became his first residence. After him the chroniclers mention a great ruler called Quinantzin Tlaltecatzin (1298–1357), who made Tezcoco his capital.

Throughout all this legend-history runs the myth of the White God in a great many different versions. The chroniclers embellished and added to it, saying that the White God had created man and light, had fashioned men from stone and turned them back into stone; had fights with other gods; stole maize from the 'food mountain' so as to give it to man.

If all this is remote and fantastic the chroniclers represent him also from a factual side: he brought the Indians their script and their calendar, as well as cotton; he taught them to cut and manufacture greenstone; he taught them weaving, and the god Bochica is reported to have left a drawing of a loom, so that men could preserve his invention. These highly practical contributions to society do not seem like the figment of a story-teller's vivid imagination: they suggest a real basis for the White God in historical fact.

7

First Fruits of Excavation

'But Nineveh, good ferryman, is destroyed: No trace of it's left, and no one can tell where it lay.'

LUCIAN (c. A.D. 150)

'From Atahualpa's castle and palace scant remains have come down to us. People's lust for gold quickened the pace of destruction, so that even before the end of the sixteenth century they had pulled down walls and recklessly under-mined the foundations of all dwellings, in order to dig for the treasures beneath.'

ALEXANDER VON HUMBOLDT
in his *South American Journey* (1799)

AFTER the soldiers of the *Conquista* the 'explorers' came, seeking gold, either on their own account or on commission from their govern-ments. They travelled all over New Spain, across the Andes, through deep valleys and the deserts on the Pacific coast. Their accounts are often the only record extant of old towns, temples and palaces. They saw the last undamaged buildings, where later travellers saw only ruins and modern archaeologists see nothing at all; for in the course of four centuries the remains of the pyramids have crumbled into mounds of earth. These first explorers were not interested in buildings or works of art as such, and they had no scruples about pulling down walls and houses, temples and palaces, wherever they could hope to find gold.

In the second half of the eighteenth century the first scientific explorers set out to see with their own eyes the ancient Indian countries described by the chronicles; they followed Cortés's old march route from the coast to Tenochtitlán. There were only a few of them at first, but during the nineteenth century more and more arrived, attracted by their predecessors' reports. And all the evidence slowly coming to light, chronicles and finds, suggested parallels between the Indians and the Old World so striking that many writers felt there could be only one explanation: all Indian civilizations must at some time in the dim past have come from the Old World.

The pyramids, it was said, pointed to Egypt, and the Aztec myth about the White God must refer to the Messiah. Some claimed that the Indians were the lost tribes of Israel; others that one of the apostles, perhaps St. Thomas, must have reached America. Many different peoples were alleged to have discovered the new continent and settled there long ago. It was also suggested, however, that the population of the whole world had originally come from America, or that the people of America had come from Atlantis, a submerged continent between Africa and the West Indies, or from another submerged continent— Mu in the Pacific.

During this period an enormous number of books and papers appeared, full of more or less fantastic assumptions and theories; their authors and the ideas they put forward have long been forgotten. But one of these authors, Lord Edward Kingsborough, has given us unique and valuable material. He collected everything he could find out about the Indian civilizations, and published nine huge volumes on them, a luxury publication designed to prove that the Indians were one of the lost ten tribes. Scholars flatly rejected his thesis, and as he had spent a fortune on this magnum opus, he ended in a debtors' jail, while his creditors waited in vain for the printing costs of the ninth volume to be settled.

The nine volumes on the *Antiquities of Mexico* were published between 1831 and 1848, the whole work costing the equivalent of 3,500 dollars—so that at the time it found scarcely any buyers. Nowadays the few libraries which boast a set of these volumes count it among their greatest treasures; it is exclusively from them that we know some of the old Inca scripts. Kingsborough also published the first edition of the ancient Maya code, which is extremely important and used to be in Dresden. Nobody knows anything of its present fate or whereabouts.

It can be said that the science of American archaeology was born accidentally one August day in 1790, when drainage workers in Mexico City were digging a hole in the road. They had dug three feet, and then hit a stone. They dug round it and tried to free it from the soil, but it took them a lot of digging and sweating before they finally exposed it. It was a colossal stone, which they had to lift from the hole by means of hawsers and pulleys; and when they got it out they saw it was no ordinary block of stone but a statue of tremendous weight and nine feet tall. They washed it in water and scrubbed off the mud, then gasped in horror at what they saw: a gruesome, barbaric figure of a goddess with snakes coiled about her body.

When this first excavation was reported there was great excitement among scholars. For they knew this goddess with her snakes: her stone image had once stood in Tenochtitlán. This proved that Mexico City was built on the ruins of the old Aztec capital. After the statue more and more evidence of a long-perished high civilization came to light in Mexico; objects made of stone, gold, silver. But most of the nineteenth-century explorers still confined themselves to isolated efforts; it was not till 1922 that archaeologists started systematic excavations.

They dug into the ground beneath Mexico City, 6,000 feet above sea level, with its thousands of inhabitants: beneath the maze of roads of a modern metropolis, its houses and skyscrapers. They took meticulous care not to undermine and bring down any of the houses, but they were on the spot wherever the foundations for a new house were dug or a new conduit line was put into the ground. Like moles they burrowed about in the dark underneath the town, hunting for old foundations or remains of houses, for Aztec monuments; and they found the great Teocalli pyramid of Tenochtitlán.

It stood in the centre of modern Mexico City, and was 100 feet high, with a base of 330 by 260 feet. Nearly the whole of its western side consisted of a double staircase with four parapets. On the platform stood two temples, small rectangular buildings, which left a great deal of clear space in the front of the platform. Close to the edge were two low stone altars. The lower end of the parapet was crowned by the stone heads of plumed serpents. In front of the former staircase leading up to the pyramid the stone of Tizoc was found, a huge stone cylinder with a diameter of eight feet, covered with relief work celebrating the conquests of the first Aztec kings.

The excavators found a big round disc-shaped stone twelve feet in diameter and weighing twenty-four tons. It had once stood on the plinth in front of the little Temple of the Sun in Tenochtitlán. This was the famous Aztec calendar stone, covered all over in bas-relief, and with the sun in its centre. All round the sign '4 mountain', with the face of the Sun-God and the symbols of the four directions, were the signs for the twenty Aztec day-names.

Gradually excavations started outside the capital as well, and in many places buildings were brought to light that were better preserved because they had not been touched by wars and destruction: these included the pyramids of Teopanzolco and of Cuernavaca, and the temple of Tepoztlan, on the edge of a volcano crater. Between 1944 and 1948 a temple was found under the forecourt of the Franciscan collegiate of Santa Cruz. At Calixtlahuaca and Huexotla round buildings were unearthed, at Tizatlan the palace of the princes of Tlaxcala and also a temple with superstructure, terraces and sculptures hewn out of the rock.

These miraculous finds produced an entirely new picture of the Indian world, which obviously could no longer be considered barbarian. The buildings reflect the Aztecs' mode of living, harsh and energetic in action, governed by an iron discipline. The art retrieved by the spade was sometimes horrifyingly savage, although the animal sculptures are realistic enough—for instance, the lying jaguar in the former main temple of Tenochtitlán—and so are the statues of old men, hunchbacks and cripples. Most of the reliefs are abstract, almost symbolic, executed in a clear, severe style yet full of movement, and never stopping at a mere imitation of nature.

When the stone statues representing flag- and torch-bearers, which once crowned the parapet of the steps of Tezcoco, were unearthed, they showed an artistic perfection equalled by very few other works in the ancient world. Rodin himself was overcome with admiration when he stood before them, and said he could never hope to create anything near their quality. They are indeed the stone monument to the Aztec's will to power—a small people which within a few decades rose from modest beginnings to become the ruling nation of Mexico.

But the excavations in Mexico brought to light traces of a people older than the Aztecs.

On the Mesa Central, the area on the northern bank of the former lake of Tezcoco, there was an old hill called Tenayuca, overgrown with cacti and bushes, its foot surrounded by several mounds of rubble. Archaeologists arrived in 1925 and started digging here to find what might be hidden under this hill. After three years of hard work they had wrested from it an unsuspected secret: a great pyramid. The pyramid had originally been over sixty feet high, with a base measuring 200 by 165 feet. Two flights of steps led up to a platform with two temples standing on it. At the foot of the steps stone images of snakes were dug up. In all, 138 huge turquoise snakes jutted from the plinth, coiling in front of low altars; they looked completely lifelike.

But this was only part of the hill's secret. When the large pyramid was dug clear, the excavators found a second, smaller, one inside it: the big pyramid had been built round the older one like a cloak. Under the second a third pyramid emerged, under the third a fourth, under the fourth a fifth. In each case the younger and larger pyramid shielded the next-smaller and older one. The building of the youngest and largest could be dated by other finds: 1507, a few years before the Spaniards came to Mexico.

As it turned out, the builders of these 'mantle pyramids' of Tenayuca were not the Aztecs but the Chichemecs, who for over 250 years ruled the Mesa Central during the period between the fall of the Toltecs and the beginning of the Aztec empire. They had been mentioned by old chronicles, but till now accounts of them had been treated as pure legend. All details about these and other pyramids were systematically compiled and compared with the chroniclers' accounts; another such pyramid was the gigantic one at Cholula, which the Mexican poet Fernando Benitez described in his book on the *Traces of Hernando Cortez*.

For Benitez the Cholula pyramid had the hidden task of 'giving symbolic expression to the holy acts of nature. The builders ... imitated a volcano. They erected a small temple. This was the tribe's first expression of power. This ... was soon covered by a pyramid, which was not erected beside the temple but on top of it, after it had been covered with earth. Layers of ashes and rubble were added to the new building ... as if after a volcano's eruption. ... The architect then designed a new pyramid within the holy precincts. ... It was simple and a little rough; two friezes with a bold volcanic motif crown the terraces. The years went by, and Cholula became the Mecca of Anahuac. ... Grave-diggers came, carrying countless mud bricks on their shoulders to overlay the building. Their steps, terraces and shining frescoes were carefully covered so as never again to see the light of the sun. On this mummy-like pyramid a new one was built, pure and graceful, like a baroque Popocatepetl, flanked by innumerable steps. ...'

Cholula, once destroyed by the Spaniards, has become a quiet, dreamy little country town, with 350 churches where once there were 400 Indian temples. Above the giant pyramid stands the baroque church of the Santa Virgen des los Remedios, on a hill with steeply rising sides, covered by undergrowth.

One day the excavators arrived here too, dug into the slopes in several places, and at length declared that the church would unfortunately have to be pulled down, since underneath it there was a monument of Mexican history more valuable than any church. The news spread like wild-fire, and the peasants of Cholula were filled with dismay. The church fathers were equally horrified at the sinful plan, and were successful in their appeal against it: the excavators were not given permission to destroy the church. 'The open struggle between the Indian and Spanish gods which has been blazing for centuries', wrote Benitez, 'has reached a new stage with the discovery and resurrection of the pyramid. The Indians' descendants have shot at the guards of the archaeological zone, in fear lest the Catholic temple on top might collapse. . . .'

Frustrated in their original idea, the excavators dug one tunnel into the mountain beneath the church, then more tunnels, and then built galleries connecting the tunnels with one another. Today there is a network of four miles of tunnel crossing the mountain beneath the church. This infinitely laborious and wearisome burrowing laid bare the old pyramid, an immense edifice built from adobes, those unburnt bricks which are called Nile bricks in Egypt because they are made from Nile mud. First they were shaped from mud, and then left to dry in the sun. Over this kernel of abobes the Cholula pyramid had once carried a mantle of stone.

It is a most wonderful experience to descend from Cholula's scorching sun into the cool and silence of the tunnel, now lit by thousands of lamps, with the tall, well-nigh endless passage in front of you, and above you the millions of cubic feet of earth from which once the great pyramid was erected in the White God's honour.

Exciting discoveries were also made in Peru, and one of the excavators, Hiram Bingham, even discovered the City of Faith, Vitcos (or Machu Picchu). For years the Spaniards had scoured every crevasse of the Cordilleras they could get to, but the vast range defeated them and they failed to find Vitcos. Others after them were equally unsuccessful, though there were many expeditions to the Andes in the next centuries.

Then in 1911 a party of explorers, including Bingham, went riding through the remote valleys of the Andes during a scorchingly hot summer. They had been travelling for weeks and had more or less given up hope of finding the lost city. One day in the Urubamba Valley, when the rest of the party had gone swimming, Bingham set off with one Indian along a steep path overgrown with bushes and trees. Panting and sweating, they cleared the path yard by yard with the machete. The peak rose 2,000 feet above the valley, and was 8,000 feet above sea level. Near the top, in the misty clouds hugging the peak, Bingham hit on a wall, hidden under thick bush, which made him forget all about his sweat and the heat. The machete struck, and out of the jungle more walls and steps appeared.

He climbed higher and suddenly saw a vision before him: there lay the ruins, huge pieces of rock built on colossal foundations. There were two temples, both open on one side, while the other sides were formed by walls rising to between nine and thirteen feet. The walls had trapezoid niches built into them, with palms growing out of the niches. The stones had been piled on top of one another, the joins hardly visible, and one of the high walls had three particularly well-made windows.

At the Inca's birthplace—so Manco, the first Inca, had said—a wall stood with three big windows. Was this the place, here where the dynasty had perished with the last Inca, long after the Spaniards had occupied Peru? Were these the three windows in the house the Inca was supposed to have come from?

Three thousand steps led up to the huge block of buildings on the summit with walls round it rising in the form of terraces. There, on the top platform, overlooking the precipice, stood a stone which 'measured the sun'—the house of the altar with the sun-dial, an obelisk carved from the rock, pointing to Heaven like a stone finger. Aqueducts led from one terrace to the next, and there were two-storey buildings among the humble people's plain dwellings. Next to the town of ruins, rock cliffs rose steeply with a sheer drop on their other side into the surrounding gorge. The 'City of Faith' which Bingham found in the Andes mountains was more fantastic than any legend.

After the first major finds it was generally believed that the soil had yielded all its important treasures. The finds confirmed the accounts of the old chronicles, and for nearly a century the misconception prevailed that the New World's only two high civilizations were those of the Aztecs and the Incas. Stories of other perished civilizations were thought to be pure legend.

But then it transpired that, historically, Aztec civilization was only a short, insignificant phase, and that there was still a mass of evidence testifying to much earlier civilizations—remains of huge buildings, temples and palaces. There were some civilizations so old that even the chroniclers did not know about them. And the new finds also testified to the mysterious White God.

PART THREE

The Civilizations of the White God

8

The Mayan Empire

AFTER the conquest of Mexico, Cortés ruled the country like a viceroy, marking out its borders, distributing the booty of gold and women, living himself on a sumptuous scale. But soon he had to launch an expedition to what is now Honduras, because Christoval de Olid, one of his captains, who had been sent to plant a colony there, had turned rebel. After subduing de Olid, Cortés returned a year later, learning of misrule and anarchy in Mexico during his absence.

The expedition to Honduras led him through extremely difficult country, and his men suffered great hardships once more. 'The overhanging foliage threw so deep a shade', he wrote, 'that the soldiers could not see where to set their feet.' And one of the men with him reported on the virgin forest of Yucatan: 'This climate eats up a man's powers and kills the women during their first confinement. The oxen lose their flesh, the cows their milk, and the hens stop laying eggs.'

On their drive across the peninsula of Yucatan (as it is known today) and through the jungles of Guatemala and Honduras, the Spaniards came across the traces of an ancient people. It was the wildest country they had ever crossed, which made it hard for them to think any degree or kind of civilization could have existed there; especially as the inhabitants of the country were no more civilized than the other peoples of Mexico. When the chroniclers asserted that these were the last miserable remnant of a great empire of millions of people—which had existed for over 1,500 years and was more than 1,000 years older than the Aztec empire—they were not believed. Although they based their accounts on what Cortés and his men had seen and heard, the accounts seemed too fantastic to be true.

In 1785, to the sound of drums and trumpets, a troop of mercenaries

of the Spanish army, under a mounted artillery captain, Antonio del
Rio, hacked into the jungle of Chiapas. Captain del Rio had orders
to find and survey the ruins of Palenque, a place entirely unknown to
him. Calderon had discovered the city's ruins a few years earlier, but
his account of them had passed almost unnoticed.

After many days, exhausted and badly stung by the mosquitoes,
del Rio and his men at last found the ruins, but they had been so
completely swallowed up by the tangle of trees and jungle plants that
for the moment a survey was impossible. Determined to carry out his
orders, he had the men bore holes into the gigantic tree-trunks, then
fill the holes with powder and blow up the virgin forest. He brought
back information and sketches, and a few finds from the jungle, and
these fell into the hands of Jean Frédéric Waldeck, former adventurer
and mercenary. When Napoleon made his famous speech by the
Egyptian pyramids, about the forty centuries looking down on his
soldiers, Waldeck was with him. After his overthrow, Waldeck went
over to the eccentric Lord Cochrane, under whose command he
fought for Chile's independence.

At sixty-six he came to Yucatan and took up archaeology. He was
proud of a talent for drawing, and found scope for this at Palenque;
he stayed there for two years, and later published blue-prints and
drawings of the old buildings, the stelae, the reliefs. He drew stelae
in the neo-classical style of his time. He 'improved' so much, that is,
that little remained of their real character: the mass of drawings he
left behind when he died in 1875 were thus an unwitting falsification
of Mayan art. Palenque was not properly rediscovered till the days of
modern archaeology, which has brought to light eighteen temples and
twenty other buildings, vast rooms let into the earth, with stone altars
and temples.

Today the wonderful temples again rise above the tree-tops, the
jungle behind them like a protecting wall; Palenque is a large island
in the midst of the immense forest. When the great temples and pyramids were built here, about A.D. 650, Mohammed had just died and the
Arabs started on their victorious march through North Africa and the
Middle East. There was nothing in Europe north of the Alps even
remotely comparable to the Mayan buildings and reliefs.

In the 1830's, a little before Waldeck published his book *Voyage
pittoresque et archéologique de la province de Yucatan pendant 1834–36*,
a certain Colonel Garlindo was commissioned by the government of
the little state of Guatemala to write a report on conditions in the
country. He remembered that one of the chroniclers, writing in about
1700, had told of a mass of ruins in the jungle of Yucatan, near the

Façade from Cambodia, with half-pillars

Mayan temple of Xlapac

Building features from South East Asia are often to be found in Mayan architecture and even extend to complete agreement in details

Step pyramids as at Sakkara, Egypt, are to be found everywhere in the Indian kingdoms

The architecture of the Mayan temple of Kabah is also reminiscent of the overloaded magnificence of an (Asian) Indian temple

river Copán and the village of that name, which Indians insisted they had seen with their own eyes. Garlindo heard other stories of ruins in this jungle, and he put into the report all he could find out about them from the Indians.

The report was read by a young man called John Lloyd Stephens, then United States consul in Guatemala, who was a keen student of ancient times, had travelled extensively in the Near and Middle East, and written two books about his experiences. He was determined to see for himself how much truth there was in the accounts of the ruins. In 1839 he set out on his quest, accompanied by a friend called Catherwood, a scholar of the Egyptian civilizations and a fine draftsman, and a few Indians. They rode through jungle and swamps, their path blocked by holly and creepers, with millions of mosquitoes buzzing round them. Oppressed by the damp heat, parched with thirst, covered with mud, their hands and faces swollen, they plodded on towards where the village of Copán must lie. It seemed incredible that a prosperous city could once have existed in this murderous country.

They found the village, a small settlement with a few miserable Indian huts. When they asked after the great ruins, even the oldest among the Indians shook their heads blankly, and the two most enterprising youths of the small community, who had explored the jungle for miles around, said they had never come across a trace of ruins. But Stephens was undeterred; he and his companions left the village and rode on into the jungle.

They were not very far from the village when they saw a big stone gleaming through the tangle of dark green foliage. With their machetes they cut a way to the stone, and soon it rose before them: a tall, narrow stone, covered all over with ornaments—like jungle literally petrified with all its creepers and plants; in the centre the figure of a man was carved out almost in the round.

They struggled deeper into the jungle and found a second stone, a third, a fourth. Altogether they found fourteen, all with the same kind of luxuriant ornament, more splendid, said Stephens, than even the most beautiful monuments of the Egyptians. The huge stones were many feet high, and in some cases the stone was hanging at an angle in the roots of a tree; as the tree grew, it had lifted the stone. The explorers began felling the trees and making clearings.

Suddenly a half-caste came running from the village. 'Hey,' he shouted at them, 'I am the owner of this piece of land, and you are damaging it.' Gesticulating wildly, he presented his documents, and followed them about, protesting with more and more vehemence. In the end Stephens was driven to put on his ceremonial uniform as United States consul—wearing it over a dirty woollen shirt without

F

collar or tie, and with mud-encrusted boots. But he received the half-caste, whose name was Don José Maria, with the dignity of a diplomat, and showed him his credentials. Impressed by the brilliance of the uniform, Don José agreed to the bargain Stephens proposed and sold his whole forest for fifty dollars. When he held the purchase money in his hand he danced for joy, as wildly as he had shouted before: this gringo must be mad to give him fifty dollars for a small piece of jungle. Then villagers of Copán arrived to look at the mad strangers and drink to the bargain struck.

They could not appreciate why Stephens was equally delighted: for fifty dollars he had bought a new world, a world of which no one before had had any inkling. He penetrated deeper and deeper into the jungle, found steps and walls, and hit on a pyramid, which he cut clear with his machete yard by yard. When he had mounted the uppermost steps, he was standing high over the tree-tops, on a big platform 100 feet above the hot, swampy ground.

Below stood Catherwood, trying to put down on the drawing-paper what he saw. Experienced artist as he was, Catherwood could not at first do justice to the strange exuberance of the forms and ornaments, the curious shapes. He kept on tearing the sheets off the easel after only a few strokes, screwing up the paper and throwing it on the ground. But in a few days he was sketching stele after stele, and the remains of the old buildings—wonderful first portrayals of an ancient civilization.

Stephens did not excavate in the wilds of this jungle. He rode on to Guatemala, to Chiapas and Yucatan, and came upon more and more evidence of the Mayan civilization. The evidence confirmed the first extensive reports of it in Waldeck's book, which had, however, made little impact. But Stephens's book, published in 1842 with Catherwood's sketches, aroused world-wide interest, and gradually one marvel of Mayan art after another was reclaimed from the jungle.

Future archaeologists also owed much to Teobert Maler, a German who had originally come to Mexico with the short-lived Emperor Maximilian: Maler wandered for years through the Yucatan jungle, accompanied only by Indians; he collected everything he could find and left a vast quantity of illuminating photographs. But meanwhile a new source of illumination was rediscovered, relating back to the years immediately after the Spanish conquest.

When the flames were devouring all the Mayan illuminated manuscripts, a fanatical young priest stood beside the stakes, fiercely spurring the Indians on to drag along more and more manuscripts. The priest's name was Diego de Landa, and he was later to become bishop of

Yucatan. In his old age he bitterly regretted his former zeal for destruction, and tried to atone by helping save the little that was left of Indian civilization. He had a search made for Indians who still knew their old signs. He got them to explain Mayan writing to him, as well as the many symbols for the days and months. Evening after evening he sat in his study and copied the signs, adding explanations whenever he could.

He asked high-placed Mayans to help him in his work, and even made friends with them, especially with a former tribal chief, King Cocom, an intelligent, cultivated, and highly reputed man. These two sat together in the bishop's study, poring over some of the books which had escaped destruction, and Cocom described the ancient lore of his people, as far as his knowledge of Spanish allowed.

A Mayan high priest's son gave further information about the Indians' history and civilization, and from all this the bishop compiled his book *Relacion de las cosas de Yucatan*. He also drew up an alphabet of the Mayan language, but this has remained more of a riddle to scholars than a help, owing to the misunderstandings which arose from language difficulties: the Indians spoke very little Spanish, and he knew practically nothing of their language. But it was a great deal that he managed to glean the symbols the Indians had used for their days and months, and to note these down. Without his work the symbols would still be meaningless signs to us, and we could not put dates to the Mayan buildings from their inscriptions. As it was, his manuscript was lost for three centuries, to be rediscovered by a lucky accident.

In the middle of the last century a young man called Etienne Brasseur de Bourbourg, after working in the Spanish colonial service, had become a priest and teacher in an Indian village in Guatemala. Back in Madrid, he took a book out of a library one day, and when thumbing through it came across a good many loose leaves which interested him greatly. He returned the book, but not the loose leaves; they turned out to be a copy of Bishop de Landa's manuscript, and the key to Mayan script.

De Bourbourg was always ferreting things out, and he made some other lucky finds. For instance, at a Mexican mart, where old books were being sold by the pound, he happened to come across the manuscript of what is still the most comprehensive Mayan-Spanish dictionary we know today. He bought it for as little as four pesos. He wrote an account of de Landa's work and explanations of the Mayan glyphs. But only a few specialists read this account and hardly anyone else heard about it, for the time of the great discoveries was supposed to be over. Nothing notable in the New World, in fact, was found between

1850 and 1880, and for a long while nothing more was published about the Maya.

The revival of interest was almost entirely due to an English scholar, Alfred Maudslay, who read up all the accounts from Central America, and was fascinated by John Stephens's travel book with its descriptions of the buildings, temples, palaces and works to be found

4. Page from de Landa's manuscript with the Mayan alphabet

in the jungle: they sounded too fantastic to be true. Although Stephens had included Catherwood's drawings in his work, he had not brought back a single find from the alleged ancient Indian cities. For Maudslay the drawings were not proof, but he felt there must be some fire behind such a mass of smoke, and he determined to find out the truth for himself. He travelled over to Central America, followed Stephens's route through the jungle, and found that Stephens's descriptions were in no way exaggerated.

Inspired by the magnificence of what he had seen, the scholar turned explorer, and visited Central America a second time, having

The 'House of the Magician', as the Indians today call the pyramid of the White God Kukulcan at Uxmal. It was the burial-place of the Mayan kings

*Arch construction in the Old World
on the principle of the 'false arch'*

Left: Delos.   *Right:* Monte Alban

Grave No. 7 from Monte Alban, Oax
where the great find of gold ornam
was made

Casemate from Tiryns

planned an undertaking new and unprecedented in the infant science of archaeology. An extremely curious column filed through the jungle: the Englishman was followed by hundreds of Indians, some laden with sacks filled to capacity and others dragging along bales of old newspapers. Centuries before, the Spaniards had come the other way, from the Indian cities to the coast, and *they* were laden with gold. There was no gold in Maudslay's sacks, but simply plaster, by the ton, so that he could take casts of everything too heavy for transport; and he needed the old newspapers for paper pulp from which he intended to take moulds. The finds were immense, filling the sacks which had formerly held plaster. The Indians rigged up litters from branches of trees, and carried these back on their shoulders with the large, heavy fragments of their own ancient civilization.

Five times more Maudslay went into the jungle, and he was in Central America seven times in fourteen years, from 1881 to 1894. He was knighted for his magnificent achievements, and infected the British with enthusiasm for archaeology; his expeditions into the jungle were financed by generous support, both public and private. The British Museum now houses the famous Maudslay Collection, archaeological finds and documents from Yucatan, the most comprehensive collection of objects from a foreign civilization ever brought back to Europe by one man. Maudslay also wrote four volumes of explanatory notes under the title *Biologia Centralii Americani*, which were published around the turn of the century.

The scholars pounced on all this material: now they could begin to study the ancient civilization. But soon they faced a baffling puzzle. Every ornament, relief or sculpture, every frieze on the temples, was covered with symbols, distributed at random all over each surface. They were repeated again and again, often whole rows of them, stone faces of men and animals, odd designs, distorted faces and demons; and then came entirely different symbols, quite unconnected with the others and without any apparent system to their occurrence.

Then somebody found de Bourbourg's work, and attention was drawn to Bishop de Landa's old drawings, the Mayan symbols for the months and days. When scholars at last came to study these, they discovered that the symbols tallied with those on all the sculptures in the temples and with the grotesque designs of the ornaments. The mystery was solved: it emerged that every ornament and fresco bore a date, and so did every building; not only the buildings but every staircase and parapet. Number of steps, height, direction, all these indicated a mathematical concept, a date.

The temple of the White God Kukulcan at Chichen Itza, for instance, was built in nine steps which together reach a height of eighty feet, and its four stairways add up to 365 stairs altogether. The temple was thus a symbolic representation of the nine heavens and of the number of days in a year. When an ornament was repeated ten times running or more, when a flight consisted of seventy-five steps, when a pyramid reached a certain height, it was no accident but a mathematical statement. The whole of Mayan art was mathematics, literally petrified, turned to stone. Mathematics, the science of their priests, was entirely in the service of their cult—a cult of the calendar.

The Maya built whenever their calendar demanded it. Every fifty-two years throughout the centuries they put a new stone mantle round their old buildings without removing the one underneath. These calendar mantles can be traced back for hundreds of years, and for hundreds of years the priests must have continually pressed the people into merciless slave labour, so as to build anew, and bigger every time —simply at the bidding of the calendar. The priests were obsessed with chronology.

Research into the Mayan calendar is still going on. It is a highly complicated system, which counted a 'ceremonial year' of 260 days and a solar year (like ours) of 365 days; the latter was made up of eighteen months each of twenty days, with another five days which were more or less 'bank holidays'. The least common multiple of 365 and 260 produced the sacred period of fifty-two years, which was taken over by other Central American peoples and became the keystone of Aztec chronology.

The Aztec priests, who were expert astronomers, observed the stars with particular care when a fifty-two-year period was ending. During the last night of the period the constellation of the Pleiades reached its highest point, and fires were lit over the bodies of the sacrificial victims. It was the time of the ceremonies of the New Fire, when the belt of the heavens (the zodiac) showed a particular position of the stars on the celestial equator, a time when comets and meteors would portend imminent calamity. There were many such portents at the end of the period which coincided with the Spaniards' arrival.

According to the old chronicles, the end of a period was also a festival to celebrate with great exuberance: everyone in the Aztec empire was obliged to pile up all the crockery they could lay hands on and smash it. The Indians must have had a wonderful time giving vent to their feelings, for otherwise they were probably not allowed to let themselves go very often. Fortunately they did not smash everything to smithereens, but left quite a few useful bits from their everyday life. When the excavators discovered these mounds of rubble, Indian rubbish-heaps, there were not only tiny fragments and splinters but plenty of large fragments which could easily be stuck together into their previous shapes of magnificent plates, bowls and vases.

The revival of archaeological interest which Maudslay's work helped to bring about in England was very vigorous in the United States as well. Large museums and scientific societies decided to follow up the traces of the Maya. Between 1892 and 1915 the Peabody Museum of Archaeology at Harvard sponsored twenty expeditions into the territory where the Maya had once lived. From 1951 to 1958 the Carnegie Institute at Washington financed excavations at Uaxactun, Chichen Itza, Kaminaljuyu, and Mayapan. The archaeologists divided up the ruins, and dug only in groups within their allotted squares of jungle. They scraped, measured, made notes, consulted geologists, analytical chemists, draftsmen, photographers. They collected and classified, fitting one tiny fragment to the next, till they had gained a fairly complete picture of the ancient Mayan civilization.

Stephens and Catherwood had found the city of Copán. Its ruins lie 130 feet above the river Copán. The 'Acropolis' is right by the steep slope down to the river, with pyramids, terraces, temples, large squares and courtyards, a town covering twelve acres. A stairway leading up from one of the courtyards is thirty-three feet wide and has sixty-two steps. The front of each step carries a relief, and this one stairway alone contains between 1,500 and 2,000 of the Mayan hiero-glyphic carvings.

The excavators discovered twenty-six Mayan temples and dozens of large stelae, in just a single city. There were nearly a hundred Mayan cities. Ten new ones were built between 435 and 534 A.D., another ten between 534 and 633, and as many as fourteen in the middle period of the Old Empire, between 633 and 731. Dozens of these cities have today been reclaimed from the jungle. As with Copán, their discovery and exploration, and the sifting of remains there, was often a laborious process. Only one of them, Tulum, was almost intact when the archaeologists came to work there in 1916. Most of the buildings were still standing, and when these had been repaired they had a fair impression of a Mayan city as it had once been.

They had a special historical interest in Tulum, for a white man had lived there, as slave of the Maya, fifteen years before Cortés discovered Mexico. This Spaniard, Geronimo Aguilar, together with some sailors and two women, had been stranded on the coast of Yucatan in 1511. Some of these shipwrecked people soon died of starvation or fever, the others fell into the hands of the Maya. Aguilar had to watch the Indians sacrificing five of his comrades to one of their gods: they cut the men's hearts out of their bodies, then ate the bodies at a solemn meal. He was too thin for them, and they put him in a cage to fatten him up. But he succeeded in escaping, and was taken into another Mayan tribe as a prisoner and slave. He adopted the tribe's way of life, but when the Spaniards came into the country he found a way to get to them and became Cortés's interpreter.

The things Aguilar could have reported about the Maya! Unfortunately he did not leave a line behind, although he was a Catholic priest who had studied theology at Spanish universities.

The stele, or carved column, which the archaeologists repeatedly came across in the ancient Mayan cities was a special sort of artifact. Hundreds of stelae have been discovered, from the simplest shape with the merest hint of bas-relief, up to stelae with their ornaments carved almost like a sculpture. The Maya were a people of the stele, as Western civilization is a civilization of the stele. Our stelae are the gravestones in the cemeteries! We have taken these over from the Greeks, and stele is itself a Greek word meaning stone, or specifically gravestone.

We can follow the stele's course throughout the civilizations of our own world, from Mesopotamia across the Nile into Greece. The falcon stele of the Egyptian king Venephes-Ezoyetis is 5,000 years old. But these old stelae were not tombstones. Their purpose was to record in stone great events and names, laws, lists of kings, accounts of victories —like the law stele of Hammurabi, the Rosetta stone from the Nile, and the tablets of the Ten Commandments.

The Mayan stelae served the same purpose; they were to remind present and future generations of great events and especially of calendar festivals. But other ancient peoples of Central America besides the Maya knew of these stones: the Olmecs, oldest people in that whole area, were already masters of the craft. The stele passed from one people to another; just as it did in the Old World, where the Egyptians took it over from the Mesopotamians, the Greeks from the Egyptians, Rome from the Greeks, and all younger civilizations from the Romans. In the course of several millennia it has apparently followed a direct path through all civilizations. The only bridge missing is how it passed from Old World to New.

The oldest Mayan city to be excavated was Uaxactun, where the first Mayan observatory was found, and also the oldest Mayan fresco. The American archaeologist William Ricketson, Jr., dug here for twelve years under the auspices of the Carnegie Institute. More than a dozen old temples emerged from the mounds of rubble; when the excavators measured and investigated them they were all almost exactly alike.

During a walk one day through the old temple town Ricketson stopped, as he had often done before, in front of the pyramid marked on his plan as E VII. This time he noticed something white and gleaming behind a crack in the wall. Putting his cane into the crack, he scraped off a bit of the white stuff, which was powdery in texture. He had it analysed, and was told it could be nothing but bits of stucco.

This was something so astonishing that he made a most unorthodox decision for a modern archaeologist: he had the old pyramid pulled down to find out what was underneath. In doing so he added considerably to our knowledge of the Mayan civilization; for what came to light was a perfectly preserved little temple, the oldest Mayan building so far discovered, and notably different from all previous finds. The excavators saw a small snow-white pyramid with a large low platform, and all its sides and steps entirely covered in stucco.

The architecture and art point to a very early stage in Mayan civilization. The human figures are clumsily carved, and look coarse and lifeless, in an attitude which is anatomically impossible. Heads are always shown in profile, body and arms frontally, legs and feet again in side-view, with the toes of the left foot touching the heel of the right. (Human figures in the ancient Egyptian reliefs are shown in exactly the same attitude.) The workmanship suggests the first beginning of stone treatment, the primitive attempts of people who were obviously working stone for the first time. This, however, contrasts with the treatment of the stucco, which is rather advanced.

But, of course, it is the use of stucco itself which is so strange a find. For stucco is not a 'natural' raw material ready to be used for building, but an artificial product based on two 'inventions'. It is roughly what we call mortar, i.e. a mixture of sand and lime, and to make it you have to know two things: how to get lime by heating limestone, and how to harden the mixture of lime and sand by exposing it to air. These procedures were already as familiar to the oldest Maya as to the ancient civilizations of the Old World.

Quite near Uaxactun was the city of Tikal. Archaeologists hacked a path through the jungle, made a clearing, and burnt down trees and plants, to be faced by colossal mounds of rubble and immense buildings, including five of the steepest pyramids that had ever been seen. Their bases were small, but they looked fantastically tall. The tallest measured 230 feet, equivalent to a twenty-five-storey house. The temple stood at the very top, towering high above the jungle. A single flight of steps outside, steep as a ladder, led up to the dizzy height. (Very similar towering narrow pyramids were found in the ancient Far Eastern city of Angkor Vat.)

Mayan art reached its highest point in the cities of Yaxchilan,

Palenque, and Piedras Negras. In the first of these it flourished from
A.D. 692 to 726—the time of Carlovingian rule, of Charles Martel,
and the Muslim conquest of Spain. Four great pyramids were unearthed here, with door monoliths which are among the finest of
Mayan sculptures. A large mural relief of warm, ivory-coloured sand-
stone, found in Piedras Negras, has a marvellous beauty, harmony,
balance, and craftsmanship; it is perhaps the most perfect single
Mayan work of art we know.

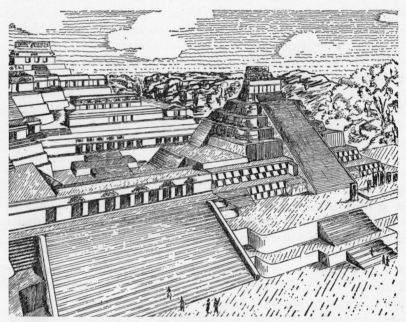

5. Piedras Negras with its broad terraces signifies a high point of Mayan
art (from Tatiana Proskouriakoff)

In 1947 crowds of workmen slashed their way through the jungle
of Bonampak, felling the trees and burning down the dense undergrowth. At length they cleared fragments and scraped rubble off the
ruins of splendid old temples and pyramids. Eleven pyramids and
three stelae, one of them twenty feet tall, were reclaimed from the
forest. Here the archaeologists discovered friezes from the classic
period of the Maya, with an artistic perfection surpassing almost all
previous finds.

In order to have a good background to work on, the old painters
had plastered over the walls. The sand of the lowest layers of this cast
was found to be coarse, but in the upper ones it grew finer, while that

of the top layer was almost as smooth as flour. The same technique can be traced in the friezes of Tiryns and Knossos.

Dzibilchaltun, so tradition has it, was a great and rich city suddenly submerged when the big lake of Boca Paila formed (in the district of Peine). The buildings on the lake's bottom were sighted and photographed from planes, and attempts to raise them are now being made, with the help of divers and frogmen.

In 1950 Ruz Lhullier was excavating at Palenque, on the platform of the Temple of Inscriptions. Suddenly he noticed a pit leading down from the middle of the platform. After clearing it he was able to descend deeper and deeper into it, and eventually found a staircase which led still farther down. On reaching what he took to be the base of the pyramid, he came upon a heavy stone door. This gave on to a sepulchral vault, nearly filled by a heavy sarcophagus, which was covered by a huge slab decorated with wonderful reliefs. The slab was much too heavy to be shifted without mechanical aid.

In Egypt, a quarter of a century earlier, Howard Carter had faced a similar problem on discovering the tomb of Tutankhamen in the Valley of the Kings: the monumental sarcophagus there was sealed by a twelve-hundredweight slab, which had to be laboriously lifted by means of ropes and pulleys. Now Lhullier had to turn engineer; and the archaeologists worked for days rigging up supports for their ropes and pulleys. At last the rope tightened and the great lid slowly rose. Breathless with excitement, they hauled in the rope by fractions of an inch. When the slab had lifted far enough to allow a first glance into the splendid sarcophagus, they saw something unprecedented: human remains, surely those of a great ruler of the Maya.

When the slab was off, the archaeologists were deeply moved. Slowly they climbed the steps, and stood, silent and awe-struck, on the platform of the pyramid which had now yielded its greatest secret. Then science reasserted itself, as they began measuring and photographing every detail of the crypt and recording it. Few places can have been so thoroughly and meticulously explored as this mysterious tomb beneath the pyramid of Palenque. New miracles of Mayan art came to light here after a sleep of over a thousand years: the stucco masks, the death-masks of the tomb, the reliefs, the many kinds of funeral offerings. Also the question began to be asked whether the New World pyramids, instead of being an invention of the Indians, might not somehow be connected with ancient Egypt, whose Pharaohs were also buried under pyramids.

As the scientific exploration of Palenque proceeded there were other surprises. Pictures of a large cross were found on a wall of one

of the temples—which was therefore named 'Temple of the Cross'.
These pictures tally almost exactly with the ones of the Tree of
Heaven from Java, which also show a demon's face between the
beams of a cross.

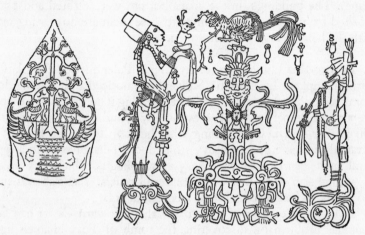

6. The Tree of Heaven from Java (*right*) and Palenque (*left*)

The frieze on the Temple of the Cross shows a reptilian monster
with a human face, and it also shows two-headed snakes held by human
arms, with human faces gaping out of the snakes' open jaws. Monsters,
dragons, hybrid-gods are common in Far Eastern art—such as the
dragons of China or the tiger with ram's horns from Chinese masks
around 1250 B.C. The Mayan fire-snake found at Palenque is very like
the mythical sea-monster of South-East Asia, with a fish's body but
paws and toes and an elephant's trunk; often shown holding human
figures in its jaws. Porches with figures of monsters, lotus walls, and
the cross-shaped 'holy arch' were discovered in Palenque's temples,
just as in the temples of Cambodia, where the holy arch was particularly common from the eighth to the tenth century A.D.

Surprisingly enough, there was another feature of civilization
introduced from the Far East: the calendar. The exact length of the
astronomical year is 365.242,198 days, and since 2772 B.C. (as will be
seen from the table) many attempts have been made to distribute this
without remainder into the days and months of the calendar year.
But there is still a difference between astronomical and calendar year,
and despite improvements with the centuries we have always had to
make occasional intercalations when the difference becomes too great;
whereas the Mayan calendar year tallied with the astronomical one to
such a degree that there was scarcely any remainder. To predict visible

Under the 'Temple of Inscriptions' at Palenque a secret passage was
found leading down to a burial chamber

This burial chamber had a beautifully worked stone floor. Taking very great care, the archaeologist A. Ruz-Lhullier succeeded in removing it undamaged

Were the human remains here those of the White God?

eclipses of the sun, the Maya used a table covering 11,960.000 days
and then starting again; modern astronomy has worked the figure out
at 11,959.888.

Comparing the Mayan with other calendars, the scholars found
that the Mayan reckoning of time must originally have come from the
Far East, for it had its exact counterpart in China, Siam and Java.
In these countries too the calendars worked through two periods of
different length, and also some of the signs of the Zodiac coincided
at the same point in the period. The presumption is that Buddhist
monks must at one time have passed on their calendar to the American
Indians.

THE MOST IMPORTANT CALENDARS

Year of introduction	Country or people	Division of the year	Duration of year in days
2772 B.C.	Egypt	Calendar of 10 months and 365 days	365.000
2500 B.C.	Mesopotamia	Calendar of 360 days	360.000
2025 B.C.	Mesopotamia	Cycle of Moon and Sun of 19 years, 12 with 12 months each, 7 with 13 months each	
1200 B.C.	Babylonia	Sun year with 12 months and 12 signs of the Zodiac	
1200 B.C.	Judaea	Moon year of 345 days with irregular inter-calations of varying length	345.000
715–672 B.C.	Rome	Numa Pompilius introduces Moon calendar with 355 days, 12 months and intercalations of varying length	355.000
46 B.C.	Rome	Julius Caesar introduces Calendar of the Sun Year, 365 days with intercalary day every four years (still used in Russia, the reason why Russian New Year is 13 days after ours)	365.250

Year of introduction	*Country or people*	*Division of the year*	*Duration of year in days*
A.D. 1582	Rome	Pope Gregory reforms Julian Calendar, and establishes the one valid today	365.242,400
App. A.D. 300	Maya	18 months with 20 days each plus 5 blank days	365.242,129
		Exact length of astronomical year	365.242,198

The scholars also proved, however, that in the very early days of their civilization the Maya used a different calendar again, one which had twelve months with thirty days each. This means, broadly speaking, that they used the old calendar from the Near East long before they took over the Far Eastern one. The Incas too used this calendar, which also had twelve months but in other respects differs considerably from that of the Central American Indians.

The Incas' astronomical knowledge was at least as good as that of the Maya. They certainly knew the Pleiades, the Southern Cross and the Zodiac. They used the old Babylonian Zodiac calendar, as we still know it today. Therefore the calendar of our time was already known to the Indian civilizations before the men from East Asia came to them.

As more and more remains from Mayan times were discovered, it became progressively easier to put dates to them, and a clearer picture of the civilization began to emerge. It showed one very mysterious facet: the quality of the art and architecture did not improve with the centuries, and fewer and fewer new works were found from the later centuries. Finally the archaeologists could state authoritatively that one of their finds was the last of the Mayan works that has come down to us. They dated it A.D. 909.

Now another astonishing fact was established: soon after that date all building activities in the ancient kingdom ceased abruptly and completely; and within a few decades all the cities and temples were suddenly deserted. It looks as if the whole Mayan people migrated *en masse*, leaving behind their prosperous cities, magnificent temples, and all the features of a highly developed civilization.

Many theories have been advanced to explain this singular phenomenon: one is that the soil was impoverished by single-crop cultivation (maize). It is suggested that the priests and 'intelligentsia'—concerned only with gods, the stars, their calendar and their cult—had overlooked material problems of preserving the soil and maintaining food upplies for a large population. Yet these people were practical enough o design magnificent buildings and also roads, the remains of which ure still used as paths today.

Earthquakes, plagues, invasions, civil war or the call of a new religion, have all been put forward as possible reasons for the great migration, but none seems to offer a wholly satisfactory explanation or the abandonment of so many populous centres in such a short period. Perhaps a plague or epidemic, for instance yellow fever, seems he most likely: it could have virtually wiped out the whole people und forced the last survivors to emigrate.

Whatever the cause or causes, the emigrants founded a new empire. While the old cities crumbled, new ones sprang up, often from small beginnings that went back to long before the migration. Here the ancient civilization flourished once more, though it did not remain ourely Mayan. It reached its highest level under the Toltecs, particularly at Chichen Itza; for after about 200 years (at the end of the twelfth century) the Toltecs conquered the New Empire of the Maya und put their unmistakable stamp on it.

The city of Chichen Itza lies in the tropical forest of Yucatan. It s supposed to have been founded as far back as A.D. 534, although the oldest Mayan inscriptions indicate a date not before 879; in any case it existed long before the migration. The immigrants now came to it from the Old Empire as they came to the cities of Kabah, Sayil, and Labna. In some cases, however, they founded cities after their arrival, as the princes of the Xiu tribe did with Uxmal.

When the archaeologists cleared the forest to reveal these cities, they found buildings unmistakably Mayan in their design, but with ornaments very different from those of the Old Empire. The fronts of the buildings were covered over and over with lavish sculptural ornaments in the shape of geometrical patterns; the stones used had been chiselled in advance. The front of the governor's palace at Uxmal, which covers an area of five acres, was pieced together from 20,000 single chiselled stones, like a gigantic mosaic. The fronts were subdivided by smooth white pillars, the walls being columns with quadrangular capitals and three-sided ledges. This style, which scholars named the Puuc style, is preponderant in Uxmal, Kabah, Sayil, and Labna.

Uxmal is not a very big city, but it makes a monumental effect because its buildings are concentrated in a small area; they are still impressive as ruins today. The largest pyramid there is the so-called House of the Magician, which the old chronicles say was erected in honour of the White God.

The second biggest city in the New Empire (after Chichen Itza) was Kabah, in the hilly country of Yucatan. Its largest building is the Palace of the Masks, built on a low platform 165 feet long, with ten rooms. The most remarkable thing in the city is a big gate, standing completely on its own, unconnected with any building. Such gates are a very common feature in the New Empire; they are all constructed after the principle of the so-called false arch, i.e. by making two piles of stones slope towards each other. They are exactly like the false arches of Mycenae, while the fronts and pinnacles of the Indian buildings—e.g. the 'convents' of Uxmal and Copán, the palaces of Sayil and Piedras Negras—also show basic resemblances to Mycenaean building.

But the general building style is even more like the style we know from the Far East at about this period. The doors and windows might be the work of a builder in Indo-China. Half-columns flanking the doors and used as wall decorations, and the ornaments of the façades, are as typical for the Mayan Puuc style as for the buildings of Cambodia in the tenth century A.D.

We know today what these ancient Mayan cities looked like, when they were built, and how long they flourished. From these facts we can produce a brief outline of Mayan history:

THE OLD EMPIRE

Our time reckoning.

A.D. 320–633	First period, with cities of Tikal, Uaxactun, Copán, Palenque.
633–731	Middle period, with cities of Naranja, Piedras Negras, Menché.
731–987	Great period, with cities of Quirigua, Ixkun, Sebal, Flores, Hakun, Tonina, Koba, Benque Viego.

THE NEW EMPIRE

987–1194	Puuc style, cities of Chichen Itza, Uxmal, Kabah, Labna, Sayil, Dzibilnocac, Mayapan, Hochob, Itzamal.
1194–1441	Period of foreign rule by Toltecs at Chichen Itza and Uxmal.
1441–1540	Period of decline and civil war; rapid decay of civilization.

Scholars still disagree as to when Mayan civilization started. The first contemporaneously recorded date of proved authenticity is that

The White God of the Olmecs, probably as rower, shows a quite un-Indian type with heavy growth of beard. This figure, found at La Venta, was first known as 'Wrestler'

The squatting figure of Monte Alban strongly reminiscent of Egyptian figures

The legend of ancient Tula or Tollan turned out to be reality. The archaeologists resurrected the city of the Toltecs. Huge warrior figures stand
near the age-old step pyramid

of A.D. 320, which appears on a jade jewel called the Leyden Plate, discovered at Puertos Barrios in western Guatemala. Next comes the 'stele 9' of Uaxactun, found in group A of the Acropolis ruins, bearing the date of 328—or rather, of course, the equivalent in Mayan reckoning, as with all these date inscriptions.

We can date a Mayan building from its style, and can also place it to some extent. Although the striking features are always the treatment of the stone and the sculptures, bas-reliefs are predominant in northern districts, caryatids and human figures are found more often in Honduras than elsewhere, and in Copán reliefs are so deeply cut into the stone that they almost become three-dimensional sculptures. Even the stelae can be approximately dated by their style, especially those at Copán: from the older ones, which still show a block treatment of the head and very prominent eyes, to the later ones, with their wonderful high reliefs and sculptures.

We know the Mayan empire and its works even better than those of the Aztecs; and we have also learnt that it is the only empire in Central America to last over a thousand years. All the others perished after a few centuries, and they are represented by only a few cities and artifacts, many of them by a single city. The Mayan empire left hundreds of pyramids, hundreds of stelae, and we already know around 120 Mayan cities. Uaxactun, a medium-sized city in the empire, had over 200,000 inhabitants in its heyday, and the population of the empire as a whole probably amounted to nearly eleven million.

9

Tula and Chichen Itza

'Alas, from Tollan, where the temple stood,
And serpent columns still are soaring high,
Our prince Nactitl left for distant lands.'
Lament of the Toltec Prince 'Ten Flower' after the White
God's departure

FRAY BERNARDINO DE SAHAGUN, one of the old chroniclers, described the land of the Toltecs, Tollan, as a paradise, where the corn-cobs reached such a size they could not be carried but had to be rolled along; where the vegetables grew as tall as palm trees, and the cotton grew coloured in the fields. The floors of the palaces were made of precious stones, their walls of coloured stucco and inlaid with turquoises.

The Indian prince (and chronicler) Ixtlilxochitl also told of the great rich city of Tula (the same as Tollan), founded in the dim past: of great temples, sun and moon pyramids, script and calendar, and a religion free of barbaric practices; of the legendary Xolotl and the assault by the Chichemecs, who completely destroyed the city.

The chroniclers gave the names of ten Toltec rulers, beginning in A.D. 856, the fifth being the white, bearded Quetzalcoatl, who reigned from 947 to 999 and eventually left his people. Then began the time of wars and human sacrifices, reaching its climax under Huamac, the tenth king, who committed suicide in 1174. After this the people of Tollan left their old city to conquer Cholula from the Olmecs and build themselves new homes in Colhuacan.

When the Spaniards arrived in 1520, they heard only the legend of the great ancient city where a White God was once King. No one knew where the site of Tula had been, and for centuries no one even tried to find it, since even its existence was doubted.

98

Then a young Mexican archaeologist, Jorge R. Acosta, became fascinated by a peculiarly shaped hill north of Mexico City, overgrown with bushes, cacti and agaves. Indians living near this hill called it 'Cerro de Tesoro' (Hill of Treasure), an alluring name which did not need to have any special significance. There were many such hills in the undulating desert country, but Acosta was convinced this one was no natural formation, and he had a hunch it might conceal something. He started digging in 1940, and found underneath it one of the most famous legend-cities of the ancient world: the city of Tula.

He discovered first that the city must at one time have been destroyed by fire (we know today it was in 1168), and there was only a shapeless mass where the main pyramid had once been. It could not be reconstructed.

As excavating continued, a five-storey pyramid was discovered, its base 140 feet long: the temple of the Morning Star, which had once stood on the pyramid's platform. It was a portico building, with a stone altar table in its shrine. The feet of the table were in the shape of small human figures; these 'Atlases', as they are called—human figures bearing a roof or a heavy table top—have been known for a long time in the Old World, including the Far East. The temple is like that of Prinias in Crete, except that it has a relief of striding jaguars, whereas the relief in the Cretan temple shows lions.

Acosta established that Tula was built in 856, when the Toltecs, a nomad tribe from the north-west, migrated to Mexico—so the old chroniclers were right about Tula's existence. Perhaps the other legend was equally true, the legend of the White God who left Tula with part of his people, the tribe of the Itza, went to the southern coast of the Gulf, and came to Yucatan, wearing the feather crown, 'the adornment of the People from the Coast'. In Yucatan he founded a new kingdom, with his capital at Chichen Itza ('at the Well of the Itza'), built after the model of Tula. Afterwards he abandoned Chichen Itza too, and sailed back to the eastern land 'on a raft of serpents'. But when he had gone his second kingdom also fell to pieces.

In 1533, when the Spaniards occupied Chichen Itza, they had their first experience of what the Mayan people were really like, and it took Francisco de Montejo thirteen years to conquer Yucatan. They had found mainly ruins at Chichen Itza and elsewhere; their conquests made the ruins a good deal more extensive. The wars lasted till 1697 before the Spaniards finally managed to overcome Tayasal, the last Mayan city—and at its capture, say the chroniclers, twenty-one large temples were destroyed.

Archaeologists started becoming interested in Chichen Itza about seventy-five years ago, but digging did not start there till 1925 under the American S. G. Morley, backed by the Carnegie Institute in Washington. The excavators soon realized that here were the ruins of what must once have been a very large city.

Film cameras were set up in front of the buildings and many thousands of feet were shot, to record everything still left of the city's former greatness and splendour. The immense ruins might have been the background for a colossal Hollywood epic, but in fact the result was more of a 'documentary' given tremendously lavish resources for its 'production' (by the Carnegie Institute). Morley was the leader of the best-equipped expedition that had ever done exploration work in the ancient Indian kingdoms; and he achieved a sort of archaeological record by working for seventeen years in the same place.

He was the right man for the job. Not having to worry at all about time or expense, he could work with the extreme thoroughness and precision to which he was inclined by training and temperament. He picked up every single stone, dug up one fragment after another, and cleaned everything with a fine paint-brush to make quite sure no damage was done. Most of the buildings have been perfectly reconstructed to what they once were.

The city extends over more than two square miles. One large terrace, which covers forty-five acres, has imposing temples on it, colonnades, a vast court for ball-games, a market square, and other paved grounds. Morris, one of Morley's assistants, spent the whole seventeen years excavating and investigating a single temple, the Temple of the Warriors. This is a pyramid with a base 130 feet square and thirty-five feet tall. The entrance to it on top of the platform is flanked by towering columns shaped like snakes, and in front of the pyramid there is a portico with sixty enormous pillars covered all round with reliefs—there are 320 reliefs on this one building alone. Up to 1,000 pillars go to make up the rest of this block of open halls, each 400 feet long.

A ceaseless throng of tourists, mostly from the United States, comes to Chichen Itza today, and you can walk across the green lawn of the ball court, past the jaguar temple with the little chapel at the back, to the north temple. You can visit the temple of the little wall-panels, the temple of the High Priest, the great pyramid of Kukulcan, and the Caracol, the huge observatory. The largest city of the Mayan world has risen again from the rubble and ruins. Once more the old chroniclers were proved right: when the Toltecs conquered the new Mayan empire, their White God spared Chichen Itza and made it his residence. A proof of this is the Caracol, originally a Mayan observatory, to which the Toltecs made alterations—one of their first building jobs after the conquest. The most impressive of the many observatories in the ancient Indian civilizations, it is a tower with seven narrow slits in its top storey for measuring the solstices and equinoxes. Here, as in all these civilizations, instruments have been found which testify to a high degree of astrological knowledge.

The White God had enough political wisdom to leave the Maya their gods and allow their priests to continue their cults—of Itzamna, their highest god (at Itzamal, his seat); the sun-god Kakmo; the moon-goddess Ixchel (on the island of Cozumel); and Chac, the rain-god. The great well, the 'Sacred Cenote', was dedicated to Chac, and he was a god who demanded human sacrifices.

The excavations at Chichen Itza confirmed that when the White God arrived it was a modest little town. For 200 years the Toltecs erected their magnificent buildings here. One of the most recent ones is the pyramid covering the Temple of Kukulcan, the highest building in Chichen Itza. This enormous pyramid, eighty feet high and built in nine terraces, was at first presumed to be the Temple of Kukulcan itself. It had outside steps, 364 altogether, on all four sides, leading up to the platform with the temple. The vestibule and shrine could be entered through a porch flanked by two mighty columns representing snakes.

When this building was first unearthed no one took any special notice of it. But afterwards, when the excavators learnt to put a date to their finds, they realized with some surprise that the big pyramid must have been one of the latest buildings of the city. It looked as if the chroniclers had got it wrong for once, for they quite clearly mentioned a great temple of Kukulcan—which should therefore have been an old Mayan building, put up long before the Toltec conquest. But then the excavators recalled the 'mantle pyramids', and opened up one of the pyramid's walls. Sure enough, there was an older structure inside, the small Mayan-built pyramid of Kukulcan, far older than all the others. Even more exciting, they found it absolutely intact under its outer shell with all its temples, altars and platforms.

When they entered the shrine of Kukulcan's Temple they were faced by a jaguar throne, a life-size jaguar, carved from stone and painted red, with eighty large and sparkling jade discs for its coat and eyes, and on its flat back a picture of the sun, a wooden disc inlaid with turquoises. This had jade beads and ornaments still on it, offerings dedicated to the gods almost a thousand years before.

Some of the most remarkable finds at Chichen Itza had been made decades before this by E. H. Thompson, a young architect who connected the Maya with the myth of Atlantis, the submerged continent. When he read a report about their wonderful buildings and art, he was struck by the contrast with the Red Indians of his time, very simple people living in miserable dwellings. He decided they could not possibly be the descendants of the ancient Maya—who must therefore have originally come from another country, for instance from Atlantis.

Although his theories were not treated very seriously, they attracted attention, and his interest in the Maya led to his being appointed American consul for Yucatan. Borrowing money from friends, he set out for the jungle in 1885, and from then on spent many years almost entirely among the Indians, riding from one to another of the ancient Mayan cities.

In 1896 he found a small pyramid at Chichen Itza to the north of the great terrace, and on unearthing the platform where the shrine used to be, he came across a pit, where the floor must at one time have opened up. There was surely a reason for this, so he started digging in the same place. The pit turned out to be filled with stones, earth—and bones.

The pit went down deeper and deeper. More and more bones came to light, and when they were eventually sorted out they made up seven human skeletons. Further down still, under soil level, the pit widened into a sizable cave which housed a tomb. Thompson was the

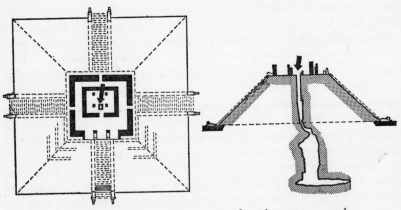

7. Under the pyramid Thompson found a strange tomb

first man to find such a tomb in a pyramid, and he was so excited that he declared it to be the tomb of the White God Kukulcan, founder of all Mayan civilization. But instead of the sarcophagus he hoped to find, the tomb held only a heap of charred bones and some objects for the dead to take on their journey.

Scholars have called this the high-priest's grave, which may or may not be correct. But at least it must have been an important man's grave, someone to be honoured even beyond death; and the grave had to be kept secret, with the pit leading down to it carefully filled up. The seven skeletons found in the pit may have been priests also, or else attendants, perhaps servants, who were either obliged to follow their master into death or did so of their own free will. From the graves of Ur we know the custom of attendants being sacrificed with their dead master; possibly the Maya had the same custom.

Chichen Itza, unlike so many great cities of the New World, had never entirely vanished; long before its real discovery by archaeologists, almost a dozen buildings towered over the tree-tops. Thompson stood on the great pyramid, looking out across the tips of the other pyramids, down a narrow path which led through the jungle and ended in the distance by the Sacred Well. The well was Thompson's original objective in coming to the city.

When there was a drought—the old chronicles reported—the people of Chichen Itza used to march through the streets singing and shouting. They were all in festive garments, including the priests, and also the virgins chosen for sacrifice to the rain-god. Slowly the colourful throng moved towards the Rain-god's Well. The priests would throw the virgins in, and as the victims struck the dark, muddy water, the crowd passed by the well in solemn procession, throwing in lavish gifts of ornaments, gold, silver, and precious stones. If there was any gold left in the land, the chroniclers declared, it must be in this well.

In 1579 Diego Sarmiento de Figueros also wrote about the well:

'The aristocracy and the country's notables would walk up to the top of the well at dawn, after sixty days of abstinence and fasting, and throw Indian women who were their property into the dark chasm. At the same time they asked these slave women to put in a plea for a favourable year in which their masters' desires would be fulfilled.

'In the late afternoon those who still could gave a loud cry, and ropes were lowered to them. They came up half dead, after which fires were lit near them and copal gum was burnt in front of them. When they came to their senses again they reported that there were many of their people down there.'

If they tried to look up—the report goes on—they were hit hard on the head. When they looked down they saw many heights and depths under the water. The people of the well answered their question about the good or bad year in store for their masters.

These gruesome accounts in the old chronicles were not credited by anyone before Thompson. He set out to find the well, having trained as a diver; and he also brought with him a Greek diver called Nicolas. His equipment consisted of a raft, a pontoon, divers' suits, pumps, a telephone, a dredger, a winch, pulleys, and a crowbar.

The well was a cavity in a rock, between 130 and 165 feet in diameter, the steep rock-faces descending sixty-five feet to the water's surface, which Thompson could see below him, red and stagnant. The dredger swung out to plunge its claws into the water, and brought up one load after another, branches, trunks, foliage. This went on unprofitably for days, until two small lumps of resinous matter were brought up with the mud. Thompson realized at once that this could only be the sort of gum the Mayan priests had burned as incense at their religious festivals. Every day after that the dredger lifted out of the mud a variety of ornaments, tools, vases, spear-points, jadeite bowls, and obsidian knives. Finally it brought up a human skeleton: that of a young girl.

Then there was nothing left for it to dig up but heavy stones, between which its claws could not get hold of anything. The time had come to start diving. The pontoon was lowered on to the water with Thompson, Nicolas and a few of the Indian workmen on board.

From down below Thompson caught sight of the reflections of the rest of his workmen, whom he had left standing round the top of the well, looking down. He also heard the sound of their voices, which reverberated strangely on hitting the water—thus supplying a natural explanation for the 'many people down there who answered questions'. He saw, too, the great 'heights and depths', the reflections of the rock-faces on the dark expanse of water.

He and the Greek got into their diving gear: 'suits of water-proof material with large copper helmets, glass goggle-eyes and air-vents near the ears, and lead necklaces almost half as heavy as the helmets. They also wore canvas shoes with thick, wrought-iron soles.'

When Thompson stepped from the pontoon on to the first rung of the ladder, his faithful Indians shook hands with him sadly, as if taking a last farewell. He pushed himself off the ladder and sank like a lump of lead, leaving behind him a trail of silvery bubbles. Then Nicolas joined him under water.

There was a layer of mud thirty feet deep, strong enough to support branches and twigs, with rock embedded in them, as he described it, 'like sultanas in a plum pudding'. Again and again rocks, loosened by the movement of the water, would topple down towards the two divers, but they always got out of the way because the pressure waves reached them first, although these hit them like a huge soft cushion and bowled them over. After shaking and swaying 'like egg-white in a glass of water', they eventually got back on their feet again and went on with their search.

They found what they were looking for: all those ornaments made of jade, gold, and alloys, both wrought and cast, cups, copper bells, carved bones. The decorations and reliefs on these articles in dicated that part of them must have come from southern Guatemala, others from Oaxaca and the west of the Mexican plateau, and from Costa Rica and Panama. Among them there were jade objects from the classical age of the Maya, wooden javelin-throwers, sacrificial knives, golden cups with saucers, bangles and finger-rings, golden bells the size of walnuts, and, above all, gold discs.

These things dated back to early Toltec times, showing Toltec motifs, Toltec battle-scenes, even perhaps scenes from the life of Quetzalcoatl, the White God. But the wrought-work was Mayan and the ornament round the edge consisted of Mayan glyphs. The snake with the sun-god looking out of its jaws was a Toltec symbol for the sky; but the dragon's head or double-headed dragon, symbol of the earth, was typically Mayan.

The modern Indians of Chichen Itza had told Thompson their fear of the Sacred Well, maintaining that they had seen great snakes and other monsters in it. He was reminded of these tales when he had an alarming experience in the pitch dark of the well.

'I felt something above me,' he wrote, 'something huge . . . slippery and slimy, pressing me down into the mire with irresistible might. For a moment my blood froze. Then I felt Nicolas pulling at the thing, and I helped him till we had freed ourselves. It was a rotting tree-trunk which had drifted loose from the mud-bank and when sinking had happened to descend on my squatting body.'

He had another experience in the well which was more serious. One day he had been sitting on a piece of rock at the bottom, feeling over a bell he had just salvaged; and he forgot to open the air-vents when he got up to put the find in his pocket. The water carried him upwards like an air-bubble, and pressed his head against the bottom of the pontoon. Half-dazed he scrambled up from underneath and got into the boat, but his hearing was affected for the rest of his life as a result of this momentary carelessness.

Most of the finds were only fragments, objects deliberately broken before being sacrificed, probably in order to 'kill' them. But there were objects of pure gold among them, and one of the golden plates shows gruesome sacrificial scenes, depicted with such realism that it gives one an exact idea of the ritual involved.

The custom of human sacrifices is common to all ancient Indian civilizations. Traces have been found in Teotihuacan of rites in which children and youths were sacrificed to the rain-god. Later on the gods were given instead the most valuable things people possessed next to their lives: rubber, jade, and quetzal feathers.

The Zapotecs sacrificed only children (also to their rain-god). The

Totonacs prepared a paste from seeds and children's blood, which they gave the people to eat when the rain-gods were angry. The friezes of Chichen Itza show eagles holding human hearts in their talons and feeding these to the sun, which is close to the earth; the skull-racks at Chichen Itza indicate the large number of victims. The Toltecs were ruled not by priests but by warriors, who alone could provide the immense number of prisoners demanded by the hungry gods.

As for the Aztecs, the Spaniards saw the evidence of this cult when they entered the temple of Tenochtitlán: walls stiff with blood, altars dripping with it, from human hearts which had been sacrificed only a short time before. If the tributes from the conquered peoples did not arrive on time, their youths and virgins were abducted by the Aztecs and sacrificed to the gods at Tenochtitlán.

Things were no different in South America. If there was drought or famine on the coast of Peru the priests would proclaim a sacrificial feast. Then the whole people, clad in festive garments, would gather round the temples, such as the shrine of Sin-An, the house of the moon at Pacasmayo. Sacrifices of children and maize beer were offered to appease the gods. On a certain day the people would climb up to the mountains, singing and dancing, along a narrow path strewn with flowers. There they were joined by the tribe's most beautiful girl, accompanied by her parents, who were also singing and dancing. Amidst cheers from the crowd, the girl would throw herself off the cliff into the abyss as a sacrifice to the fertility god.

Before a battle was waged, or when the Inca was ill, children and youths were selected for sacrifice to the gods; they were first given great tins of cocoa to make them drowsy, and then led into the temple to be slaughtered like cattle. In the Inca's triumphal procession a conquered ruler, lying on a litter, was exhibited naked to the people of Cuzco, surrounded by kettle-drums made from the skin of his nearest relatives.

The later Incas, however, gave up the practice of human sacrifices, and substituted llamas; a llama was killed and burned at dawn every morning in the temple of Cuzco. But at Pachacamac the people stuck to the old customs. When the burying grounds were eventually opened up, more and more skeletons of young girls were found, even laid out in rows next to one another, together with the golden ornaments they had worn on their last journey.

At first sight these barbaric human sacrifices might seem evidence against the existence of a White God or White Gods: if white men came to the Indians, bringing a high civilization, they would surely have made it their first task to eradicate such customs. But in fact the civilizations of the Old World had these customs too.

The people of India, and even the Romans, offered human sacrifices at the time of the full moon. The Egyptians sacrificed red-haired men to their god Busiris. In Persia—in the fifth century B.C.—Xerxes sacrificed his nephews to the gods. The ancient Germans sacrificed their prisoners of war to their god Ziu, and people even sacrificed their own children to Wotan, god of death.

As early as 3911 B.C. the ancient Egyptians made an annual sacrifice of a young girl to the Nile. In 2550 B.C. sacrifices of attendants were made in the sepulchral vaults of the kings, and around 1550 B.C. human sacrifices were also known in the Shang civilization of China. Particularly bloody sacrifices, mainly of new-born children, went on in Canaan for a very long time, until the Israelites were forbidden them by Joshua, Moses's successor. A cemetery has been unearthed outside the gates of Jerusalem with many graves of sacrificed children.

The Minotaur also asked for human sacrifices every nine years at the rate of seven youths and seven virgins from Athens alone. At Carthage thousands of clay urns were found with the remains of children and gifts for them to take on their last journey. The sacrifices of children continued in Carthage till its fall, and as late as 409 B.C. a Carthaginian general sacrificed 3,000 Roman prisoners-of-war at one go. Even the Etruscans were still sacrificing Roman prisoners in 307 B.C.

So if white men came to the American Indians in the first two or three millennia before Christ they would have been quite familiar with human sacrifices. They may even have introduced such practices to the Indians—as part of their 'high civilization'.

A white man was king of the Toltecs. He resided for ten years in their great city of Tula, but then left Tula and conquered the New Empire of the Maya, making Chichen Itza his capital. He is supposed to have arrived there between A.D. 967 and 987. The two cities are 770 miles apart as the crow flies. He came from the area of Chakanputan, south of Campeche, and sailed across the Gulf of Tabasco to the coast of Yucatan.

The Maya called him and his Toltecs 'the foreign speaking' or 'people from the coast'—they wore the old head-dress of the Olmecs, the feathered crown. He put his stamp on all the buildings of Chichen Itza, his new capital, for he was an architect and an artist. He was a shrewd politician and governor; and a conqueror, for many years at war with the Maya, as we know from tales and pictures that have come down to us. Again, he was a scholar and astronomer, but also a good business man who organized the trade in cotton and cocoa in his kingdom—the largest kingdom which ever existed in Central America.

This white king was called Quetzalcoatl, and he is beyond doubt a historical personality, even though his life and work have given rise to many legends. His name was also current with other peoples, and it was given to pioneers of civilization right up to the time of the Aztecs.

The Maya in the New Empire still looked to Kukulcan as White God and their first teacher, although he had been dead for many centuries; to them Quetzalcoatl was a foreign conqueror and oppressor. There were thus two White Gods being worshipped at Chichen Itza, for the Toltecs deified their white king. He was the living White God, and his symbol was the plumed serpent. The symbol is found on all Chichen Itza's buildings, a ubiquitous piece of history in stone.

The north temple there is remarkable for the reliefs on the vaults of its ceiling, and these show long rows of priests and also warriors, standing round a jaguar throne or sitting on cushions; only one of

8. The reliefs of the White God of Chichen Itza show a
quite un-Indian type

the priests has a long beard. Other reliefs in the city show the same bearded old man, and his features have nothing Indian about them—they are unmistakably European. He could be Quetzalcoatl himself.

It was no wonder that Kukulcan and Quetzalcoatl were sometimes identified long afterwards, for the former means 'serpent swimming in water' (Kukumaz, as several Mayan tribes called him, means 'heart of the sea'); while Quetzalcoatl means 'serpent covered with the feathers of the Quetzal bird'. He is often represented as a plumed serpent, but often as a fabulous monster with a snake's body and a crocodile's jaws. If depicted in human shape, he has a crown suspended over his head, shaped like a Quetzal bird pouncing, and a mask over his face from the coils of a turquoise snake.

These symbols are not so strange for a White God as they may sound: the feathered serpent was a very old symbol for the rain-god among the Indians. Everything depended on the rain, it governed all the natural powers: the sea, water, the sky, the clouds and the lightning, the whole world of plants and animals. The highest rain-god was

symbolized by the Quetzal bird and the snake. On the reliefs his priests
are often surrounded by a frieze of feathered serpents symbolizing the
terrestrial waters. The feathered serpent is the symbol for water, rain,
and vegetation, for everything that 'makes things sprout'. Because the
Zapotec god Xipe made the vegetation sprout, he also wore the symbol
of the feathered serpent. But among all the ancient Indian peoples the
White God was the pioneer who made civilization 'sprout', and could
therefore be compared to the effect of rain on vegetation.

Originally these symbols were attributed to the Mayan Kukulcan,
but many centuries later they were transferred to Quetzalcoatl, the
White God of the Toltecs. The knowledge of astronomy and the
entire wisdom of the priests go back to Quetzalcoatl, but he was a
warrior king and (unlike Kukulcan) became a warrior god. The
Toltecs identified him with the warlike god of the morning star (sometimes calling him Ce-acatl, that god's name), and the feathered serpent
became a symbol for the sky and for the god of the Zodiac. As god
of the Zodiac, Quetzalcoatl was represented by the Aztecs with a
crocodile's jaws and often with a bird's beak.

The buildings of Chichen Itza show certain influences from the Far
East, for instance the artistic motif of the lotus. Lotus blossoms and
leaves are depicted very often, even the whole plant, with the rhizome
(stem) used as a decoration. The lower room of the jaguar temple has
a frieze containing the lotus motif with stylized rhizome.

At Chichen Itza, just as in India, this motif often serves as a
border round an imaginary landscape, and as a frame for other motifs,
e.g. human figures. Even the figures' movements and postures are
like those in India, only their attire is different. The Toltec frieze of
water-lilies at Chichen Itza is like the water-lily ornament of the temple
town of Amarâvati on the east coast of southern India. The motif
originated in the second century A.D. and spread from Indo-China to
the Malayan peninsula and Indonesia. The Toltecs of Chichen Itza
took it over from their Mayan predecessors.

The lotus throne and sceptre, and the motif generally, occurred in
Indian and South-East Asian art up to the later periods, although
transformed with time into a purely decorative shape. They were
often combined with other motifs: in South-East Asia and Cambodia
for instance, between the ninth and eleventh centuries A.D., the lotus
rhizome at Chichen Itza jutted out on either side of a demon face.

From Indo-China and Indonesia we know representations of the
lotus plant growing from the jaws of a macara, a mythical sea-monster
with a fish's body and an elephant's trunk. Exactly the same image of
a stylized fish with a scaly body, at both ends of a lotus motif, is found

at Chichen Itza; the monsters here are even shown in the same position
as in India. Clearly men must at some time have come to the New World
from east Asia and introduced their native artistic motifs. The lotus

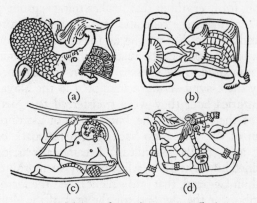

(a)   (b)

(c)   (d)

9. (a) Makara from Amarâvati (India)
   (b) Makara from Chichen Itza
   (c) Lotos-shoot motif from Amarâvati
   (d) Lotos-shoot motif from Chichen Itza

motif was particularly in evidence during the period of India's greatest
expansion, the first 600 years A.D. It was from there it perhaps passed
to Central America, probably between the third and fifth centuries A.D.

We have already come across other features of pictorial art,
common to both sides of the Pacific, such as the 'false arches' found in
the temples of Cambodia and with the Maya. In Cambodia these were
current mainly from the eighth to the tenth century A.D., as were the
cross-shaped sacred arches and the feathered serpent. In American-
Indian art this is the symbol of the sky at night, devouring the moon
rabbit; and the same motifs occur in Chinese pottery from the earlier
bronze age.

These people from East Asia must also have brought along some
basic traits of their native iconography. The second century A.D. saw
the first Asiatic representations of gods standing on squatting human
figures, or sitting or standing on tigers and jaguars. Exact copies of
these motifs from Hindu and Buddhist art recurred with the Maya,
particularly at Palenque.

The disc of the sun as a quoit, the mussel shell with a plant, the
figures of Vishnu—all these appeared on both sides of the Pacific either
in identical form or with so strong a resemblance that they cannot have
originated independently of one another. Then again, the ancient
Maya knew the umbrella as a mark of dignity and a symbol of rank;
and the umbrella hails from South-East Asia, where it was already

known in the third millenium B.C. The friezes of Chacmultun in
Yucatan show two types of umbrella as they are still used today in
India and South-East Asia. As we have seen, fans, litters and certain

10. *Left:* God on the tiger throne (India)
Right: Mayan jaguar throne

religious concepts are other features common to the civilizations on
both sides of the Pacific.

The link between them must have started roughly in the middle
of the Mayan classical age, and must have been particularly strong
during the beginnings of their New Empire. The lotus motif at
Chichen Itza with the human figures and the mythical sea monsters
goes back to about 500 A.D., when the school of Amarâvati was en-
joying its greatest popularity. But the combination of lotus flower with
demons proves that such a link must also have existed much later on,
from the ninth to the twelfth century.

A further proof of this is the Mayan Puuc style, with decoration of
house-fronts, and door-frames with half-columns which look as if
they were turned on the lathe or consisted of several spools. They are
characteristic of the art of the Khmer empire in Cambodia in the tenth
century A.D. It was not till around 1200 that these Cambodian influences on Indian art ceased, when the empire perished and the links
were broken.

To get to Central America, these men from South-East Asia could
only have come across the Pacific. It is a terrific distance for them to
have covered, but we know from old records that they were excellent
sailors and had big, seaworthy ships. Ptolemy described how in the
second century A.D. East Indian ships sailed across the Indian Ocean
to Malaya and Indonesia. It is also known that in the third century
A.D. a transport of horses—which would have needed large ships—

reached Malaya and Indo-China. About A.D. 400 the Chinese monk Fa-hien sailed on a ship with a crew of 200 from Ceylon straight to Malaya and afterwards reached north China on a similar ship. As the American expert Walter Krickeberg has pointed out, such ships with crews of up to 200 men were larger than Columbus's ships under sail 1,000 years later.

These ancient travellers from East Asia probably sailed north along the coast, then by way of the Kuril and Aleutian Islands towards the north-west coast of the American continent, then due south along the American coast to Mexico. Or they may have gone north round Hawaii, then to the Californian coast, and from there to the south. Hundreds of far smaller ships have crossed the Pacific. During the eighteenth and nineteenth centuries, for instance, many Chinese junks were even swept across accidentally and washed up on the American coast.

So for centuries men made these voyages from South-East Asia to Central America. It has been suggested that they were probably merchants and a few monks. They must have had some strong incentive to make them sail across the Pacific, and their voyages would certainly be planned—presumably with a return to their own countries included in the plan.

If there were monks among them, it is rather puzzling that they did not bring Buddhism with them; or, if they brought it, that it did not get a lasting foothold in the New World. There may be a parallel in the fact that the Chans in Annam were under strong Hindu-Buddhist influence from the second to the fifteenth century A.D., but all traces of these religions vanished when the kingdom collapsed in 1471.

At any rate most scholars are agreed that men from east Asia discovered America long before Columbus. It was therefore 'discovered' at least four times: first by nomad hordes who crossed the Bering Strait over 10,000 years ago; then by merchants from South-East Asia between A.D. 300 and 1200, thirdly by Vikings, starting out from Iceland and Greenland, who founded a colony in Vinland, and finally by Columbus.

As we have seen, it may have been five times, not four. America and Asia are divided by 10,000 miles, and the trade-winds blow away from America. If men from South-East Asia nevertheless crossed the Pacific to Central America during the first centuries A.D., other men might surely have come over a few centuries before, across the Atlantic. America is only 1,500 miles distant from the Canary Isles, and on the Atlantic the trade-winds and currents persistently carry sailors towards America. So the Atlantic would be a much more favourable route for White Gods coming to America.

The lavish design of the warrior temple of Chichen Itza, with its colonnades
and the 'thousand pillars', is reminiscent of Egypt

The pyramid of the White God Kukulcan at Chichen Itza. Thanks to long years of work by archaeologists and restorers visitors to this ancient Mayan city can go unimpeded to the buildings of a perished civilization

10

Other Ancient Peoples of Mexico

'The ruined city lay before us, like a ship wrecked in the
middle of the sea, her masts lost, her name disappeared, her
crew drowned; no one can tell where they came from, to
whom she belonged, how long she had been on her voyage,
or what was the cause of her sinking.'

STEPHENS, on seeing Copán

THE interest aroused by the excavations of the ancient Mayan and
Toltec empires, confirming so much of what the old chroniclers had
reported, led the scholars to re-examine minutely the diaries of the
Conquista generals; and Cortés's diary had much to say of the Zapotecs,
a people feared particularly for their gigantic spears. Their king paid
homage to Cortés after his victory over the Aztecs, but the mountain
Zapotecs put up a stiff resistance, and indeed carried on a bitter struggle
with the Spaniards for nearly a century. When the Spaniards conquered Tenochtitlán, Cortés was made a 'Marques de Valle' (Marquis
of the Valley). The valley referred to was Oaxaca, situated among
these mountains, where most of the gold and silver was mined.

The Zapotecs had migrated to the area—the plain north-east of
Oaxaca—early in the first century A.D. Later they ventured farther
south-east till they reached the sea, their territory now extending
from the Isthmus of Tehuantepec right to the Pacific. They lost parts
of this when the Chichemecs invaded the Valley of Oaxaca shortly
before the Spanish conquest. The Aztecs kept a garrison in the city of
Oaxaca, but never managed to suppress the Zapotecs entirely.

The chronicler mentioned cities, temples and palaces in the
Zapotecs' large kingdom, but these must have perished long before
the Spaniards landed in Mexico. They did find there a small remnant of
the ancient people, men with richer and more beautiful clothes than

H

those of other Indians: these men wore robes reaching down to their feet and covered all over with embroidery; and their headgear was a feather crown.

The chroniclers also referred to a 'place of nourishment' and a 'place of the dead', and to the city of the great old priests. Moreover the Spaniards, travelling through the defeated country soon after the conquest, had found the ruins of large old buildings near the city of Tlacolula, among them a palace with four rooms above and four below ground, the latter containing a vault and several tombs. These were the ruins of Mitla, the Zapotecs' second great city.

Mitla was rediscovered in 1895. Excavators brought to light, among other palaces and buildings, a 'palace of colonnades', consisting of three courtyards and an interior one, a kind of patio, walled in on all four sides. All three courtyards are paved with mortar, hard as flint, and surrounded by long halls with three doors opening on to the courtyards; the doors are framed by mighty monoliths. The panelling is made up of a great many stone slabs with patterns chiselled into them, giving the whole wall a mosaic effect—the patterns' main feature being geometrical lines and shapes.

The most impressive colonnade, measuring 120 feet by 20, with a roof supported by huge round stone pillars, has a passage leading from it to the walled-in patio and the chambers where the chief soothsayer, the Uija-tao, probably lived. There were similar colonnades at Chichen Itza—and also in ancient civilizations of the Mediterranean, e.g. the palace court of the castle at Tiryns and the staircase of the living quarters at Knossos in Crete.

Mitla was built when the Zapotecs left their biggest city, the old temple city of Monte Alban, which was discovered under rubble and deep undergrowth in 1931 by the Mexican archaeologist Alfonso Caso. Digging on a mountain ridge near the modern city of Oaxaca, rising 1,300 feet above the Valley of Oaxaca, he first unearthed steps and terraces leading up to a large level platform. On this platform, about 2,300 by 825 feet, stood the remains of the old temple city, the great pyramids and also monumental buildings decorated with reliefs and script characters.

The city was founded around the time of Christ's birth, when the first Mayan cities were being built; in fact Monte Alban even had close relations with the Mayan cities, as can be seen from buildings, sculptures, the script, and the calendar. There was also a lively exchange of culture with another ancient people, the people of the city Teotihuacan.

Monte Alban had ball courts very similar to ones which existed in the Old World, with exactly the same flights of steps from which apparently the games were watched. Caso also found a work of art which was very unexpected for America: a 'genuine Egyptian'. This was a statue of a squatting naked man with a turban, more reminiscent of Egyptian statues than almost any other product of a non-Egyptian civilization.

The Zapotec style in Monte Alban, Mitla, Xoco, and Cuilapan was replaced by an entirely different one in the fifteenth or perhaps already in the fourteenth century. A young warrior people, the Mixtecs, took over what they found and merged it with their own ideas of civilization and art. At Monte Alban they simply cleared out the Zapotecs' graves and entombed their own dead kings in the vaults, decorating the vaults in their own style, also the monoliths on the doors and the walls of the crypts and passages. The decorations were paintings, which have been called 'illuminated manuscripts in fresco', and, to judge from these, Mixtec history lasted from 692 to 1519.

Besides the Mayan cities and Monte Alban, some of the Totonac cities were also in existence in the first century A.D. Cempoalla, mentioned earlier as destroyed by the Spaniards, was a Totonac city, but, according to the chroniclers, quite a late one. Long before this the Totonacs had lived in El Tajén (Tajén means 'lightning'), which in its heyday was said to have been one of the largest cities in Mexico. One chronicler's account referred to a pyramid in the depths of the jungle, which the natives called El Tajén. A traveller saw it in 1785, but archaeological interest did not centre on this pyramid till 150 years later.

In 1935 a small expedition led by Garcia Payon hacked a way with machetes through the highland jungle near the city of Papantla, in the Vera Cruz area. Luxuriant creepers, bamboo thickets and the tendrils of the thorny palms made every step a laborious struggle. Bizarrely shaped roots, perched in the air, hung down from the branches, and the giant trees with their dense foliage let very little light through to the ground. Some sunlight reached the higher branches, and thick clusters of orchids and bromeliae were growing on these. Vanilla spread from branch to branch and tree to tree, drawing everything into its web.

Payon and his men fought on for days, till in the dark of the dense green jungle they caught sight of a big mountain. Under the bushes, palms, and vanilla tendrils, this suggested the outlines of a pyramid, and it was in fact the great Tajén. They cleared it from its surroundings with great care, for it had suffered badly from the jungle's musty air and the undermining effect of thick roots. With a base 115 feet square, it had seven steps and was about eighty feet high. It was built differently from any which had been seen before, having little square recesses built into the walls of its steps—a niche pyramid.

When the whole site on which it stood had been cleared, the excavators saw that it had once been surrounded on all sides by buildings; in the north and south these were ball courts, which had walls decorated with ornamental ribbons.

On a small hill another pyramid was discovered, the so-called Little Tajén, and close by it the colonnade building, the largest building in the ancient city. These were clearly later works than the great pyramid—which shows East Asian influence. Both in its structure, and in being a niche pyramid, it is very similar to the pagodas of the ancient Burmese city of Pagan. The ornaments of the Tajén style, especially on clay vessels—and the interlocked dragons with short, sickle-shaped wings—are almost indistinguishable from the late Chou style of China in the fifth or fourth century B.C. The round mirror of China was also found in the Tajén civilization, but made of pyrites, whereas in China the material was bronze.

The chroniclers also referred to the Michuaque, the 'people who have fish', who were said to have lived in Michoacan on the banks of Lake Patzcuaro—a lake 6,700 feet above sea level and abounding in fish. Christoval de Olid, one of Cortés's officers, wrote that these people —the Spaniards called them Tarascans—conquered large areas around the lake and built their cities there, they were excellent goldsmiths and true artists in producing feather ornaments, and that even in Spanish times they still supplied the church with priests' vestments made of feathers. They were also fine painters, embroiderers and weavers, master stone-cutters, carpenters, wood-carvers, obsidian and metal workers.

Their founder and legendary first king was called Tariacuri, and the kingdom reached its peak under his great-nephew, with the alliance of three cities: Tzintzuntzan, Ihuatzie, and Patzcuaro. He extended the kingdom's borders in victorious battles with the Aztecs, and the Tarascans were then the Aztecs' equals. But his son had to pay homage to Cortés after the fall of Tenochtitlán, and ended on the stake in 1532 for failing to hand over his state treasury; in fact de Olid had seized it from the treasure vaults of Ihuatzie the year before.

Until a natural calamity occurred, little attention was paid to the Tarascans in later centuries, athough some of their strange buildings were still standing, reasonably well preserved, near the little Mexican village of Paricuti: five steep 'temple terraces', with five Yacatas on them—that is, buildings partly round and partly square.

One day in February 1943 a peasant was ploughing his field, quite close to these terraces, so that he could sow new maize. Suddenly

Snake pillars flank the entrance to the temple on the Kukulcan Pyramid

The colonnade at Mitla

The colonnade at Knossos

the ground opened in front of him, swallowing up his plough and team of oxen. He fled back towards his village in panic, and when he turned round once more he saw red-hot lava masses belching from the ground and pouring over his field. After ten days the volcano had reached a height of 1,000 feet, a burning mountain which buried everything beneath it.

When the volcano subsided archaeologists began looking for Tarascan remains in the fishing villages of Lake Patzcuaro. There were more than twenty of these villages, and they still exist today. On the banks of this lake the great ancient city of Tzintzuntzan, hidden so long under earth and forest, was now dug up. Among the remains found were step pyramids: the steps were so steep they looked more like walls, and the rungs so shallow they were barely noticeable.

The city's largest building was a high mud terrace, about 1,400 by 900 feet, with steep walls. The terrace was reached by a flight of steps 325 feet wide, and at the foot of these a chieftain's tomb was excavated. In it were funeral offerings, ornaments as beautiful as any that have been found since—copper and gilt half-moons, bells shaped like terrapins, filigree work made from fine wires soldered together, and little masterpieces in obsidian, the hard stone which has been called the 'Stone Age Steel'. The craftmanship shown by all these ornaments excelled even that of the Zapotecs.

The chieftain's tomb was surrounded by other graves, with remains which allowed only one conclusion: attendants had followed their master into death, human sacrifices made to a god king.

But the glories of Tzintzuntzan and Tajén, of Monte Alba and Mitla, of the Mayan cities, were outshone by one tremendous city, Teotihuacan, 'the place where the gods were made'—so mighty in its time that according to the old legends white giants had come in the dim past to raise its buildings to their towering height.

The chroniclers go on to tell us that it was a city of powerful priests, inhabited first by the Toltecs and finally by the Aztecs; that there was a wide, mile-long road leading right across the city, often interspersed with steps because of the slightly rising ground, with temples on either side of it. The road was referred to as the 'Via Sacra' or 'Way of Death', and it runs into an open square at the foot of a big pyramid dedicated to the moon, just east of the road; to the west rises the even bigger Sun Pyramid.

Cortés's army, on their escape from Tenochtitlán, passed Teotihuacan in July 1520, when it was already a vast city of ruins—it extends over eight square miles. The ruins were never swallowed up by the jungle like the ancient Mayan cities, and it is only just north of the modern capital, Mexico City; so that a modern archaeologist, Manuel Gamio, who excavated there from 1917 to 1922, had only a twenty minutes' tram ride to and from his site. Yet the ruins of Teotihuacan, which many believe to be the most ancient city in Mexico, lay more or less unnoticed on their treeless plain until 1905—when Leopold Batres started digging up the building which the Indians called the Sun Pyramid. Later on, Gamio dug a tunnel through this to uncover the citadel.

The Sun Pyramid, with sides measuring 740 by 725 feet, has the same foundation measurements as the Cheops Pyramid, but is only 215 feet high, half the height of the Egyptian one. It is built from adobes and covered by a thick cast of stones and mortar. The Moon Pyramid, which has also been resurrected, is 140 feet high, with sides 400 by 500 feet.

Oddly enough, the old chronicler said nothing about the citadel (excavated by Gamio), a pyramid built in six steps, consisting of an older kernel and a later superstructure. It rises from a big platform, which carried fifteen smaller pyramids as well. One side of its front is still preserved, and both plinth and frieze are decorated with recurring reliefs of the plumed serpent, which end in protruding snakes' heads sculptured in the round. Originally the pyramid contained 366 images of snakes' and gods' heads, brightly painted, eyes inlaid with obsidian —it must have been a fantastic sight.

Between the snakes another religious symbol is repeated at regular intervals, the butterfly. This is also found on a clay vessel from Teotihuacan; and all the other ancient Indian peoples, including the Aztecs, were familiar with the butterfly symbol. The *Codex Borbonicus* shows a dance of death round a sort of mast, with mummies of the god Xolotl hanging from the top; and the mummies are decorated with butterfly symbols.

Now Evans, at Crete, found very curious clay objects in the palace of Knossos. They look almost like a modern tie with a knot, and have been called 'ritual bows'—used in ritual acts to show that the priestesses represented gods. But they have also been taken as symbols of the departed. So it seems possible that the Indians of Teotihuacan may have received this symbol from the Cretans.

The excavation of the immense city is still not quite completed. Between 1932 and 1935 Sigvald Linné dug up a site of ordinary dwellings, and between 1942 and 1945 Pedro Armillas found tombs, weapons, jewellery, tools, pottery, and splendidly preserved murals. The excavators also found walls blackened by smoke and charred beams; from these traces they have established beyond doubt that the city was destroyed by fire in A.D. 856 (by the Toltecs).

All the finds, in fact, buildings and sculptures, ornaments, utensils, and characters, could be put together piece by piece to form a mosaic of the city's history, and thereby trace one of the most ancient Indian civilizations of Central America. An archaic civilization still existed in the Valley of Mexico when the city was built; and on the city's site there had also been a primitive settlement. But these early stirrings of a civilization were followed without transition by the style of Teotihuacan; the change was so abrupt that presumably a different people must have settled there.

The city's large buildings, such as the Sun and Moon Pyramids, were erected during its early period, between A.D. 100 and 300, and it had its heyday between the fifth and sixth centuries. Its defeat by the Toltecs was probably due to the degeneration of its dynasty. After its fall the inhabitants fled to Azcapotzalco on the western bank of Lake Tezcoco, and there the old civilization brought forth new blossoms.

When Teotihuacan was resurrected by the archaeologists, and its buildings and works of art compared with those of other peoples, the comparison showed that it must once have been a very important centre of civilization. Its technical achievements, patterns and ornaments exerted their influence over a wide area, ranging over the whole of Central America. The closest ties existed between the city and the Maya, and it influenced Mayan civilization and art down to the smallest details. Possibly its people founded a sort of colony there on the highlands of Guatemala.

The Zapotecs also were greatly influenced. Their rain-god at Monte Alban is depicted in very similar shape as at Teotihuacan. The mythical butterfly, too, recurs on their helmet masks and their vessels; and the two civilizations have the maize god in common. The Totonacs have the same intertwined and twisted band ornament so characteristic of Teotihuacan, and the butterfly is found on their stone yokes.

These remarkable common factors everywhere suggested that all the ancient civilizations of Central America must have derived from the city of Teotihuacan. But other discoveries, made at about the same time, shed an entirely new light on their origins.

In 1928 archaeologists excavating on the northern bank of Lake Tezcoco found rubble heaps between twenty-three and forty-six feet deep. On clearing these they could distinguish between three very different 'layers' of civilization: a very old one at the bottom, an intermediate one during which the population must have changed, and the most recent one on top, contemporary with the highly developed civilization of Teotihuacan.

Other rubble heaps on Lake Tezcoco yielded first Aztec remains, then a thirteen-foot-thick Teotihuacan layer, and finally, at the very bottom, a five-foot archaic layer with the very beginnings of civilization.

Archaic civilization existed roughly between 3000 and 1000 B.C. Simple tools, containers and ornaments found here from this period point to the fact that certain articles, e.g. shells worked into ornaments, must have been introduced from the Pacific and also from the Atlantic coast—so there was trade with the peoples in the south. The presence of jade alone is evidence of this.

The pottery finds attracted special attention. The archaic clay sculptures showed a realism never afterwards achieved in Mexico. They were primitively shaped human figures with a hyper-small waist, the limbs indicated only by stumps. This sculpture reached its peak in the art of Tlatilco, representing women with buxom bodies, big breasts, and plump bottoms. There were also the specimens of what has been termed 'pretty lady': figurines of women with elaborate hair-styles, coquettish dancers, sitting mothers with children, women with a little lap-dog. Among the male sculptures were ball-game players, masked figurines, hunchbacks, and also men with short beards. Despite their primitiveness, these works testify to the dawn of a civilization, just as the works of the archaic period in Greece were the first step towards the glories of Greek art.

Apart from the man-made finds, the excavators in these archaic depths discovered something rather sensational: a thick layer of fine alluvial mud, with clay vessels, tools, statues and pottery embedded in it.

In 1900 Zelia Nuttall, a famous archaeologist of the time, was digging in Zacatenco. She remembered that other excavators had found such thick layers of mud, and also that Sir Leonard Woolley had hit upon something very similar at Ur; his Babylonian finds proved that there had once been a Great Flood, the flood of the legends, which had submerged all human settlements. By Lake Tezcoco, Zelia Nuttall found the traces of the American Great Flood. Holding in her hand the primitive finds she had dug up from the mud, she let her eyes roam over the Valley of Mexico, and had a vision of the landscape as it might have looked about 3,000 years before.

There was the big lake, and on its banks the simple little huts of the men living in this valley. It was raining. It rained for days, for weeks—one single never-ending cloud-burst. The surface of Lake Tezcoco rose, the huts on the banks were flooded, the people fled up to the mountains. It kept on raining, the lake's surface rose every day, and every day they had to climb higher up the mountains to save their lives. Anyone who stayed in the valley was lost.

The rain did not abate. Streams came flowing down the mountains, then they turned into rivers, torrents of water, mud and stones. Frightened to death, the people crept into miserable shelters they had made from leaves. The animals sought refuge with them. They had left their huts, their utensils, everything they possessed, and now it was all lying at the bottom of the lake, which had risen by sixty feet and was now filling the whole Valley of Mexico. The people living at Copilco on the lake's west bank also had to flee, and it was their clay vessels that were retrieved from the layer of mud 3,000 years later.

Those who got away from this place of horror and survived on the mountain-tops, or fled to other lands, told tales of the Great Flood, and these became part of the Indian people's myth. In the Aztec legends the third age of the world perished in the Flood. Men from the archaic period carried the myth to Peru when they conquered its north coast and founded their little kingdoms there.

In the Old World we have the Gilgamesh epic of Mesopotamia and the Sumerians, the legend the Greeks took over in their story of the Flood which only Deucalion escaped. This Deucalion was Noah, and so was the God-fearing Tapi of the Indian myth, mentioned earlier in this book. Archaeologists discovered long ago that both Gilgamesh epic and Indian myth go back to real natural catastrophes.

A thousand years later the Valley of Mexico saw its second great catastrophe.

The people who had fled from the Flood had come back. Their descendants were still telling tales about it, as if it had happened in their own lifetime. It took 500 years for the waters to subside and the lake to sink to its former level.

Now there were again settlements on the lake's banks. The people had tilled the soil and caught fish in the lake. But they were living in constant fear, because the ground beneath them would not calm down. It shook often, and the great volcano of Ajusco spat steam, smoke and fire. The mushroom of smoke over the crater became ever higher and bigger. Flames blazed skyward, and one day the volcano burst. A stream of liquid lava came pouring down Mount Xitla, reached the valley, and flowed on, expanding all the time, advancing slowly, burning and covering everything under it.

Through the dark of the night, through the black rain of ashes dimming the sun in full daylight, the people fled before the red-hot river, as it poured over their settlements, across fields and the graves of their dead. Only their pyramid of Cuicuilco was too tall for the lava masses to swallow it entirely, and today two-thirds of the pyramid still rise above the ocean of lava turned solid.

Thirty-two square miles had turned to stone before the eruption had spent its force and the lava cooled down. A stone ceiling of between twenty and twenty-five feet thick covered the traces of former human life in the south-west of the Valley of Mexico. These traces were discovered by the archaeologists when they dug galleries under the layer of lava.

The pyramid of Cuicuilco, lying in the southern outskirts of Mexico City, was freed from its stone mantle. It is a round building, sixty-five feet high and 450 feet in diameter. Its outer cast consists of pounded mud, which at its base has a protective covering of unhewn stones, joined together without mortar. Steps lead up to the platform which carries a rectangular altar. The pyramid is surrounded by several concentric rings of graves. It was built only a few centuries B.C., so the volcano must have erupted somewhere around the time of Christ's birth or a little earlier.

Even more important for the archaeologists were finds from a definitely archaic period—statues, figurines and vessels—which showed such great artistic skill they could have come from only a highly developed civilization. They were too old to be attributed to any of the peoples of Central America: not to the Aztecs, the Toltecs, the Chichemecs, the Maya, the Totonacs, the Zapotecs. For the history of these peoples had been laboriously traced back to about A.D. 300. Could the Indians have had a high civilization, so far overlooked, older than any of the known ones?

For years this question remained the greatest riddle of Mexico.

11

The Olmecs and their Inventions

'It was my turquoise: I had it of Leah when I was a bachelor;
I would not have given it for a wilderness of monkeys.'
SHYLOCK in *The Merchant of Venice*

ALMOST every one of the old chroniclers related the legend of the age-old country of Olman, most ancient of the Indian kingdoms, a paradise where cocoa and rubber grew and rare birds were flying about—the Quetzal bird, the kotinga, trupial and spoonbill. The country abounded in jade, turquoise, gold and silver. The people there, the Olmecs, were clad in robes and magnificent ornaments; on their feet they wore sandals made of leather, or sometimes of rubber. They worshipped a goddess of the earth and a goddess of the moon. They were familiar with secret sciences and had a magician for a king.

Everything great had originally happened in Olman, all discoveries and civilizations had come from there. These and other marvellous things the chroniclers related of Olman, and until this century such tales were treated as pure legend.

Until near the end of last century almost every artifact found in the ancient Indian kingdoms could be attributed by its style to the people that made it. But in 1884 Alfredo Chavero reported finds on the coast of the Gulf of Mexico so strange that they could not belong to any of the known civilizations, and he could explain them only by the immigration of men from a different Old World civilization. They were stone heads of colossal dimensions and axe-heads with faces on them, the features a mixture of man and jaguar. After this Noguera found a little green stone figurine at Michoacan, and Vaillant a clay figure of the same type at Gualapita. Neither of these could be placed, but they seemed to be in the same style as a stone sarcophagus discovered at Tres Zapotes many years before.

123

Then came another find (made about 1910) in the same style, from near San Andres Tuxtla, west of La Venta: a small jade figure. But this had a date inscribed on it, and the date could be deciphered, because it was very like the Mayan glyphs, which had by then become known Transposed to our reckoning, the jade figure carried the date of A.D. 162—the oldest date discovered till then in Mexico and Yucatan

This meant that similar finds could now be classified and attributed to a very ancient people, and it proved—even more sensational—that such a people already had a script. Now the scholars boldly declared that the remains found were those of the Olmecs, celebrated in the old chronicles, the bringers of civilization to all Mexico. They had lived along the coast of the Gulf, between the Alvarada Lagoon to the south of Vera Cruz and the Terminos Lagoon at the borders of the Yucatan peninsula and in what is today the district of Tuxtla. Their traces were also found at Morelos, Guerrero, Puebla, Oaxaca, and Chiapas. Their capital must have been somewhere in the enormous swamp area of Mexico's Atlantic coast, and a succession of archaeological expeditions set out to discover this city, but they all returned without even finding any clue as to its site.

An American, Matthew W. Stirling, who came in the early thirties, seemed likely to be equally unsuccessful, although he worked very systematically, exploring every hill that might have a building buried underneath, questioning the natives, trying to get a hint where to start digging. For weeks he and his assistants roamed the country in all directions and found nothing.

One day he saw a wooded hill rising in the middle of a swamp. It must have once been an island in a big lake, where the water had gradually evaporated over a very long period, turning the lake into a swamp. Stirling asked the natives what they knew about this island and what its name was. They told him its name was La Venta; that was all he could get out of them. But he had a strong hunch there was something special about it. He determined to go over to it and see what secrets it might be hiding.

When he and his companions reached it, they had the same experience as Stephens had had at Copán: they saw walls gleaming through the dense foliage of the mangrove wilderness, and suddenly they were standing in front of a high building. Its shape showed that it must once have been a pyramid, the centre of a cluster of buildings and squares with bigger and smaller mud pyramids grouped around it. This was indeed the Olmecs' capital: La Venta.

When Stirling started digging there, he made many puzzling discoveries. North of the pyramid, at a depth of twenty-three feet, he came upon a mosaic of serpentine chips, with thirty-seven axe-heads

The thousand-pillar hall at Chichen Itza is in principle like the colonnade of Knossos

Palace of Knossos

The young maize god of Copán. This representation has suggestions of both East Asian and Mediterranean influences

also made of serpentine, laid out crosswise on the mosaic. On closer investigation he found that the single parts and chips of the mosaic were carefully embedded in asphalt.

Asphalt was a trading commodity of the area between the rivers Euphrates and Tigris, where the soil was rich in oil; and from there it reached the civilizations of the Old World. The Cretans used asphalt, in their art of incrustation and their tarsia style of painting, in order to fix all the single parts of inlaid work to one another and to their base. The famous game-board of Crete, about a yard square, has pieces of gold, silver, ivory and rock-crystal, circles of rock-crystal lying on gold-foil. The eyes of the Cretan bull-tritons (goblets in the shape of a bull's head) are of rock-crystal with scarlet pupils and framed with jasper. All these components are carefully embedded in asphalt.

The excavation of ancient Crete is still going on, and quite recently, when the old ceremonial caves were being explored, altars were un-earthed with heaps of bronze and gold axes lying or hanging near them—just like Stirling's find at La Venta.

He also found huge altars there, weighing from twenty to fifty tons. They were hewn from immense blocks of stone in such a way that their upper part jutted out like a table-top; and they were covered in reliefs on all sides, the jaguar motif prevailing. The niches of one of the altars contain statues with crossed legs, sculpted in the round. They are holding on a rope two men in fetters who are represented in bas-relief on the altar's sides.

In a second altar's niche the main statue holds a dwarf on its lap. Dwarfs carried in arms by adults recur four times on the altar's sides, and they are shown in the attitudes of unruly children. These reliefs have a workmanship and feeling so like certain reliefs at Monte Alban that they have been attributed to the same master.

The stone used for the altars came from the Tuxtla volcanoes, and had to be brought from there to the island in the former lake, a distance of eighty miles as the crow flies. How the Olmecs managed this trans-port is a mystery which has never been solved.

Another mysterious find among the ruins of La Venta was an immense human head in stone. As Stirling and his assistants went on digging, they came on half a dozen such stone heads. One of the smaller ones is six feet tall, with a circumference of eighteen feet; others reach a height of eight feet. At first the excavators took them for gigantic statues, only the heads sticking out of the ground—although this would have made the whole statues about the height of a ten-storey house. But it soon turned out that there were no bodies attached to the heads, which were supported by only a stone plinth. Statues far over life-size were found at La Venta, however; one is holding a bowl and wears a comb in its hair. A giant figure, with a mask shaped like a jaguar's face, once stood on the edge of the crater of the Tuxtla volcanoes.

The realism of these statues, which is as remarkable as their size, was hardly ever achieved in later times, and it became the model for sculptures in all the Central American kingdoms. It is equally astonishing that the statues do not represent Indians. Though they are men who have many features in common, pointing to one particular race, it is not the Indian one; and these men wear a helmet with flaps protecting the cheeks.

The White God wore a helmet. The Aztec prince asked Cortés for a mercenary's gilt helmet because it was like the one which had been worn by the White God. Remains of helmets have been found on Crete, and so have representations of them, plated with boar's teeth, which show the cheek protection. They were adorned with a horse-hair plume, as shown also on an ivory relief from the city of Mycenae. Perhaps this was the kind of helmet the White God wore.

If the White God's helmet could go back to the Olmecs, the feather crown too might have originated with them. Their country was described as a 'paradise of tropical birds'. Quetzalcoatl, exiled from Tollan, went to this coast and wore 'the adornment of the people from the coast', the crown of feathers of the Quetzal bird. It was the same as the famous crown of Montezuma II, kept today in the Ethnologica Museum at Vienna; and such Indian feather crowns can be admired in many museums.

But we know other feather-work as well from the Indian civilizations, an art medium capable of extraordinary beauty; gossamer feather embroideries; smaller and smaller feathers assembled into a carpet rug or coat; feathers of a metallic brilliance mixed with others ranging from the lightest to the darkest blue, from the palest to the richest yellow; feathers green, brown, purple, red and orange, joined together to make patterns of the most delicate shading and the softest silkiest, almost weightless, cloths. These feather coats were so wonderfully beautiful that long after the *Conquista* the Spanish bishops still had their vestments made from feathers by Indian women who had formerly embroidered the robes for their own rulers.

No feather-work was found during the excavations in Mesopotamia, Egypt, or Crete; but the Cretans were certainly familiar with this craft. In the legend of Icarus (originally Cretan) his father Daedalus made wings from feathers so that the two could escape from the dungeon of King Minos, who had summoned them to build the maze; their jailor found feathers, wax and straps which they had left behind in their empty cell.

The old chroniclers said the Olmecs came from Olman. The meaning of 'Olman' is given as 'country of rubber'; and if the Olmecs wore sandals of rubber they may have invented the rubber ball too, perhaps ball courts as well, and the ritual ball-games. For the oldest courts were found in their cities, similar to those of the civilizations which followed theirs.

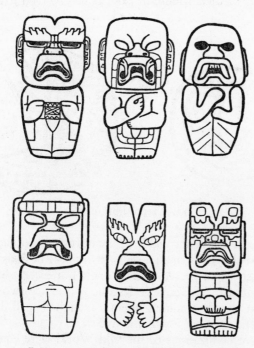

11. Jaguar men from the Olmecs, showing
their votive axes and jade figures. They
were masters in working jade—like the
Cretans (from Crickeberg)

The jaguar motif also goes back to the Olmecs, passing from them to the Maya of Uaxactun, to Teotihuacan, to the Toltecs and the Aztecs. The Olmecs were so dominated by this motif in their art that it has been called a 'jaguar mania', and they depicted all types and stages between man and beast. The ancient Cretans had a similar mania, only with them it was lions: hence the many lion-masks found in the Cretan civilization and those which followed it.

Another thing found in La Venta was also typical of Crete: little talismans of jade, the opalescent bluish or emerald-green stone to which all the Indian peoples attached a tremendous value. They cherished it more than gold or silver, it was their most precious possession, and after life itself the most precious gift to be offered to the gods.

Very big finds of jade were made in the Olmecs' territory. They were masters in working it, and the craft passed from them to all the civilizations of Central America; the subject peoples of the Aztecs still paid some of their tribute in jade, as can be seen from the Aztec tribute lists.

12. Cretan lion masks

One tomb in La Venta yielded a treasure-trove of jade objects— ear-rings, animal figures, axes; a great many bare designs only lightly scratched in, so as to preserve the stone's glittering, smooth, semi-transparent surface. At Cerro de las Mesas—eighty-two jade figures were found in one spot, among them a trough-shaped dug-out with paddles, and the figure of a weeping dwarf.

The ancient civilizations of the Old World were equally familiar with jade. Confucius called it the stone of virtue, and it was greatly valued in China. The Phoenicians were masters in working it, and as traders made the stone known all over the world of their time. Jade vases and ornaments from Crete or Mycenae reached the court of Thothmes III of Egypt around 1500 B.C.—they had been brought in by Phoenicians, who in exchange took ivory from Africa back to Crete. Hathor, the cow-headed Egyptian goddess, one of whose temples stood on Mount Sinai, was a goddess of jade and turquoise. But green jade was specially important in Crete; Cretan women adorned themselves with jade talismans. To this day Cretan peasant women wear pierced Minoan signet stones on a ribbon round their necks—and they will not sell the stones at any price.

Similarly, chieftains of the wild Indian tribes on the Amazon still wear such stones on ribbons round their necks, and absolutely refuse to part with them: it is the only thing they do not use for barter. Perhaps

The uncanny Sacred Well at Chichen Itza. Its sheer walls go down
sixty-five feet to the shimmering green water below

The skull-rack at Chichen Itza: expression of a warrior people's conception of religion

the search for Confucius's 'stone of virtue' was one of the reasons why men from the Far East came to America.

The same might apply to another material used for jewellery: amber. The dredger brought up a great deal of amber from the sacred well at Chichen Itza, and amber jewellery has been found in nearly all the Indian civilizations. In the Old World only the Phoenicians traded in amber, bringing it from the Baltic. But long before that the Cretans, whose ships had also brought it from the Baltic, were using it for jewellery. So perhaps the Indians' amber, like their jade, came from the Old World.

Old World origins can be proved for the Totonac stone yokes and the so-called Palmas, both of which were taken over by the Totonacs from the Olmecs. The Palmas are three-cornered stone pillars with a recess at their base. They are decorated with birds, standing or kneeling men, often with closed eyes, sometimes presented like 'humanized' birds, snakes, butterflies. The composition and arrangement of the figures are the work of a master, and the same applies to the stone yokes discovered during the excavations on Mount Tajén.

These yokes, made of basalt, andesite, diorite or serpentine, are shaped like horse-shoes, and represent animals or birds, sometimes also human beings, though these often wear animal or bird masks. The head is at the base, the arms and legs at the sides. They are clearly connected with some ritual for the dead, since offerings for the dead have been discovered between the sides. The yoke may have been meant to pinion the departed to the ground, but its significance has never been explained for certain.

Some of the Olmec yokes have the two sides connected by a crossbeam, a shape known from representations in ancient Egypt, where it was also part of the ritual of the dead. The Egyptians referred to this symbol as 'Ankh'; it was their symbol of life—the life after death. The Olmecs could scarcely have invented the same symbol in the same context by mere chance.

Olmec and Totonac axes have been found in entirely different shapes from the ceremonial ones: axes with perforated blades, which have animal and human figures, sometimes acrobats, worked into the opening and fitting beautifully into its curves. We know such an axe from ancient Egypt: it has only the outline of the blade left, while the animal figures worked into this frame are arranged just as skilfully to harmonize with the given space and curves.

When the scholars compared the different styles of the finds made in the last decades they were forced to the conclusion that all the stone

I

craftmanship of the Central American civilizations originated from th
Olmecs. The Olmec also invented reliefs, sculpture in the round, an
the stele. Their stelae were such masterly creations that they serve
as models to all the peoples that came after them; the art of the Olme
stele can be traced almost without gaps through a whole millennium
The Maya took over stucco as well as stelae from the Olmecs, wh
had discovered how to make mortar for building pyramids. Othe
Olmec inventions were the pyramid itself, the big stone altars, th
sarcophagus, the use of asphalt, probably feather-work and the rubbe
ball; and the script.

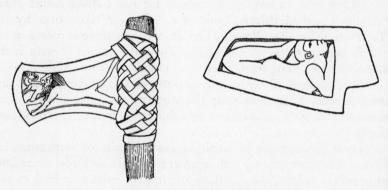

13. Ceremonial axes, both with edges bored through: from Egypt
(*left*); from the Olmecs (*right*)

The Olmec script, the oldest Indian script so far known, is pre
served only on some few stelae, which are entirely Mayan in style
The Olmecs gave the Maya their script and probably their figur
symbols. Therefore, since the Mayan characters were Cretan symbols
the Olmecs must have known the Cretan script.

Indeed the Olmecs' civilization, short as was the time it lasted, i
almost unique in history for the strength, range and durability of th
influence it exerted. When it was destroyed by force, it passed to th
Olmecs' nearest neighbours, the oldest Maya, the Zapotecs at Mont
Alban, and the people of Teotihuacan, which the Olmecs had als
built. The Totonacs and Tarascans took over the Olmecs' building
and building components, and the Olmecs built the great city o
Cholula, which was still flourishing at the end of the twelfth century
A.D. when the Toltecs reached that area.

The Olmecs must have come to Mexico in the first years of our era
and built then their cities of La Venta and Tres Zapotes. This can b
seen from two very early inscriptions on finds at the latter city. On
has been mentioned above: a jade statue inscribed with a date th

equivalent of A.D. 162—a clumsy figure with bird's wings, and a duck-billed but otherwise human face. The other is a fragment of a stele dated the equivalent of A.D. 31, its reverse decorated with a jaguar mask.

The features on the Olmec statues prove that the Olmecs were not Indians. They must therefore have been the White Gods of Mexico, who later went to the Maya and the Zapotecs and became the White Gods of those peoples too (see table on page 199).

But although their civilization has a great many traits in common with our own ancient civilizations, they cannot themselves have brought these traits over from the Old World. For when they arrived in Mexico, many of the 'inventions' they introduced—the knowledge of asphalt, ceremonial axes, jade, the 'jaguar motif'—had long been forgotten in the Old World. The same applies to the script: the high civilization of Crete had then been extinct for 1,500 years, and the Cretan script was no longer known.

Therefore the Olmecs must have received their civilization and their script from an Indian empire much older still, which flourished outside Central America, somewhere where the Cretan script was known and used, where art and engineering had gone on developing for hundreds of years. What the Olmecs knew of these things when they arrived in Mexico, they could not have acquired from one day to the next but only by long experience.

Was that mysterious empire in South America? Did the Olmecs once migrate from there?

12

Ancient Peoples of the Peruvian Plain

THE Peruvian plain has no impenetrable jungle to swallow up buildings or whole cities in a few decades. It is an arid, sandy strip only eighty miles wide, but stretching about 1,000 miles along the Pacific coast. If you fly over it you will see hundreds of pyramids: over seventy of them among the ruins near the mouth of the river Jequetepeque, in what was probably the ancient city of Pacatnamu; dozens more in the ruins of another big city, which was once called Chan-Chan.

Like the pyramids of Hauwara and Illahun on the Nile (and unlike most of the ones in Central America), all the Peruvian pyramids were built from adobes. They are step pyramids, with an outside staircase leading up to the platform which carries the temple.

In Mexico the myths of vanished cities were for centuries the chief or only evidence of those cities' existence. In Peru most of the ruins are still standing today just as they were when the first Spaniards entered the country. So Peruvian archaeology has developed in a very different way. Instead of having to fight through the jungle, as in Mexico, anyone with a spade could see plenty of ruins and start digging at once. It became quite fashionable to go to Peru for a short dig, perhaps out of mere curiosity; and finds were made almost everywhere the soil was scratched. But of course many serious archaeologists came as well, and with their painstaking research they contributed an enormous amount to our knowledge of the ancient civilizations. They were particularly successful working on the burial grounds near the coast. From a vast number of details they built up a picture of the ancient Chimu empire.

According to the chroniclers, the Chimu people created this empire by federating many small kingdoms, like those of Quito, Lambayeque and the Chira Valley. These were founded by men who

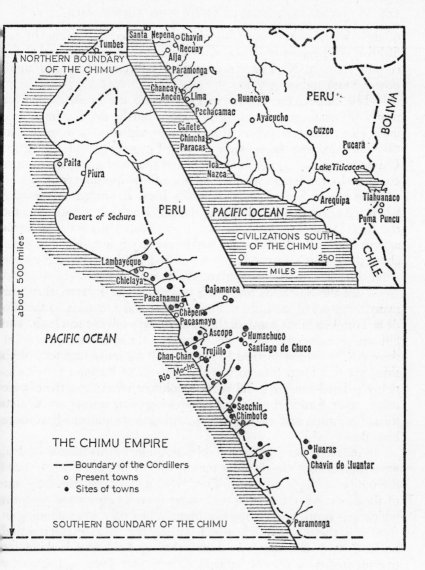

The map shows labels including:

Tumbes, Santa, Nepena, Chavin, Recuay, Alja, NORTHERN BOUNDARY OF THE CHIMU, Paramonga, Chancay, Ancón, Lima, Huancayo, PERU, BOLIVIA, Pachacamac, Ayacucho, Cañete, Chincha, Cuzco, Paracas, Pucará, Paita, Piura, Ica, Nazca, Lake Titicaca, Desert of Sechura, PERU, PACIFIC OCEAN, Arequipa, Tiahuanaco, Puma Puncu, CIVILIZATIONS SOUTH OF THE CHIMU, 0 250 MILES, CHILE, PACIFIC OCEAN, Lambayeque, Chiclaya, Cajamarca, Pacatnamu, Chepen, Pacasmayo, Ascope, Humachuco, Santiago de Chuco, Chan-Chan, Trujillo, Rio Moche, Secchin, Chimbote, Huaras, Chavin de Huantar, Paramonga

THE CHIMU EMPIRE
- - - Boundary of the Cordillers
○ Present towns
● Sites of towns

SOUTHERN BOUNDARY OF THE CHIMU

about 500 miles

had come on rafts from Mexico's Pacific coast, probably driven out of their country by the Great Flood, of which they brought legends with them.

The Chimu too were originally small kings or tribal chiefs who settled in their fortresses and temples along the river Moche. They at first called themselves Mochica, and this was also the name of their language. In the course of the centuries they defeated all their neighbours and ruled over the whole coastal plain. After this they were called Chimu, which means 'ruler', an extension of the name of one

133

of their kings—'the great Chimu'—who reigned at the end of the fifth or the beginning of the sixth century A.D. and expanded the empire enormously. For centuries they collected more and more power, more and more gold.

Their empire, the biggest in Peru before the Incas, existed for nearly fifteen centuries, and their history can be divided into three main parts: the first period from their immigration and settlement till about A.D. 500; the second a period of prosperity under the great Chimu kings, lasting till about 1000; and the third going up to their conquest by the Incas round the middle of the fifteenth century.

The chroniclers recorded that the Incas destroyed this empire when the army of Chimu Capac, the last king, lost a battle against the Inca Tupac Yupanqui. In fact it was probably a popular revolt against the small ruling class, as well as military defeat, which brought about the empire's downfall. Its art and civilization survived for some while after this, to disappear gradually in Spanish times.

When the Spaniards first came to Peru under Pizarro, they saw many remnants of the Chimu empire. There was a fortress on the Rio de la Torteleza in the south of the country, on a hill 165 feet high. The hill was surrounded by ramparts with a fort for an entrance; the other three corners of the fortress had been built up into outer forts with sides 130 feet long. Pizarro saw this fortress of Paramonga with its richly painted ramparts and walls absolutely intact; and there were many other fortifications equally imposing, monuments to Chimu former greatness and military power. All such monuments have since been destroyed.

In 1602 loot-hunting Spanish soldiers, under a man called Montalva, were approaching what is today the city of Trujillo, when they noticed the outline of high pyramids. They were particularly struck by one of these, sixty-five feet high and rising from a large, wide platform which was another sixty-five feet high. When they were standing in front of it, they saw that it was built entirely from mud bricks: it would be hard work breaking this down, they realized, and looking for treasure underneath. They immediately set about diverting the nearby river Moche in the pyramid's direction, and left that to do the work: the walls collapsed according to plan. Treasures came to light under the ruins, and disappeared into the soldiers' pockets. They found and pillaged silver table-ware and platters made from an alloy of gold and copper. They found a figure of pure gold 'standing an inch high from the belt and looking like a bishop', as one of the chroniclers described it.

Heavy falls of rain completed the walls' disintegration, and only a vast amorphous mound of earth was left, in which form the ruin has survived to our day. Fortunately the Spaniards did not think the so-called Pyramid of the Moon, the smaller pyramid next to the tall one, important enough to be worth pulling down. It concealed a different sort of treasure—mummies in graves—which modern excavators were to recover intact.

The Spaniards found a particularly rich booty in the Huava del Toledo, the old tomb of the Chimu kings: golden goblets, figures, and a fish of solid gold, their metal content alone worth the equavalent of £800,000. In the temple of Moche the Spaniards pillaged gold and silver to the value of 300,000 gold pesetas. From another temple Escobar Corchuelo and his companions stole gold and copper worth 500,000 pesetas—'not counting the loot they kept secret', as one chronicler put it.

Travellers in the following centuries found the residence of the kings of Chimu, the old Chan-Chan, which for some reason the Spaniards had left untouched. This city covered six square miles, and lies between Trujillo and the Pacific, about five miles north of the river Moche. It used to be a port, but is no longer on the sea owing to alluvial deposit.

Among the ruins, the foundations of two very large walled-in palaces were discovered. The so-called 'big palace', a colossal building with sides 1,300 by 1,650 feet, contained a large water reservoir. In front of the palace was a building which was at first called the prison, because it had many small rooms which were taken to be cells. The second, smaller, palace, its site nearer the sea, was surrounded by a double wall with a parapet, and here too the remains were found of a building with many small passages and 'cells'. Both palaces had courts, halls, dwellings, and planned gardens. The 'hall of the arabesques' in the bigger palace has become famous for its relief patterns with rhombic decorations in strict hieratic order, reminiscent of chess-boards.

The 'prison' buildings were divided into rooms by huge stones, and the rooms contained dress materials, mummies, human and animal figures, fragments of wooden idols, and mother-of-pearl shells. So these buildings could not have been prisons; they must have served ritual purposes. Snakes were kept in them—living gods: the snake palaces of Chan-Chan may have been the scene of the 'trials by ordeal' which occurred in all the ancient Indian empires.

Living men were flung to snakes, ferocious beasts, and scorpions (this was still the custom with the Incas at the end of their empire). An Indian might be tortured if he denied an accusation, and if this brought no result he would be thrown to the beasts. If they spared him for two days his innocence was considered proved.

Similar customs, of course, prevailed in the past empires of the Old World. A German emperor made his wife walk on red-hot iron slabs to find out if she had been faithful to him; and, even more closely akin there is the story of Daniel:

'. . . Then the king commanded, and they brought Daniel, and cast him into the den of lions. Now the king spake and said unto Daniel, Thy God whom thou servest continually, he will deliver thee . . . Then the king arose very early in the morning and went in haste unto the den of lions. . . .' To his astonishment he found Daniel alive 'Then said Daniel unto the king, O king, live forever. My God hath sent his angel and hath shut the lions' mouths, and they have not hur me. . . .'

There is a legend with a slightly different version. Before being thrown into the den, Daniel provided himself with pitch and hair which he worked into the shape of baby chickens and threw to the savage beasts. They devoured the 'chickens', believing them to be alive, but it apparently gave them indigestion and made them lose their appetite. Alas, there is no legend of an Indian Daniel.

The snake, creature of the water and the underworld, looks down from all Chan-Chan's walls. There are so many snake representations that the city must undoubtedly have been the city of snake ritual. The very name is evidence, for Chan was the Mexican name for snake. 'Na Chan' meant House of Snakes, and 'Na' meant house in Chimu as well as in Mexican.

The Chimu ritual was one of water. Throughout their lives these people had very close ties with the sea. Water was their element, its symbols being fish and snake, which in pictorial art often figured as symbols for the play of the waves. Incidentally, a very similar ritual existed in ancient Egypt, where the goddess of Buto used to be a live cobra kept in temples.

Chimu pottery and goldsmith's work survived the destruction of their cities, and both are extremely accomplished. The pottery recovered from Chimu graves is to be found today in nearly all the great museums. The head-shaped jugs carry the features of men, women and children of the people, sometimes also the hard, determined faces of their kings. Such jugs are common to all Indian civilizations (as they were also found in Troy, Etruria, and Mycenae): the nose and features are in relief, and there may be little arms and legs as well, or even the entire body.

A very peculiar piece of pottery was specially popular with the Chimu: double jugs, connected by a tube, with only one spout They are like the double jugs of the ancient Mediterranean civilizations, as are the Chimu's pottery urns, shaped like houses; we know such urns from Crete and Etruria.

The kings whose faces we see on some of the clay jugs once ruled in the realm of 'Wotan'. Pedro Corzo, a pilot who sailed up and down the Peruvian coast for four years, reported that everywhere in the temples he had found wooden or stone statues of a god called Guatan. The name means whirlwind, an equivalent to the old Germanic name 'Wotan', the ancient god of storm—and the Maya called him Votan.

On a clay jug from Ratinlixul in Guatemala there was a representation of the god of the moon as king of night and darkness, with the glyph 'ahau' added, meaning 'master and king', and 'votan', meaning 'interior of the earth'. This god was also worshipped by the Maya, the Mixtecs, the Zapotecs, and the Aztecs. He was held in particularly high esteem by the Maya because he had the gift of the oracle.

Our modern soothsayers, the astrologers who work out horoscopes in the newspapers, use a system based on the ancient Babylonian signs of the Zodiac. Egyptians as well as Babylonians believed in oracles, and so, of course, did the Greeks. People came from great distances to consult the famous Delphic oracle—author of that highly 'oracular' answer to Croesus, last king of Lydia, who asked if he should march against the Persians. 'If you cross the Halys,' he was told, 'a great empire will be overthrown.' He found out too late that it was to be his own.

The counterpart of Delphi in the New World was Rimac, a short day's journey on foot from Pachacamac, which is near today's Lima. The chroniclers recorded that the inhabitants of the Rimac Valley worshipped a god of human shape who when consulted disclosed the future like the oracle of Delphi. White-robed priests, who lived as celibates and never partook of salt or pepper, carried out his ritual. Before starting out on a military expedition, or even a hunt, kings and chieftains would consult the oracle at Rimac, which was known all the way to the Cordilleras.

Nearly as famous was the oracle of the god Pachacamac, after whom the chieftains of Guismancu had named their capital. (Guismancu was a small country on the coast of Peru south of the Chimu empire.) According to the chroniclers this city was bigger than ancient Rome, and in its temple a black devil had spoken to the people. In the temples of Guismancu, which became places of pilgrimage for the population, the priests foretold the future from behind gold masks.

The oracles of the Peruvian coast were so famous that in order to annex them the Inca Pachacutec once mobilized an army of 40,000 men. He took the god Pachacamac along to Cuzco. The victors seized a few idols from one of the temples, such as a gold dog and a golden fish, but did not touch anything else. The pilgrims were still flocking to the former shrine when the first Spaniards arrived.

'It was a city of a considerable population', Hernando Pizarro wrote, 'and many of their houses were firmly built. The temple of their tutelary god consisted of a row of buildings which, enclosing a cone-shaped mountain, looked more like a fortress than a place of religion.' All the city's buildings, incidentally, were made not of stone but of adobes.

When Hernando Pizarro was refused admittance by the priests, he forced an entry. 'Followed by his men,' his aide's account runs, 'he squeezed through the pass leading to the open square at the summit of the mountain. On one side of the mountain stood a kind of chapel. It was the shrine of the fearful deity. The doors were covered with crystal decorations, with turquoises and small corals.'

When the Indians tried to prevent Pizarro from entering their shrine the city was shaken by an earthquake, and they fled in fear of the White Gods. Pizarro pulled open the door to the holy place and entered with his men. But instead of a hall with gold and precious stones offered to the god Pachamacac by his worshippers, the Spaniards found only a small dark room, a cave—the place of sacrifice. In the darkness of the remotest corner they made out the image of the god, a horrible monster made of wood with an almost human head.

In disappointed rage they pulled the wooden idol from its lair, dragged it out into the open and smashed it to pieces. Then they cleared the ground and erected a large cross of stone and mortar in its place. The priests had hidden away most of the rich booty the conquerors had been looking for; only a small part of it, to the value of 80,000 castellanos, fell into their hands. For a long time after this the faithful would come from far and wide to visit the old shrine, and its continued existence was a thorn in the flesh of the Spanish priests. But the stream of pilgrims gradually dried up.

Today there are only ruins left of this city of the oracle with its palaces and temples, roads and squares, and its thousands of graves. In the graves were mummies, another unexpected treasure for the archaeologists.

When Pizarro's men had stripped the gold frieze off the temple of Cuzco and rushed into its hall, they noticed strange bundles leaning against the walls. These were mummies, wrapped in precious materials, with masks of gold, silver, wood or clay over their faces. Their eyes had been replaced by the eyes of cuttle-fish. These 'state mummies', the bodies of the Inca rulers, were attended by priests and carried through the streets on every solemn occasion.

Besides the mummies in the temples, every important family's house contained a large room with the ancestors' mummies lining the walls. They were thought to give supernatural inspiration, so festivals were celebrated in this room. Vaults of mud or bricks or stone chambers were built for the mummies who were buried neither in the great temples nor in the houses. Alternatively, a large clay vessel would simply be put upside down over the mummy's head, or it would be covered over by shelters made from wood and reeds. Sometimes the mummies were tied together into bundles: perhaps an epidemic had killed off a lot of people at the same time, or else one of the group may have been the master, and others were his attendants who had to follow him into death.

According to the chronicler La Calancha the dead were usually buried after five days. They were washed, and their knees were pulled up so that the chin rested on them. They wore ordinary clothes under robes and shawls or covers made of reeds, or sometimes wicker-work or animals' hides or mats. The corpse was sewn into these, and bales of grass or seaweed were wrapped round the bundle to avoid its being damaged during its transport to the temple.

Nothing is known about the Peruvian method of mummification, except that the viscera were removed. The Peruvian civilizations did not have the Egyptian custom of using natron and resin packs and anointing with oil—since the climate favoured a natural process. A dry climate and saliferous soil can in themselves lead to mummification if the dead body is in contact with the ground. But this was not the case with the state mummies.

Mummies were known not only to the Incas and in Peru but also in Colombia. When excavators opened up a cave in Ganchavita, they found mummies, each wearing a small gold crown, with funeral offerings lying round it, cloth, gold figures, ornaments and emeralds. It was surprising that mummies should have been found here, a country with a climate most unfavourable for conservation. But chemical analysis has established that resins and oils were used—so the methods of mummification were almost exactly the same as in ancient Egypt.

For many generations after his death a man could play an important part in his descendants' lives. This was a source first of bewilderment and then exasperation for the Spanish judges in the law-courts at Cuzco, set up entirely after the Spanish model. They had enough trouble in the first years with the language difficulties, as they knew very little of the Indian languages, and the Indians understood hardly any Spanish. They also noticed that the courts were always filled with Indians to the last seat: anyone who had a complaint to make or was a party to a law-suit would evidently bring along all his relatives to the capital.

As the judges looked more closely from their dais at the crowd o spectators, they saw a lot of extremely old people sitting huddled with veils or masks over their faces. After the verdict had been announced the Indians sitting next to them would shoulder these aged people like a bundle and make for the exit. Every morning when there was a court-day at Cuzco, crowds of Indians would hurry in from the mountains so as to secure seats for themselves and the people on their shoulders. Eventually the judges discovered that these 'aged people' were dead bodies, the family mummies who always had to be present when an important decision for the family was to be expected.

It took a long time to get rid of this deeply rooted custom by strict prohibitive laws; the laws were so much resented that at one point they nearly led to the entire collapse of Spanish jurisdiction. Meanwhile for years after the *Conquista*, many a judge had to read out his verdict to a court where half the people 'present' had been dead for generations. In reports sent to Spain the judges quite often let off steam about these gatherings of mummies, and the reports, fortunately, were preserved for posterity.

Mummies were found also in the burial grounds of another ancient people on Peru's coastal plain, the people of Nazca, Ica and Paracas. The ruins of this civilization, several temples and fortresses, are in the Valley of Chincha. The fortress of La Centinela, for instance, was built over during the times of the Incas, but its eastern part, built from adobes, is much older.

It was this people which constructed the vast irrigation system for which the country was famous in Inca times. Like the Chimu, they must have originally migrated to the Peruvian coast from Meso-America, but they had to lead a harder life here than the Chimu. Fighting the wild tribes in the mountains, they became a warrior people, who offered fierce resistance to the Spaniards. They never accepted the Sun religion, but continued to worship Moon and Water long after their conquest by the Incas. We know them less from the great cities of ruins than from the ancient burial grounds on the coast, with the evidence of amazing arts and crafts to be found there.

At Ancon, for instance, the dead were buried, often on top of one another, in simple holes in the ground. The mortal remains in these graves have long disintegrated, but the funeral offerings— weapons, ornaments, pottery and materials—have survived, and today form part of museum collections all over the world. In the graves of Nazca some of the finds go back to before the beginning of our era, in the upper graves to the times of the Incas. At Paracas cave-tombs have been found, often containing as many as fifty skeletons, and whole cities of the dead, hewn twenty feet deep into the stone, with room for up to 400 corpses. These were put into cells in a squatting position, wrapped in thick layers of material; and the funeral offerings here are particularly plentiful.

Very strange creatures are depicted on the pottery and textiles of this early civilization: animals like cats and dogs but with several heads on top of one another; cat-heads, wearing beards, and snake bodies surrounded by lightning flashes; snake bodies intertwined; parrots, owls, fishes, frogs, men with puma masks, and human heads with snakes. There were also images of weeping gods with tears running down their faces—they hold severed heads in their hands as trophies.

Another peculiar find was the interlocked dragons with short sickle-shaped wings (mentioned earlier for Tajén) characteristic of the Chou style in China. The Chinese may also have brought copper to the New World, for this was first discovered in America in the so-called 'Gallinazo' civilization of about the same period; and a contemporary Chinese state, conquered by the Yüeh dynasty in 473 B.C., had a civilization of copper. The 'Mochica' or 'Proto-Chimu' people also show signs of Chinese influences, which ceased after 333 B.C. (when the Yüeh were overthrown by a new dynasty).

This is the third time we have come across proofs that men from the Far East reached America: influences traceable for the Maya at Palenque, the Puuc style of the Mayan 'New Empire', and at Chichen Itza; then for the Totonacs at El Tajén; and now for the coastal civilizations of South America. But many other finds on the Peruvian coast, particularly the textiles, point quite clearly to the ancient civilizations of the Mediterranean.

The tombs at Paracas are famous for their textile remains. In these tombs, twenty feet below ground, hewn out of red porphyry, besides clay vessels, weapons and gold ornaments, mummies were found: hundreds and thousands of them, wearing masks of wood, copper, silver or gold, adorned with gold and precious stones and wrapped up in either feather-work or materials. The feathers were fastened to a web, and there were often many thousands of them, making up a veritable feather carpet.

The shrouds woven from wool or cotton, sometimes lengths of twenty yards or more, can be seen in the Lima National Museum. Unique to the Nazca civilization, they have a fairy-tale beauty and are among the great achievements of Indian applied art. They show regularly recurring patterns, such as images of two-headed men with square faces, pumas with human heads and feet shaped like snakes, stylized birds, and mythical creatures. These woven-in images, which look as if they were painted on to the material, are the first instances of a secular art of representing men—i.e. with man, not god, put into the foreground. The Nazca civilization probably started during the first seven centuries A.D., its last emanations reaching as far as 1400.

The archaeologist Nevermann, who has written several treatises on the craft of Indian weaving, came to the conclusion that the Indian civilizations were familiar with the remarkable ikat method of applying patterns to material: this is based on the principle of wrapping parts of the warp or woof with raffia, leaves or waxed thread, before the weaving process starts, in order to keep them clear of colour. The dying is done afterwards, and when the material thus prepared is woven the design takes shape. We know this method from peoples of South and East Asia, as well as of the Mediterranean.

But the Indians also knew and used the batik method, i.e. weaving the cotton first and then covering the design with melted wax. The dye is then absorbed only by the uncovered portions, until the wax is dissolved in boiling water or scratched off, when a net of fine veins appears on the material along the lines where it has broken. Both batik and ikat techniques must surely be imports from the Old World, where they have always been much favoured.

From Greek mythology we know Cerberus, the three-headed dog with the skin of a snake, who guarded the entrance to Hades, and the aged ferryman, Charon, who took the souls of the dead across the river which flowed nine times round the underworld. The Greeks put a small coin, an obol, into the mouths of the dead, as a fare for Charon. In Egypt too the god of death was depicted, like Cerberus, with a dog's head.

In Aztec mythology Xolotl, god of death, companion to the setting sun, wore a dog's head—though the slim wolf-like animal of the Egyptians has turned into something more like a pug. He took the dead to the underworld, which had the river Chicunauictlan flowing round it nine times. He was also one of the incarnations of the White God Quetzalcoatl, who went down to the realm of the dead and appeared again as Xolotl. For a long time much of this supposed mythology was thought to be an invention of post-Spanish times; but when the mummies from the Peruvian coast had been unwrapped from their beautiful shrouds and were submitted to a thorough medical examination it was found that they had a small thin copper disc in their mouths—'the obol for Charon'.

Vases with strange designs were also retrieved from the tombs: designs of a cormorant trained for catching fish—such training of cormorants had been known in China from very early times; and designs of men 'planting fish'. They are digging holes into a ground while crossing a field and putting fish into the holes together with a seed of maize. This shows the rite of 'fish manuring', a custom so old it has otherwise come down to us only from Babylonian representations.

Then there were the animal mummies, discovered in the graves of the Peruvian coast, mostly dogs, parrots and guinea-pigs. We know from Egypt the holy graves of the Apis bulls, the cat graves of Bubastis, those of the sacred crocodiles of Ombos, the ibis graves of Ashmunein, and the ram graves of Elephantine. All these contain state sarcophagi where the Egyptians used to keep dead animals in their temples as 'living gods'. The Chimu city of Chan-Chan, as we have seen, contained the residence of *their* living god, the snake.

So much evidence the mummies provided that white men must have come to the Peruvian plain in very early times. But there is stronger evidence still, amounting to positive proof, from plant life, particularly cotton and the sweet potato, and possibly maize as well.

All plants, like every other living thing, develop from a cell formed when the male sperm merges with the female egg-shell. The new cell usually contains in its nucleus half a set of the father's and half a set of the mother's chromosomes. But it may receive one or several sets of chromosomes from the father and mother: it is then called diploid (twofold) or tetraploid (fourfold). These polyploid cells are of special significance when plants are cross-bred, and mainly affect the blossom. Many horticultural experiments are aimed at cultivating polyploid specimens with particularly big blossoms from familiar plants.

Often there is no noticeable outward difference between a polyploid and a normal specimen. But the cell's nucleus shows the cross-breeding distinctly, and this is the case with the cotton of the Indians. It has a double set of fifty-two chromosomes, twenty-six large and the other twenty-six exceptionally small; so it must be a cross between one parent with large and another with exceptionally small chromosomes.

One parent of the Indian cotton is the American cotton—growing wild—which has twenty-six small chromosomes. But the other parent does not exist in America and must have been imported. It comes from Europe, where the cotton's cell nucleus always contains twenty-six large chromosomes. So the cotton of the Indian civilizations is a cross between European and wild American cotton.

When the scientists studied the cotton of Melanesia, Micronesia, Australia, New Guinea and Polynesia, they found that this also contained twenty-six large and twenty-six small chromosomes. It could not have come from Europe (where all the cotton has twenty-six large chromosomes), so it must have reached those areas from America.

But where did the Indians get the cotton seeds from Europe to cross with their own wild cotton? These could not have been brought during the migration of people from Asia by way of the Bering Strait, since this migration lasted for thousands of years, and anyhow cotton cannot grow in very cold conditions. It must have come by some other route, and gone direct to regions with suitable conditions for its growth—certainly not by what is today Alaska and Canada.

It cannot have travelled in the sea, for sea water would have destroyed its germinal power. Nor could birds have been the carriers, for they do not eat cotton seeds. So man must have brought the seeds to the New World. The cotton examined came from the early civilizations of the Peruvian coast, which go back to a few centuries B.C. Therefore the Indian civilizations must have already known European cotton at that time, and crossed it with their own wild cotton.

As to maize, the chroniclers related how the god Quetzalcoatl stole it from the 'Food Mountain' and brought it to mankind. Scientists held divergent opinions about where maize originally came from: some say the Middle East and parts of Asia, some Polynesia, some South America. It is supposed to have been planted or cultivated from wild plants in the south of Mexico and in Guatemala as far back as pre-archaic times.

If the area with most varieties of a cultivated plant or a related species is the least likely to be where the plant came from, then Brazil should be the home of maize, for it occurs there in more varieties than in any other country. Anderson and Stonor claim to have proofs that maize existed in Europe before Columbus: could it have been the return present the White Gods brought with them when they went back to their old country?

It is easier to trace the route of the sweet potato, which certainly travelled across the Pacific, though we cannot be sure in which direction. The name of Cumura for the sweet potato can be found in the entire Pacific area, and derivations of it were current among the Aztecs and the peoples of Panama and the Caribbean. At any rate this points to the fact that an exchange of civilizations took place across the Pacific, perhaps in both directions, long before Columbus discovered America.

The chroniclers said the White Gods 'made the cotton to grow coloured'. Several scientists claim to have established that there was naturally coloured cotton—brownish or even blue—growing on the Peruvian coast. If so, the White Gods, in their cross-breeding, achieved more than modern agriculture, which has not yet succeeded in cultivating blue cotton. But it could mean also that among other things which they taught the Indians was the art of dyeing.

The walls of the palaces of Mitla are adorned with stone mosaics. They are very like the halls of arabesques at Chan-Chan in the kingdom of the Chimu

Snakes' heads and mythical butterflies on the façade of the very old central
temple in the so-called Citadel of Teotihuacan

The first Spaniards were astonished to see the kings who came to meet them wearing robes of ancient or Tyrian purple, equivalent to our crimson. This was the colour of the Incas, and the llamas sacrificed daily to the sun at Cuzco were adorned with crimson ribbons. 'With wool of that colour', said La Calancha, 'the Inca was crowned Just as crimson was the chosen colour of our popes and cardinals, purple here was taken to signify majesty and sovereignty.'

In the Old World Tyrian purple was the colour of the Phoenicians, who varied it from pale violet to pale pink and lilac. In their colonies too, such as Carthage, this colour was obtained from a whelk-like shell-fish called murex. Heaps of murex shells can still be found today in Kerkuan, near Carthage. Phoenician ships took Tyrian purple to the entire Mediterranean area.

There are scientists who maintain, having studied the distribution of the murex shell, that it could have come to the Indian civilizations only from the Mediterranean. But others point out that there is also a whelk species which yields the dye in the waters of the Isthmus of Mexico. So this question has not yet been settled.

It is significant, of course, that, like our own potentates, the Indians also chose purple of all colours as a symbol of 'majesty and sovereignty'; for they were familiar with other natural dyes such as indigo and cochineal, and with complicated ways of dyeing textiles, such as the alum-bath, which for a long time was a closely guarded secret of the Phoenicians (and presupposes a knowledge of chemistry). Some centuries B.C. the Phoenicians, having noticed that certain materials were hard to dye because they would not take colour, discovered how to treat the materials first with an alum solution, preparing the fibre in such a way that it took the colours desired. This process is still widely used in dyeing today.

Purple and alum-bath, cotton and sweet potato, the obol for Charon and the dog-headed god of Hades: these and many more parallels were discovered or confirmed by the finds on the Peruvian plain, proving once again that men from both the Far East and the ancient Mediterranean civilizations must have come to the American Indians. Now we must follow the White God's traces still further, to a very old Indian people living high up on the plateau of the Andes.

K

13

The Great City of Tiahuanaco

THE two parallel mountain ranges of the Andes, the Cordilleras
both of which reach a height of nearly 25,000 feet, run from north to
south, and cast the mould for the whole Pacific coastline of South
America. Between them is the corridor of the Sierra, which goes on
for thousands of miles, reaching from Ecuador right down to Argentina. It is over 500 miles wide round Lake Titicaca. Farther north
near Cuzco, it narrows down to 200 miles, and still farther north to
little more than 100.

It is wild, bare country, with not a tree to be seen anywhere
the sort of landscape one could imagine on the moon. Framed by the
cones of snow-covered volcanic mountains, the vast plateau, 13,000
feet above sea level, is traversed by low chains of mountains with
bizarre lava rocks, and cleft by gorges and fissures criss-crossing the
rocky ground—evidence of continued volcanic activity. It is the land
of the ancient Aymara and Colla, the country round La Paz, capital
of modern Bolivia.

At the foot of the western (the Maritime) Cordillera, with it
sheer slopes, the Peruvian coastal plain begins. One wide river, the
Santa, breaks through the Cordillera to flow into the Pacific. But the
plain is so dry that many rivers which have started up in the mountain
ooze away to nothing before they reach the sea. The Amazon and
several of its great tributaries have their source in the mountains of the
east Andes, the 'Montaña'. Virgin forest starts here, the 'Green Hell'
as it is called, and stretches for thousands of miles.

With the jungle to its east and the Pacific to its west, the Sierra
lies between its mountains, a lonely, silent, hostile steppe, where the
condor circles the sky on enormous wings. The days are sultry, the
nights icy cold. Only a few valleys lie lower than 7,000 feet, and with

146

their near-tropical vegetation they are like oases in the desert of stone. But when the sun rises blood-red above the eastern Cordillera, it turns the desert into a fairyland. The bare rock shines first a brilliant red, then brown, yellow, blue. In the clear, pure air the outlines of the mountains can be seen across immense distances, and the sun makes the snow-caps of the volcanoes on the horizon look a fantastic blue.

Everything seems motionless, dead—except for some of the volcanoes. Now and then they disgorge fire and lava, and the land of silence is shaken by earth tremors. Houses start tumbling in the cities of La Paz and Cuzco. But the houses and buildings which were standing before the Spaniards took possession, those of the Incas and from even earlier times, still defy the earthquake. This was once the realm of the White God Viracocha.

During the first half of the thirteenth century Mayta Capac, the fourth Inca, led his army against the Aymara. After a long march from Cuzco he and his men reached the highlands round Lake Titicaca, where they came upon the remains of an ancient city: a group of huge buildings the natives referred to as Tiahuanaco; another group, to the south-west, they called Puma Puncu; and there was a third, Achuta, farther to the north.

A pyramid rose as a big dark silhouette against the evening sky. Its sides, hollowed out by the rain, still showed distinct traces of steps leading up to the platform. The plinth cast in stone was half buried by mud. On the immense platform at the top there were only the remains of a temple left. In front of it an enormous monolith gate towered into the sky. Its columns had the heads of gods carved into them—the old gods of Tiahuanaco keeping watch over the ruins.

In the sacred precincts, surrounded by quadrangular basalt columns, there were also remains of a wall left on the platform; these were hewn from granite and decorated with reliefs. Some of the walls were still standing, stone slabs piled on top of one another. Others had tumbled, and the colossal blocks of stone lay scattered all round. A flight of steps leading to the sacred precinct was still intact. Its foot had once been lapped by the waters of the lake, and boats had moored here to land tribute and visitors to the capital.

The Inca stopped here, had his litter put down, and ascended the steps. He saw little pyramids rising between tumbled columns and idols; the stone vaults underneath these were the resting-places for the bones of those who had once ruled the country like gods. Alone except for his highest dignitaries, he walked among the ruins of the city his ancestors had lived in, so legend said, over a thousand years before.

After the Spaniards had conquered the Inca empire, and become

masters of South America, expeditions kept going out, chiefly to look
for gold. Some reached the barren plateau of Lake Titicaca, and found
not only huge stone slabs, which did not interest them, but gold nails
in the slabs, which did.

After this a great many people began coming to Tiahuanaco. Most
of them were merely after booty, which it was easy enough to find
there, and snatched up whatever they could lay hands on. But some
wanted to look at the ruins, and they were the men who later compiled their chronicles, describing what they saw. Here, for instance,
is the Inca chronicler Garcilaso de la Vega on the ruins of Tiahuanaco:

'The most beautiful structure is a hill created by the hand of man.
The Indians aimed to imitate nature by this work. In order to prevent
the masses of earth from collapsing, they secured the foundations by
well-built stone walls. From another side there are two stone giants
to be seen. They are clothed in long gowns and wear caps on their
heads. Many large gateways have been built from a single stone.'

Diego d'Alcobaca wrote that amidst the buildings on the lake's
bank there was a paved court eighty feet square, with a covered hall
forty-five feet long going down one of its sides.

'Court and hall are one single block of stone. This masterpiece
has been hewn into the rock. . . . There are still many statues to be
seen here today. They represent men and women, and are so perfect
one could believe the figures were alive. Some seem in the act of
drinking, others look as if they were about to cross a stream; women
give children the breast. . . .'

Jimenez de la Espada says that a particular building in the city was
one of the wonders of the world: stones thirty-seven feet long by
fifteen feet wide had been prepared, without the aid of lime or mortar,
in such a way as to fit together without any joins showing.

Travellers from later centuries and from recent times have contributed their own descriptions of the city's ruins. One of these buildings is known today as the Calasasaya. It is a low mud terrace, 13
feet high, 420 feet by 390 in wen. A flight of wide steps leads up to it. The
structure is believed to have been originally at first surrounded by great
stone columns which stood on top of a wall at intervals of sixteen feet.

Cieza de Leon, one of the chroniclers, wrote of a huge building
'with a patio fifteen spans square, and walls more than twice as tall as
a man. On the opposite side stands a hall measuring 45 by 22 feet, with
a roof built exactly like the roofs of the Temple of the Sun at Cuzco.
This hall has many big gates and windows. The lagoon of the lake
laps the stairs leading to the vestibule. The natives say the temple is
dedicated to Viracocha, the creator of the world.'

D'Orbigny describes a great building with covered galleries on

Court of the
Pyramid of the
Sun, Monte Alban

*The places of worship in the Old and New Worlds are closely related
to each other*

Stairway of
the Palace of
Radamanthos,
brother of
King Minos, at
Phaistos, Crete

When the 'great Kajen' was released from the grip of the jungle, a niche-temple appeared, which has its counterpart on the other side of the Pacific

its western walls. A Swiss traveller called Tschudi, very well known in his day, interpreted the building as a fort; while Arthur Posnansky—a modern authority we shall be hearing more of in a moment—regarded it as an unfinished 'Gran Palacio'. Posnansky also says that on the artificial hill there was a building 225 feet by 210, to which he refers as the 'Sanctissimum', the Holy of Holies. In the literature on this building the stone columns are treated as the remains of a sort of colonnade encircling the Temple of the Sun.

A synthesis of all these details suggests that the Calasasaya was a great flat pyramid, which only served as a refuge when the lake flooded its banks. Its stairs led up from the water. The structure on the large platform, most of which was empty, consisted of a vestibule with gateways facing the stairs, and a long building, the palace; both vestibule and palace had stairs. The entrance to the palace was a gateway on its long side, probably the one which is today called the Gate of the Sun. The Gate's remains show distinctly that it used not to stand where it does now, and from the way it is worked one may deduce that it once formed part of a building.

The rulers and priests were divided from their people by a wide gulf. Their palaces and halls must have had a magnificence equal to those of the Pharaohs and Babylonian kings in the Old World. The walls and the recesses in the halls were filled with statues made of gold, copper or bronze; the pillars were decorated with reliefs. The walls were also hung with stone and clay masks, precious gold and bronze ornaments, and were adorned with large-headed old nails; the holes for these can still be seen today. Thousands of the nails have disappeared, but there are many on view in the Bolivian Posnansky Museum at La Paz, and the stone masks are hanging on the museum's walls, just as they used to do in the palace of Tiahuanaco.

Imagination boggles at the amount of gold that must have been pillaged from Tiahuanaco. The pieces still to be seen in South American private collections are truly magnificent: gold statues of gods, weighing between four and six pounds, gold animals and birds—ducks weighing six pounds; gold cups and plates, goblets and spoons. There are dozens of gold spoons, with pointed ends and an ornament where the bowl joins the handle.

The gold 'talent' used as a weight in the ancient civilizations of the Mediterranean was the shape of a duck, so perhaps the people of Tiahuanaco knew the Old World's currency unit, just as they knew cups, plates, spoons and goblets.

The British archaeologist Evans had been studying hieroglyphs for years when he found some strange characters pointing to Crete.

He went to Crete, saw ruins and enormous mountains of rubble, and started digging (in 1900). Gradually he unearthed the civilization of the island where Rhea, the earth mother, gave birth to Zeus; where Minos, son of Zeus, had reigned, that mightiest of kings; and where Daedalus had built his legendary name.

Evans went on digging for decades. He found the maze of Knossos. He found the remains of a palace that once covered nearly six acres. The great court was a huge quadrangle, with towering adobe buildings on all sides, their roofs resting on columns. There must have been several storeys containing halls and other rooms. The palace once had whitewashed columns and walls decorated with stucco and murals. One day he discovered a room let into the earth, at first taken to be a bathroom. Further digging showed that there was a room behind it, twenty feet by thirteen, surrounded by stone benches on three sides, and with a throne standing at one of its narrow sides—the throne of Minos. He had found the audience-chamber of the royal palace of Knossos.

Posnansky found the White God's audience chamber at Tiahuanaco. It is a building west of the Calasasaya, oddly enough with double walls. Max Uhle refers to it as 'El Palacio', B. L. Romero as 'Tribunal de Justice' or 'Palacio del Inca'. Romero said the building consisted of four platforms and had ten large gateways. Ciezo de Leon wrote of two large statues standing near the Calasasaya and of a building near them with walls of mighty stone. Naidallac stated that the outer walls enclosed a platform with a large rectangular room dug out of it in the centre. The walls of this 'pit' were lined with great stone slabs, carved with reliefs of human figures. From the lay-out of the ruins it can be seen today that the building was surrounded by an outer wall which enclosed a large raised terrace. The 'dug-out' in the centre of the terrace was surrounded by a gallery several yards wide. The many gates and windows mentioned by the chroniclers must have been in the outer walls.

Even less is left of the 'small enclosure', as Joyce calls the smaller building east of the stairs leading to the Calasasaya. Posnansky refers to this as 'Palacio' and it is alleged to go back to Tiahuanaco's early period. Its walls, too, enclosed a room let into the ground, which had stone walls adorned with many human faces. Most of these heads were carved into the stone slabs the walls were then lined with. There is no trace left of steps leading down to this lower room, but everything points to their having existed.

The whole lay-out of this building is so like the 'Palacio de Justicia' that presumably both served the same purpose. When they were first discovered they were taken to have been bath-houses, just as Evans had done with his find on Crete. But Minos's audience chamber is no more than a closet in comparison with those of the ruler of Tiahuanaco. It is 13 feet by 20, its antechamber only 6 feet by 10; whereas the bigger Tiahuanaco audience chamber is 160 feet by 125, and even the smaller (and older) one is 85 by 100.

Evans came upon a 'modern' drainage system in the palace of Knossos: there were subterranean ducts to drain the water from basins and privies, the only difference from our modern installations being that the water had first to be poured in from a jug. These drains were large enough to allow a man to walk through in order to clean them. The system of supplying water from extensive 'cross-country' aqueducts is known not only from Crete but also from the Hanging Gardens of Babylon, where the water for wells, fountains and gardens was brought from a long distance by stone conduits.

The builders of Tiahuanaco were as much drainage experts as were the ancient Cretans. The city had an aqueduct to supply it out of stone pipes with sparkling fresh drinking water from the mountains; and it had an extensive drainage system as well. The conduits built from stone slabs may also have supplied water for gardens, but there are no traces of such gardens left.

Even the ruins of Tiahuanaco were still a majestic sight—until the end of the last century; then the city suffered its second destruction. For the ruins were treated as a quarry for building blocks: the ancient walls, the stone statues, were blasted with dynamite, smashed up with the pick-axe. The fact that anything has survived at all is largely due to the devoted work of Arthur Posnansky, a German engineer at La Paz, himself the owner of a large brick-yard; he died only a few years ago.

When he first came to Tiahuanaco he was fascinated by the ruins. He was no trained archaeologist, but had the sure instinct of a man with a feeling for 'the soul of stones': he realized that these were the remains of a very ancient and mighty civilization, probably unique in the whole of America. For years he vainly wrote articles and pamphlets condemning the work of destruction.

He spent all his leisure on the site, photographing every stone, every fragment he could find; he was the first to make a blue-print of the ruins' lay-out. Then he succeeded in getting the town of La Paz to found an open-air museum; he built this himself and put in it whatever he could save from Tiahuanaco. He excavated at his own expense, paying out of his own pocket the workmen who helped him shift the huge blocks and statues in order to preserve them. The museum became a place which today gives at least some inkling of the city's former greatness and high level of civilization. But the archaeologists of the day blamed Posnansky for having removed these few remnants from the site so that no one could tell where they had originally been standing. Later on people began stealing gold spoons and plates from the museum, and he was powerless to stop them.

Meanwhile he had to watch other expeditions arrive with a government permit to dig. As soon as his back was turned, they would start using the dynamite and then cart away the fragments. He saw them burrowing among his ruins, digging up foundations, hacking them to pieces, then covering up with earth the havoc they had created. He could do nothing but photograph everything that came to light before it was destroyed.

A bitter and disappointed man, he at last confined himself to writing about his wonderful finds. He contended that the plateau of Lake Titicaca must have been the cradle of all mankind, that here at Tiahuanaco he had found the origin of all civilization. He had taken the measurements of the Gate of the Sun and worked out that it must have served an astronomical purpose, a kind of calendar stone; to which he attributed a date of 16,000 B.C. In making these claims he undoubtedly let his obsessive enthusiasm carry him away. They became the weak spot of his archaeological work, and his enemies took their chance to brand him as a charlatan.

But whatever his later errors, he preserved a priceless record for future generations, particularly with his photographs.

They show the great stone slabs lying on top of one another or side by side, with niches and blind windows carved into them, as for instance on the reverse of the Gate of the Sun. They show the remains of the magnificent drainage system; they show the colossal idols being dug up and carted away; they show the monoliths and stelae, the sculptures in the round, and the reliefs. These photographs still convey some small impression of that magnificent civilization—all record of which, but for Posnansky, would have been irretrievably lost. His work can be fully appreciated only by someone who goes to Tiahuanaco today.

The antiquated narrow-gauge carriages travelling from La Paz jolt on their rails. Only the engine, wood-fired, is newer; it spits and hisses and spews up thousands of bright sparks from its funnel. The train crosses desolate steppe. The Indians have let down the flaps of their wool caps and are sitting huddled in their ponchos. They are Aymara who have turned their meagre harvest into money at the capital, and are now coming back to their villages with what they have bought.

The train gets emptier and emptier. Then it stops in the middle of the steppe. A board announces that the place is called Tiahuanaco. There is a small church, a cemetery—surely one of the grimmest cemeteries in the world—and a few miserable Indian huts; otherwise only an expanse of barren stone, without any vegetation at all, in the dead plateau, naked under the dazzling sunlight.

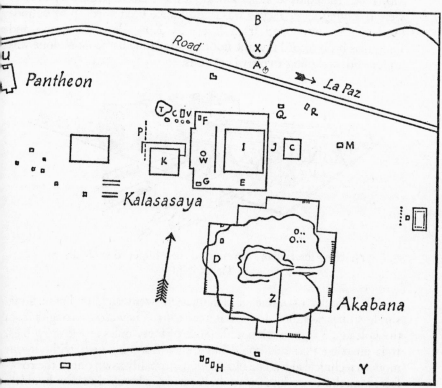

14. Arthur Posnansky measured the ruins of Tiahuanaco and drew plans, which is all we have left today to give us an idea of this buried city. Today the Gateway of the Sun is at F

Close to the village there is a strange sight: a big stone gate rises straight out of the desert, with a few square stone columns and large flat stones lying beside it: with some imagination you can recognize these as the remains of a flight of stairs. In the background you see a mountain—but a mountain of mud. It is hard to picture this as the great pyramid of Acabana which it once was.

Today you can see nothing from here of Lake Titicaca, now sixteen miles away from Tiahuanaco. The lake's surface keeps receding year by year, and its former bank stands out like a low dam, reaching right to the walls of the ancient city. This is all that remains of Tiahuanaco, once one of the mightiest cities in the world.

Fate has been much kinder to Tiryns, that ancient city of the Peloponnese in southern Greece. For 3,000 years (from 1200 B.C. to A.D. 1800) the colossal stone blocks of the walls described by Homer were left lying here. Tiryns was said to have been piled up by round-eyed giants, summoned from Lycia by King Proetos. Strabo and Pausanias both record that the floor of one of the bathrooms alone was a monolith weighing over twenty tons.

15. How the Indians transported their huge stone blocks into Tiahuanaco

The blocks of stone at Tiahuanaco were equally huge: some single stones weighed 100, even 200, tons. They were brought from the volcanic Kiappa region, a distance of forty miles as the crow flies. It is amazing that this could have been done by men without our modern technical aids. The blocks were probably sawn out of the rockface, a method also known to the Cretans, who used to saw boulders into ashlars with bronze saws. How the blocks were then transported can still be seen from the holes in some of them. Probably they were put on rollers, i.e. heavy round trunks, and slowly pushed along.

As with the pyramids in Egypt, thousands of men must have worked for hundreds of years to erect the enormous buildings of Tiahuanaco, slave labour forced to build on an ever larger, taller, more powerful, scale. Like the Egyptians, they piled the single stone blocks on top of one another without any joins showing. But the Tiahuanaco buildings have a special feature, the use of copper rivets, which is known from only two places in the Old World, Assyria and Etruria. The stone blocks of the walls were fastened together with pegs. Little holes were bored into the slabs, and copper poles, put into these holes, were then flattened at both ends, thereby turning them into a sort of rivet.

Other parallels with the Old World in architecture and building techniques include the audience chambers, rooms let into the ground; the little round hole in the top slabs of graves (exactly as on Egyptian tombs); and the technique of 'cast' and 'packing'. From the pyramids of Tiahuanaco up to the latest Aztec pyramids they all contain a mound, a kernel of mud, which is covered by a stone cast.

16. A Tiahuanaco death-chamber. The ceiling shows the same small hole for the bird of death present in the burial ritual of the Egyptians

Then there are the double, parallel walls at Tiahuanaco, with a cast of large stones outside and the gap between the walls filled in with mud. This method too was used in the Old World, in particular by the Cretans, whose way of building can still be distinctly traced in an old harbour they constructed on the mouth of the Nile. They built a jetty 200 feet wide consisting of two parallel walls of hewn stones, and the whole space between them filled in with rubble.

All that has been found at Tiahuanaco shows that it was a city of artisans and craftsmen: carpenters, builders, stone-masons, painters, potters, blacksmiths and weavers, bronze-founders and metal-workers. Besides their workshops the city must have had technical centres planning and directing all projects for buildings, aqueducts and drainage.

The 'balsas' also, the boats plying on Lake Titicaca, may very well go back to the Old World. Both in construction and in material they are amazingly like the Egyptian papyrus boats we know from reliefs.

Many guesses have been made as to the derivation of the name Tiahuanaco. Some have taken it to come from the stem 'tia'; 'tia wanaca' would mean 'this is from god'. The word for god is very similar in the languages of many different countries, even civilizations, e.g. 'tien' (Chinese), 'theos' (Greek), 'teotl' (in Mexico); the Aztecs had their 'teocallis' (temples), and before them the ancient city of priests was Teotihuacan. The similarity seems more than coincidence, and perhaps when the white man first came to the Indians, they called him something like 'theos', having heard him called this by his men.

But there is also another promising suggestion: in the language of the Aymara 'tia' means something bright and big, a thing shining, the horizon; and 'Wanaca' is the name for king in Cretan Linear B. 'Tiawanaco' might therefore mean 'shining king'—an apt description for the White God of this great city.

When was the city built, and for how many centuries did it flourish? The problem of its age will be considered later. As to when it perished, we can tell only approximately (the dates advanced vary between A.D. 100 and 800), though we know that Mayta Capac, the fourth Inca, found it in ruins in the first half of the thirteenth century. It was destroyed by force—this can be seen from the ruins—military defeat no doubt aggravated once again by internal revolt. The legends say that the White God of Tiahuanaco started a war with the Cari of Coquimba, and lost it; the wild Indians killed all the men of the city, so that only the women and children survived; but the White God managed to escape with a small band of his followers.

A troop of Spanish mercenaries in search of gold came upon the tallest pyramid they had ever seen; the Indians called it Acabana. When the Spaniards heard that they were facing the ruins of the White God's city, they of course expected to find great treasures there and set to work: 400 Indians were ordered to push the remains of the ancient temples down into the depths. For weeks these men were busy digging a crater into the mountain, piling up the earth they dug out or shovelling it down over the pyramid's sides.

It is not known whether the treasure-seekers found what they had been hoping for, but their traces are still visible today—the artificial lake in the centre of the platform where the temple once stood. For the crater filled with water in the course of time. It is 265 feet in diameter, and takes up only a small part of the platform; which shows how vast the platform must be.

The first travellers who saw the mountain of the old pyramid were deeply impressed, even awe-struck. Naidallac described it as a fortress made of mud, about 150 feet tall and built on square foundations.

Figure from Monte Alban

Figure from the Peruvian coast (taken from Groth-Kimball, *Kunst im alten Mexico*, Rascher-Verlag, Zürich)

The Indians were fond of depicting bearded types. They themselves hardly ever had beards

Double jug from Peru; there are similar jugs in Crete

Left: an Olmec head; *right:* a head from the Egyptian El-Amarna period

Amazing similarities

Jaguar god from Tiahuanaco

Jade statuette of a figure with duck's bill, showing Olmec characters and the year number equivalent to A.D. 162 (San Andres Tuxtla, Vera Cruz)

Pablo E. Chalon states that its sides measured 600 feet, and that it was built in three steps of strong concentric walls. At intervals of thirteen to twenty feet large stones were leaning against the slope at a slight angle, the gaps between packed with smaller stones so as to secure the whole wall against shifting.

Even today the pyramid still stands fifty feet high, and at one time, judging by the masses of earth that have slid down or been washed away, it must have been at least 100 to 165 feet. Excavations have so far been undertaken only on a very small scale, and have yielded a lot of sculpted stone blocks. Posnansky's photographs give an idea of the gigantic blocks the steps were built from. On the top of the hill as it is today there are the remains of three buildings erected from hewn stone slabs; among them there were also slabs with reliefs. The size of the blocks shows the pyramid's enormous dimensions, as big as any of the Mexican pyramids from later times. From the finds and the chroniclers' records the pyramid must have been not a fortress (as was at first assumed) but a large temple, apparently built from ashlars which formed a mantle round the mud kernel and secured the steps.

This was not the only pyramid the soldiers burrowed in. A little over half a mile south-west of Tiahuanaco they found a bigger one still, the 'Puma Puncu' (Gate of the Puma) or 'Punca Puncu' (Ten Gates). Here were the largest stone ruins of the whole region, enormous boulders weighing between forty and fifty tons lying about in great profusion, even slabs of 100 or 200 tons. They were remains of the mantle or else of the buildings which once stood on the pyramid's platform.

'In Puma Puncu', wrote Bernabé Cobo, 'there is a large square mud terrace of two steps, with its sides secured by big stones. The terrace is twice the height of a man, and its sides are a hundred paces long. It can be reached by a flight of stairs leading up from the east, at the top of which there is a stone building 24 by 60 feet.... This seems to have been a hall. It must have stood in the centre of the large building, which was a temple and is 154 by 46 feet, with walls constructed of huge stones.... These walls have tumbled. But on one side of the building a big stone gate is still standing, and on the south side a large window, carved from a single stone, has been preserved.'

Puma Puncu was a gigantic pyramid of three or four steps, with terraces carrying large buildings. On the third platform the remains of a big gate were discovered, the so-called 'Gate of the Moon', and on another platform the remains of another four large gates.

A third step pyramid, also very big, was found on the coast near Secchin. Like the others, it consisted of a mud kernel with sides secured

by large stones. Secchin was part of the Tiahuanacan empire, and so
was Cuzco, later the Inca capital.

The earliest similar buildings in the Old World were the step
pyramids of Mesopotamia between the rivers Tigris and Euphrates.
They were originally earth mounds serving as 'hills of refuge' during
the frequent floods. From them developed the Babylonian Ziggurates,
in which several mud terraces, each of diminishing size, were piled
on top of one another to make a step pyramid, with a temple standing
on the top platform. These buildings were an expression of the idea,
also prevalent in the Indian-Buddhist world, of the 'Meru', the Mountain ascending to Heaven. Many ancient peoples sacrificed to their
gods on the mountains, and pyramids represented artificial mountains.
They were therefore temples, not tombs—and the Bible's 'Tower of
Babel' was a step pyramid, with a temple on its platform which probably contained an altar table.

The Egyptian pyramids were of different origin. They had neither
platforms nor temples, and their side walls were plain, at least in
later times. Their interior contained a chamber in which the Pharaoh's
bones rested, inviolate for eternity under a stone mantle of millions
of cubic feet. The chamber was accessible by a low passage through
the stone, which was filled in with earth after the ruler had been entombed. These pyramids had no outside stairway leading up to the top.

The pyramids of the New World are step pyramids, with an outside stairway leading up to the platform; they have a temple on top
for which they really serve only as a plinth: in other words, we are
back to the idea of the artificial mountain. The pyramid was first built
from mud and protected against weather influences and pressure of
earth masses by a layer of rough stones. Such basic shapes of pyramids
have been discovered, round as well as rectangular. Later these artificial
mountains were built from rubble and adobes; and they were covered
with a mantle of carefully shaped stones or secured by a stucco cast of
calcined mussel shells and sand. Clearly their outer appearance is like
that of the Old World step pyramids; but the resemblance may go
further than that.

When archaeologists are unearthing a new find, they very often do
not know what it is they have discovered. They interpret and compare
the objects, sometimes arriving at the most varied explanations of
the same thing. Even Schliemann could make slips: once he dug up
what he took to be an alabaster vase, and it turned out to be an ostrich
egg.

Similarly a very large duct was found at Tiahuanaco, which was
referred to as the Cloaca Maxima, and leads to what used to be the
centre of the Acabana Pyramid (as shown in Diagram 14). On this

spot, according to Posnansky, there was a little stone chamber, which he took to be a cistern, with an arrow square opening like a door at both the north and the south end of it—though these doors certainly do not suggest a cistern. The duct started at the south door, and Posnansky thought it served primarily to drain off surplus water from the stone 'cistern'.

But the duct was far too big for such a purpose; little grooves at the sides of the cistern would have been enough, if any rainwater drain was needed at all in this not very rainy climate. Seeing the difficulty, Posnansky suggested that in times of war the duct may have been used to dispatch patrols and spies unseen or let them into the fortress. But in that case the duct should have come out far enough away from the fortress to be out of the enemy's sight; whereas it ends just at the foot of the pyramid, exactly where the enemy would have been posted during a siege.

In fact the little stone chamber was probably the tomb over which the pyramid was erected, and the Cloaca Maxima was neither drain nor spies' tunnel, but the passage leading into the burial chamber— exactly as with the Egyptian pyramids. It was not straight, but followed the lines of the pyramid, sometimes running nearly vertical, and then horizontal again. Today it is completely destroyed, except for its end-piece. From Indian legends it has become known that this once formed part of a passage; and the tradition as to its real purpose has led to a myth—still current among the Indians of the area today—that it was a subterranean passage leading from Acabana as far as Cuzco.

Minos, King of Knossos, sent his son Androgeus to take part in the Olympic Games at Athens. Being the strongest, Androgeus defeated all the other contestants. Aegeus, King of Athens, was furious with envy and killed him. Minos exacted a terrible penance: he launched a surprise attack on Athens with his fleet and conquered the Athenians, who thereafter had to send the flower of their youth to Knossos every nine years, seven young men and seven virgins, as a sacrifice to the Minotaur, the Cretan monster. When the sacrifice became due for the third time, Theseus, son of Aegeus, sailed to Knossos himself. Ariadne, daughter of Minos, saw him and gave him a sword with which to fight the monster and a ball of wool. He killed the monster, and with his wool found his way out of the maze.

Was the terrible Minotaur the bull of Minos, a sacred beast kept in the palace like the sacred beasts in the temples of Egypt; like Apis, sacred bull of Memphis? The sacred bull, 'servant of the god Ptah', lived in the temple and was looked after by the priests. When he died, he was buried with great ceremonial in the subterranean gallery of

the Serapaeum in the Memphite necropolis, Sakkara, where ever since
Rameses the Great all sacred bulls rested together. After his death a
new sacred bull was found with similar markings.

The Egyptians had other 'animal gods' besides Ptah. The god
Khnum was a ram, the god Horus a falcon, the god Thoth an ibis,
the god Sobek a crocodile, the goddess of Bubastis a cat, and the
goddess of Buto a cobra. In all temples dedicated to these gods the
living god was kept and worshipped in animal form. When the animals
died they were buried in temples worthy of kings and gods. Tiahuanaco
provides parallels with this.

In the old pyramid of Puma Puncu a small stone gate was discovered, carved from a single block, with an opening 24 by 15 inches
—too small for a man. But it was big enough for the puma which had
given the pyramid its name. The god of the puma was not only kept
there but worshipped in animal form, the living puma which could
pass through the gate into its enclosure. There the puma lived as a
god, and the great pyramid was decorated with his images, realistic
representations which Posnansky found as he passed through the
ruins. Later on statues were discovered, sometimes representing a
puma and sometimes a sort of puma-man, an animal in human form.

Nearly every large town in Europe contains an obelisk, that strange
needle-shaped stone monument, a little pyramid towering on top of a
slender four-sided pillar. The obelisk comes from Egypt, where it
was extremely common, and these 'fingers of the sun' used to stand
outside the Egyptian temples. Two of the tallest, built by a powerful
Pharaoh, are in front of the temple at Heliopolis. Obelisks were known
at Crete, for there are two of them shown in frescoes on the sides of
the sarcophagus of Hagia Triada; and obelisks also stood outside the
temples of Tiahuanaco. In addition, twenty-one human figures in
stone, sixteen stelae, and forty-eight sculptures altogether, have been
salvaged from the horseshoe-shaped temple of Pucara in Peru. These
statues are more rounded than the 'cubist' forms of Tiahuanacan art
but otherwise the two styles tally exactly. The Pucara pottery, too, is
like that of Tiahuanaco, showing the same winged creatures, the
hybrids of man and beast, catlike creatures, hunting trophies and
condor heads, fish heads and llamas.

Tiahuanaco, the capital, clearly had a great influence over its whole
empire, as can be seen from the ruins found extending right down to
Peru's coastal plain. On the coast near Pisco Professor J. Tello, the
Peruvian archaeologist, dug up the ruins of two large cities, one of
which is said to have had over 40,000 inhabitants. Unlike the other
cities on the coast, these two are all of stone: their houses, their temples

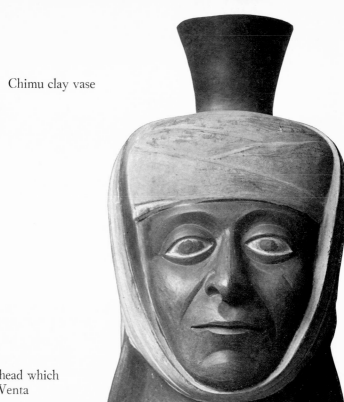

Chimu clay vase

The Olmec giant head which once stood at La Venta

Gateway at Persepolis

Gateway at Tiahuanaco

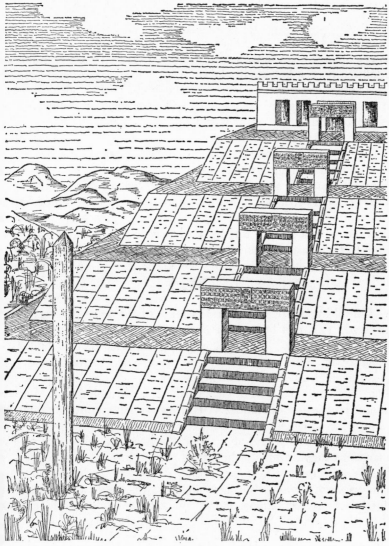

7. There is an obelisk in front of the Pyramid of the Moon at Puma Puncu

heir tombs. And archaeologists kept coming across the Tiahuanaco
iguar on the coast. The highland style, in fact, is so much in evidence
t three particular places that the Tiahuanaco civilization is thought
o have flourished there even after the fall of the capital.

Among the few things which survived from the capital were the
tatues of the gods in the temples; and Posnansky could salvage only

a few of these. Today the museum at La Paz houses some of thes
huge statues, much more than six feet high, covered all over wit
reliefs, among them figures with turbans on their heads—the turbar
significantly, is a Semitic headgear.

There is another Semitic feature, the prefix 'pacha', which is foun
in several of the gods' names, such as Pachacamac or Pachatata, go
of the sun and keeper of the world, and Pachamama, great goddess o
the city, mother of the earth, goddess of fertility, sometimes goddes
of the sea with symbolic attributes of fishes, condors, fish heads an
winged human creatures. Her big statue, with turban-like headgea
from Tiahuanaco's second period, is preserved, while from the city'
third period Posnansky found a further statue of the goddess in th
little temple east of the steps leading to the Calasasaya—here too she i
crowned with a sort of turban. Pachamacac was the god who late
came to the coast and remained so powerful that the Incas stole hir
to incorporate him with their own gods; indeed he became thei
highest god.

On all important sites of ruins some of the great gateways hav
survived. This is a little surprising, since a gate, the place where
wall has been broken through, might be expected to be a building'
weakest part. Three gates have been preserved, or at least can be re
constructed, from three different ancient civilizations of Europe an
Asia: the Babylonian gate of Nebuchadnezzar, the lion gate at Mycena
and the Hittite gate of Hattusa. All three gates have animals or fabulou
monsters as ornaments.

There are also sacred animals on the huge monolith arch at Tia
huanaco, which towers on the barren plateau in solitary magnificence
This is now commonly known as the Gateway of the Sun, though th
name is very recent. D'Orbigny in 1839 was the first to refer to it
allegorical representations of the sun and the condor, and in 189
Mitre described the 'picture of the sun' on the gate of Tiahuanacc
The gate is carved from a single block ten feet high and over six fee
wide: it is the largest carved monolith on earth. At the front its vertic
walls rise sheer, crowned by a frieze extending along its whole widtl
A stylized jaguar with human features is enthroned over the arch'
centre; holding the symbols of thunder and lightning, it carries
nimbus round its head. Jaguar, condor and cobra are represented o
the frieze, which also shows several rows of winged creatures on to
of one another on either side.

Few single works of pictorial art have been studied so extensivel
as this gate, and the studies made have confirmed beyond doubt th
tremendous influence which Tiahuanaco exerted. The characterist

symbols and shapes of ornaments named after this city found their way from here into all the other American-Indian civilizations. For instance, noses in the shape of a spiral or disc recur everywhere in Indian art, from Peru across the Cordillera to Mexico, in pottery, knife-handles, textiles and stone carvings: this symbol started at Tiahuanaco. So did the weeping god, a symbol of rain and fertility found from Guiana to the Andes, right across the Amazon country, as far as Argentina and down to the Pacific coast. Everywhere in Peru we come upon the weeping god—faces bathed in tears—formerly misinterpreted as representing the sun suffering.

There were the remains of more big gates on the great pyramid of Puma Puncu. One of them, the Gate of the Moon, must have been a magnificent sight: it is a monolith similar to the Gateway of the Sun,

18. Archaeologists have constantly studied the Gateway of the Sun at Tiahuanaco. Even buglers are among its ornamentation

also with a frieze in relief, but with fishes instead of the condor and with no winged creatures depicted. Its reliefs still show little boreholes, particularly in deep-set places; these served to fasten plates of silver—the colour of the moon—which lined the relief's hollowed-out parts. Puma Puncu was dedicated to the goddess Pachamama, who may have been also the moon goddess.

In the 1840's, when A. H. Layard was excavating the great palace of Assur-nastir-pal II (c. 884–859 B.C.), he discovered on the hill of Nimrud no fewer than thirteen pairs of winged lions or bulls and giant animals: these were the immense statues of the ancient Assyrian astral gods of Marduk. With the Egyptians these fabulous creatures, which we call gryphons, were lions with birds' heads. The Cretans too had genies, demons in animal shape, hybrids of man and beast with wings, goats with horns and wings. The Etruscans had the winged typhon with snake feet, and other winged creatures, such as the vulture demon Tuchulda.

The Gateway of the Sun at Tiahuanaco has a similar creature

represented, with a man's body, a bird's head and wings: a sort of cousin of the ancient Mediterranean gryphons. Representations of such creatures are found also in other parts of the great Tiahuanacan empire.

Again, from Greek mythology we know Tritons, Nereids and Sirens—human figures with the body of a fish, with scales and a tail; and the Phoenician god Yam was a god with a fish tail. Little statues found at Tiahuanaco and all over the plateau show the same kind of hybrids, worked from gold and silver: women with fish bodies and tails, their breasts particularly conspicuous. Similar statues were un-

19. *Left:* Cretan gryphon. *Right:* An Indian sphinx from Calle de Trionfo

earthed in Argentina, such as a god with a snake's body and without a mouth—an image like those current in Troy, ancient Persia, and with the Celts.

Witches too, or something like them, were known to the Incas. Although they had not started riding on broomsticks, one Indian chronicler has drawings of creatures with horns and wings floating through the air, the same as on representations from Mediterranean civilizations. All these imaginary creatures can scarcely have made their way across an ocean entirely unaided.

One creature found in the Tiahuanacan empire, not fabulous but prehistoric, has given archaeology one of its greatest puzzles, so far unsolved. About 1920 Professor Tello was digging up vessels from the ruins of the two coastal cities mentioned above as part of that empire, when he came upon jugs with representations of a five-toed llama.

Llamas now have two toes, but at a very early stage of their evolution they had five, just as our horses and cattle once did—though this fact only became familiar after Darwin's *Origin of Species*. At any rate llamas at this very early stage must have been known to the Indians, which was remarkable enough. But then Tello discovered the skeletons of llamas, all with five toes; so the Indians must once have kept five-toed llamas in their temples.

The evidence could not be denied, yet it seemed to threaten the very foundations of accepted natural history. Tiahuanacan civilization was certainly very old, but by no stretch of the imagination could it be as old as the five-toed llamas: in *their* day saurians and giant lizards may still have existed, but there were certainly no human beings yet. Could the Indians have found 'living fossils', somehow left over from primeval times—like the recent discovery of the coelocanth—and because of their unique appearance regarded them as sacred animals to be kept in the temples? It sounds far-fetched, but no satisfactory explanation has so far been given for this extraordinary phenomenon.

The five-toed llamas do not help us at present with the age of Tiahuanaco, which indeed is very hard to assess. The pyramid in the capital has almost entirely collapsed, as have the buildings in other parts of its empire: from this poor state of preservation we can infer that they were among the oldest buildings in South America. On first consideration it would be easy to guess that they and the empire are older than they are, simply because of their style. The period of colossal building in the Old World ceased about 1200 B.C., so immigrants to America must have brought this style across before then. And if they introduced the building method of the pyramids, or even the concept of the pyramid as tomb, they would have done so while the method and concept were still current at home, i.e. not much later than 1700 B.C., when the last great Egyptian pyramids were built.

But Tiahuanaco cannot have been the first city which white men built on reaching America. Strangers cast up on those shores for the first time would not at once have moved to an icy plateau 13,000 feet above sea level, far from the coast and in the midst of the most forbidding country. Their descendants, however, were not looking for fertile soil or a mild climate but for something which did not exist in the valleys and was to be found in only a few places on earth. Tiahuanaco was the only New World city of its time which had tin (just as Bolivia today owns most of the world's tin), and bronze was produced from copper and tin: its site was chosen because of the deposits of tin found there.

When the Spaniards invading the Inca empire landed on the island of Puná opposite the city of Tumbez, they saw objects made of bronze for the first time in America. Afterwards they 'met' plenty of these in their battles with the Incas, whose weapons were of bronze. The Incas had learnt how to make bronze alloy from peoples they had conquered, the Aymara and Colla, who had known the technique centuries earlier. They had in turn taken it over from an earlier people, and later created a regular metal industry at Potosi, where their furnaces would glow from the mountains day and night. 'There was such a great number of them', the chronicler Cobo recorded, 'that the mountains looked as if they were illuminated.'

The Aymara's 'tutors', who discovered the secret of making bronze, once lived at Tiahuanaco. Bronze was used there when copper was still the staple metal everywhere else in the New World. But pure copper was also worked at Tiahuanaco, though only to make things it was particularly suitable for, such as the nails to join the single stone blocks of the buildings—what we should call rivets today. The ends of the soft copper poles were very easy to flatten.

Tiahuanaco was the first and for a long time the only New World civilization that knew bronze. A full thousand years after the city's fall there was still no metal worked in Mexico—not even copper. Tiahuanaco skipped the copper age and leapt right into the bronze age. Bronze travelled from them to the other peoples of the continent, first to their nearest neighbours and then to the coast of Peru. They used to burnish and furbish bronze, they were familiar with soldering and silver-plating, malleating and embossing, wire-drawing, and even such a rare process as damascening. The Tiahuanacan bronze tools are shaped like those in the Old World, and their stylized animal figures in bronze are almost exactly the same as such figures from the Caucasus

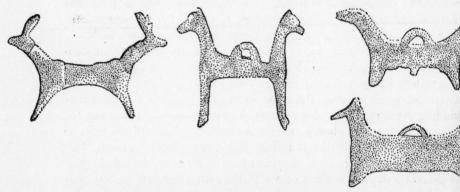

20. Bronze-cast figures of double animals from the Caucasus area and the Tiahuanaco empire
   (a) Kedabeg-Kalakent, Georgia
   (b) Luristan, Persia
   (c) Copacabana and Tiahuanaco. (Taken from Heine-Geldern)

The oldest bronze objects we know are Egyptian sculptures going back to about 2500 B.C. at the earliest. Stylized figures of men and animals found on Sardinia have been dated about 1900 B.C., the time when the bronze age started in Western Europe and the time of the first high civilization in Crete. It was in Crete that bronze first became linked with the spiral, the ornament used by all later imitators as soon as they started working bronze: almost every find of that period from

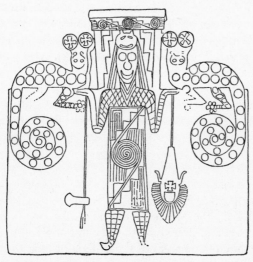

21. Bronze altar (or breast-plate) from Tiahuanaco with the Cretan spiral and the arrangement of two animals at the sides of a higher
centre-piece, which is characteristic of the Old
World civilizations

all over Europe shows the Cretan spiral. Bronze was superseded by iron in the Mediterranean civilizations about 1200 B.C., but whatever immigrants came to America after that did not bring the new metal; for even when the Spaniards arrived the Indians knew nothing of iron.

The Tiahuanaco empire used the bronze spiral extensively, but bronze cannot, of course, have come directly from the Cretan civilization, which had perished centuries before the tin deposits of Tiahuanaco were found. For the introducers of bronze we must probably look again to the Far East. One of the early coastal civilizations of Peru was reached and influenced by the Chinese, as we have seen, some time between 500 and 400 B.C., and this link snapped about 333 B.C. when the Chinese coastal empires went under. But the connections

were not broken off altogether, they were taken over by new civilizations of the Far East: the Dongson civilization of Tongking and
Annam, which belonged to the bronze age. Its influence can be traced
already in the Mochica (Proto-Chimu) civilization of the Peruvian coast
in the fourth century B.C., and it extended as far as Chile and Argentina.

Particularly strong traces of this influence have been discovered
in the mountains of Argentina and Bolivia, where there were deposits
of tin. Some metal objects from the Dongson civilization are remarkably
like metal work from South America, and men from the Far East must
certainly have influenced Tiahuanacan civilization, at least up to the
first century A.D.—when connections were severed because the
Chinese conquered Tongking and northern Annam.

There was bronze at Tiahuanaco by the first century A.D. at the
very latest, and it must have taken several centuries for all the city's
buildings, temples and statues to go up. This would suggest that the
city itself was founded somewhere between the fifth and the first century
A.D.; and archaeologists, on other grounds also, have generally agreed
to such a date.

The inheritance of Tiahuanaco was taken over by the Aymara,
an Indian people of near-savages. Perhaps they were the people
originally ruled by the White Gods; they may have rebelled, chased
their rulers away, and destroyed the city in the process.

They inhabited large areas of the Bolivia of today and round Lake
Titicaca, settling there about 1000 B.C. Their country extended as far
as the primeval forest and the peaks of the Andes, and to the mines of
Portosi in the south. They were conquered by the Incas only in the
fifteenth century A.D. after violent struggles. Three generations of
Incas had to wage war against this people of peasants, herdsmen and
masters of metallurgy. Their bronze weapons, vastly superior to those
of the Incas, inflicted terrible wounds on the invading enemy, who left
6,000 dead on the battlefield after a single day's fighting.

The Inca rule came to an end, but the Aymara and Colla survived,
and with them the ancient myth of the great White God and his mighty
city. They still inhabit the area round Lake Titicaca, and when a white
man visits them today their greeting is still 'Viracocha', the name once
given to their highest god. They will show their visitor the only
remains left of the White God, a great gateway on a desolate highland,
and a huge artificial hill behind it, the shape now so faded that you
can scarcely recognize the great pyramid it once was.

Old masters leave a stamp upon their paintings so that even without
a signature the expert can tell at once who the artist was. Works by his

pupils or originating from his workshop will also bear his stamp: style, choice of colours, technique, conception; and it will remain more or less imprinted on even the later output of his former pupils.

The Olmecs were the pupils of such a workshop. They migrated to Mexico at about the beginning of our era. Judging by the great number of things they brought with them, they must have come from a much older country with a civilization presumably going back to springs in the Old World. Such a country could only have been situated in South America. They could not have acquired their high skill in stone masonry from the Chimu on the Peruvian plain, whose civilization was one of clay. But there were certainly master masons living at Tiahuanaco, so the Olmecs may well have come to Mexico from there: many features of Olmec art are very like the Tiahuanacan style and forms.

Tiahuanaco itself was not a civilization transplanted direct from the Old World (or the immigrants would not have built pyramids and other colossal buildings, a style long obsolete). They must have carried on a tradition brought over centuries earlier. The first White God, in fact, must have come to or founded an empire a thousand years older than even Tiahuanaco. Such an empire did exist.

14

The Chavin Civilization—and the Ancient Gods

'For wisdom and reason they could find no better image
than a man's head, for strength, a lion's body, for omnipresence,
a bird's wings.'
LAYARD on the images of the Assyrian astral gods

AT THE end of the nineteenth century, when European archaeologists
were digging up ancient burial grounds near a village on the Peruvian
coast, an Indian boy watched them lifting human skulls out of the soil.
They showed him the square holes in the skulls, marks of trepanning,
and the bulge of bone matter formed round the edges, indicating that
the patients had survived the dangerous operation. The boy asked
whether the white men too could open up skulls this way. The Europeans admitted with a smile that they couldn't. 'So the Indians were
cleverer than you are,' the boy said.

The boy was Julio Tello, and all his life he felt a great pride in his
ancestors' achievements; it was this which prompted him to take up
archaeology. The only notable American-Indian archaeologist, he
undertook and organized over fifty expeditions throughout Peru, and
presented his country with six museums of anthropology and early
history. He led his last expedition into the jungle as late as 1941 and
died in 1947. With great skill and very limited resources he had
devoted himself to the task of discovering the most ancient of the
Indian civilizations, which he called Chavin—because the greatest of
the ruins from which he 'resurrected' it were near the village of Chavin
de Huantar, 600 miles north of Lake Titicaca at the foot of the mountain ridge, but still 10,000 feet above sea level.

These ruins were of a magnificent temple-fortress, with terrace
steps leading up the slope to it from the river Pucca. Its walls, tapering

170

upwards like dams, are built from square and oblong stone blocks. The cornices have representations of jaguars, condors, and snakes with menacing fangs. There is a flight of granite steps going up to a rectangular pyramid with a side flat top. The shrine on the platform above contains a round sacrificial stone bowl, standing on four legs, which was probably used to catch the sacrifice's blood. It has a groove leading to a block carved with the god's image in a jaguar shape, so that the blood would run down the god's face.

The part of the temple today called the 'Castillo' had an ingenious system of air conduits carrying fresh air to every room in the building; a similar air-conditioning system has been discovered at Knossos. Underneath the temple of Chavin, just as at Knossos, there were crooked passages, lined with small square stones, tall enough for a man to stand in. In a few places they widened out into niches, which had ceilings supported by stone pillars and recalled the niches in much later buildings, such as the hall at Mitla and the Temple of Viracocha near Chacha.

Two of the chroniclers referred to the Chavin site as 'one of the most famous ones, like Rome or Jerusalem with us'. According to Professor Tello (though scholars since have disagreed) the Chavin civilization began between 4000 and 3000 B.C. and was in its prime about 1500 B.C. That was the era in the Old World of the palace of Knossos, the Cretan sarcophagus and bronze spiral, of the Hittites, and of Thothmes I in Egypt. During the next century there was a female Pharaoh on the Egyptian throne, Queen Hatchepsut, who launched great expeditions across the sea.

Chavin was not only the first high civilization of the Andes; it covered the widest area as well, probably extending right from the jungle to the sea—from the sources of the Amazon to the Pacific— and even the Pacific islands. On the eastern slopes of the Cordilleras, in the Urubamba Valley and on the upper course of the Maranão river, a temple fortress near Tantamayo probably belonged to the Chavin empire, and so did the colossal building on top of which the Incas erected their fortress of Machu Picchu. In the fourteenth or fifteenth century the Inca Tupac Yupanqui was defeated in a war against the Chachapoyas; he encountered great mountain fortresses defended by men of white skin who hurled huge blocks at the attackers. These Chachapoya fortresses show clearly the influence of the Chavin civilization, with their representations of jaguars, their drawings of the sun, and their conical tombstones in the shape of human figures. There are such Chavin features too in the old civilizations of Colombia, particularly the empire of the later Chibchas, which consisted roughly of today's Colombia.

Besides the 'original' temple near the village of Chavin de Huantar there are many other monuments to the Chavin civilization: the ruins of temples and other buildings, hundreds of stelae and statues, and thousands of smaller works of art. One of these Colombian sites of ruins is Moniquira, where the remains of an old palace have been found, with great round and oval stone columns and obelisks. Another is Lavapata, with the so-called Piscina, a room let into the ground with sculptured walls, which was probably a bathroom. The most striking of the reliefs that have survived here is a double cornucopia with a human face between its horns. San Agustin on the source of the river Magdalena (in the north-western tip of South America) has statues up to thirteen feet high, showing human figures which wear a kind of flat hat, very like Tiahuanaco statues, or huge idols and heads with head-bands round them—quite in the style of the Olmecs.

Finally there is Neyta, where Lopez came upon a tomb with an immense statue of a jaguar in front of its entrance. Later he found more statues, of llamas, monkeys, toads, of a man and a woman, and a big well-polished stone slab—four feet merging into a central pillar—which (he recorded) it took fifty men to lift. These Chibcha statues, and the motifs on them, are very like those of Chavin and Tiahuanaco. After thoroughly investigating the works of art produced by the Chavin civilization, the archaeologists found that it had already used practically all the symbols which were to occur in the younger civilizations—including all those on the Gate of the Sun at Tiahuanaco.

The most frequent Chavin finds were stone statues of their gods, many of their heads resting on a stone plinth—just like the heads produced by the Olmecs. All these Chavin gods have pointed fangs jutting out from their mouths, and they are either holding snakes in both hands or have hair composed of hissing snakes. The most striking statue is the Lanzon of Chavin de Huantar, a stone jaguar rampant, with hair ending in snake heads, fangs pointing from the mouth, and another set of 'teeth', equally predacious, on top of the head. This statue has been taken for a gorgon. Gorgon is the name for the masks made of copper or gold—dancing masks, ritual masks used as protection against magic—which existed in a great many early civilizations all over the world. These gorgon masks are very similar everywhere, but the Lanzon is the only 'gorgon' stone sculpture, and in execution it is far superior to the primitive masks. In detail it is so extremely like the Gorgon of Syracuse that one can scarcely help believing in a connection between the two: hair, mouth and nose are almost exact copies.

The snake recurs on all the Chavin walls and statues, and could be a ymbol coming from the ancient Mediterranean civilizations. Snake, eagle and panther were their symbols for the gods: panthers were the emblems of Artemis, mistress of the beasts of Asia Minor; eagle and snake watched the holy olive-tree of Astarte. In these civilizations as well, gods are often depicted in repulsive shape, terrifying creatures with snakes instead of hair dangling from their heads, winding in

22. *Above:* Gorgon from Athens and godhead from San Augustin, Colombia. *Below:* Gorgon from Syracuse and Lanzon from Chavin de Huantar

front of their faces and entwining their bodies. The Sumerians had a goddess or earth mother they represented as a snake, and the Cretan goddesses carried a snake in each hand. The symbol of the snake associated with the earth can be traced back to Crete as early as 2500 B.C. The Cretans considered the snake a good spirit, and made clay bowls and tubular vases to be filled with milk for snakes. The Etruscans had an underworld peopled with snakes and demons; Charu, their god of death, who accompanied the souls on their last journey, was depicted with a nose like a bird's beak and with snake hair. The Jews knew a demon called Jaldaboth, in the shape of a snake; and certain gnostic sects made a snake cult out of the Middle Eastern and Chaldaean conceptions of snake gods combined with the serpent from the Garden of Eden.

In ancient times, according to an old Indian tradition, a fleet of balsa boats from the north arrived on the Peruvian coast. A mighty king came ashore with his retinue and his people, and they built a city with a temple a little way inland. Inside the temple there was a statue which they called Yampallec, a monument to their great king Naymlap.

Naymlap reigned peacefully for many years, and at his death was buried under the hall of his palace; but the priests told the people that he had flown away. He was succeeded by his son and afterwards by another eleven kings. But the twelfth king decided to remove the statue from the old temple and erect it in another place. Thereupon a great rain started falling from the skies, as it had never rained before, and the people were afflicted by a famine; so that, led by their priests, they rose against the king who had brought such misery upon them and threw him into the sea. Thus ended the dynasty of the kings of Lambayeque; but their empire came under the suzerainty of the kings of Chan-Chan, and later of the Incas.

For a long time no trace of the Yampallec statue could be found. Then in 1870 it was discovered by a traveller called Antonio Raimondi who was exploring the remotest parts of Peru. When he reached the valley of the river Pucca, he came upon the huge green monolith in the old temple-fortress of Chavin de Huantar and took it to Lima where today the National Museum houses the wonderful treasures of the ancient Peruvian civilizations. Raimondi knew nothing of the myth about King Naymlap, nor, of course, did he know the significance of Chavin. In fact it was only recently that Professor Hans Leicht pointed out the identity of the Raimondi monolith with the ancient idol of Lambayeque.

The sculpture is a tall, narrow slab, decorated all over with reliefs. It shows a jaguar standing on its hind legs like a man, has a man's body, a jaguar's claws, and a head which is part jaguar and part bull (with bull's horns), pointed fangs and hair ending in snakes' heads. Such representations of gods as a cross between man and beast are characteristic of Chavin art and its successors. They also occur often in the ancient civilizations of the Mediterranean: in their lion masks for instance, we find every shade of mixture between man and beast (as in the Olmecs' tiger faces).

The bull is a very common element in the mixture.

Babylonian parapets show colossal stone bulls with human heads. There is the myth of Zeus assuming the shape of a bull to abduct Europa. Seals from Elam (north of the Persian Gulf and east of the

river Tigris) show human beings with bulls' heads—the bull is standing on his hind legs with a leather apron and human shoulders and
arms. This representation goes back to the fourth millennium B.C., and
it was from Elam that the bull ritual originated, passing from there by
way of Mesopotamia and Asia Minor to the coast of Phoenicia and
Canaan, and coming to Crete by way of the Nile.

Other Indian works of art strike a more familiar note, being

23. The Raimondi monolith from Chavin

straightforward and entirely in human form; for instance the Spring
God Xochipilli, usually referred to as the Prince of Flowers; the young
maize gods, such as those of the Maya of Copán; and the old maize
gods of the Chimu. But since Indian art was primarily religious,
depicting scarcely anything but gods, most of their idols and symbols
seem very strange and savage to us, their meaning incomprehensible.
Such are the statues with masks in front of their faces, gods without
heads, gods with snakes, birds in human shape and other creatures
neither man nor beast.

The oldest Indian gods are those of vegetation, the earth, fertility spring and flowers, maize, the water and rain. Gods of the moon have been found on the coast. Gods of the sun are pre-eminent everywhere as the father and king of the gods and creator of the world—like Pachacamac at Tiahuanaco. There are also fish gods, gods of the night of river sources, of the interior of the earth, and of war. The Maya had a war-god painted with black dye, a god of the north star, with a monkey's head, a god who had a snake for one of his legs, and a god of death with a skull for a head and his chest open. The more recent Indian civilizations, the more gods there were; for the younger conquering peoples, originally savage warrior tribes, took over the traditional gods of the older, priest-ruled empires. Thus the Aztecs and Incas' pantheons include nearly all the gods of the Indian empires

The gods of our very early civilizations, Babylonian, Sumerian Egyptian, Phoenician, were just as numerous and 'specialized'. In the different areas they were very much the same gods, with the same functions, bearing the same symbols, represented in the same way. As early as 3370 B.C. the Sumerians had a goddess or earth mother whom they represented as a snake. This Great Mother was in all religions the consort of the king of the gods. The ancient moon god of Nineveh was called Sin—and in Peru the Chimu called their god of the moon Sin An.

In the Old World, as in the New, the rulers were revered as sons of the gods, and in particular of the sun. In Egypt around 2550 B.C. the king was the highest god, a son of the Sun-god Re. In 1385 Amenophis IV introduced the ritual of the Sun-god Aton as the only ritual to be observed in the country, and called himself Echn'aton. In China about 1050 B.C., the Chou dynasty claimed to be descended from the sun, in Assur the king was deified, and in Crete the priest-king enjoyed a degree of veneration that made him the equal of a god.

The Incas in the New World had a ritual similar to that of Aton Their highest god was the sun, and the ruling Inca was his son, ever since the sun had revealed himself to Manca Capac, founder of the dynasty. Sun-worship was the state religion, and people came streaming in to Cuzco from all over the country for their national holiday the festival of the sun, a day which would be fixed by the priests. Before sunrise the Inca went to the main square of Cuzco, where the royal family, the nobility and the people had already gathered. They stood silent and still, their eyes turned towards the east, waiting for the great moment when the first brilliant red rays should shine forth above the peaks of the Cordilleras. Then everybody sank to the ground in prayer. The Inca alone remained standing, holding a golden bowl in each hand. The bowl in his right hand he first offered to his father.

On the desolate highland plateau of Bolivia, where once Tiahuanaco stood, there are three stone statues of kneeling gods. The turban is found here too as headgear

The Gateway of the Sun, the last remains of the White God's city

he sun, then poured the maize wine from it into the groove leading to
he Temple of the Sun. He would himself drink from the bowl in his
eft hand, then offer what remained to his retinue.

Then he walked towards the temple at the head of the great pro-
ession, and there he offered both the golden bowls as a sacrifice to
he sun. The face of Viracocha gleamed on the altar, flanked by the
mages of sun and moon. At the close of the ceremony a black llama
vas slaughtered, and its entrails were handed to the priests so that
hey could find out if the sun was satisfied. So they too had the strange
ustom of observing the entrails, which we know in the Old World
rom the Etruscans, and after them the Romans.

When men from the Old World arrived in countries with a more
primitive civilization, they obviously brought not only their arts and
rafts, their scientific and technical experience, but also their religious
onceptions and their gods. When the Spaniards came to the New
World, they could not be expected to renounce the Christian faith and
adopt the primitive Indian beliefs; and the attitude of these earlier immigrants must have been similar. They too would not have adopted the
imple stone-age rituals they found, renouncing their own beliefs, but
would have introduced these in the countries they conquered and made
hem take root there.

So although some of the Indian gods may have arisen indepen-
lently, originating for instance from totem worship, we may conclude
hat there were a great many which came from the Old World, especially
rom the Mediterranean and the Middle East.

M

15

The Goldsmiths

'History affords no parallel of such a booty—and that, too, in the most convertible form, in ready money, as it were— having fallen to the lot of a little band of military adventurers, like the Conquerors of Peru.'
PRESCOTT in *The Conquest of Peru* (1848)

'They laughed all over their faces. They grabbed at the gold like monkeys, laughing at the sight of this excrement of the gods. For they were very thirsty for gold, longing for it, starving for it, and they snuffled it up like pigs.'
FRAY BERNANDINO DE SAHAGUN

'Apart from their worth alone, the valuables were so fantastic in their novelty and originality that they seemed priceless. Nor is it likely that any of the princes known to us on earth possesses things of such or near such value.'
CORTÉS in his letter to the Emperor Charles V on the Aztec treasure

WHEN the chieftain Chibcha of Guatavita came to the throne, he wa anointed with oil and resin and dusted with gold powder till he sparkle as if made of pure gold. He was El Dorado, the gilt one. Gilded in thi fashion, he descended from a raft into the sacred water of the lake, an the water rinsed the gold dust off him again. The people standing o the banks threw their gifts to the gods into the lake: gold, preciou stones, gold statues.

The Spaniards had heard the old tale of El Dorado, the gilt king and they had long been looking for this special land of gold. In 156; under Jimenez de la Quesada, they found it here with the Chibcha On reaching the Lake of Guatavita they literally fished for gold. The dragnets brought up a gold alligator, thirteen gold toads, many golde

178

fishes, and three statues of pure gold, representing monkeys. All this disappeared into the mercenaries' bags and sacks.

Two decades later Spaniards again cast their nets into the lake, and again they made a good haul. In 1818 a traveller called Cochrane salvaged more gold figures and statues when he fished the lake for the third time, and after this there were many new expeditions to the land of gold.

About the same time as de Quesada's first fishing of the lake, another troop of gold-hunting mercenaries, under Pedro de Heredia, were marching through Colombia to the valley of the river Cauca. As they penetrated deeper into the country, they came upon an old Indian people ruled by a woman. She gave the strangers a friendly welcome, showed them her palace and the great temple, where there were twenty-four large statues of gold, covered entirely in gold foil. In the sacred grove surrounding the temple the Spaniards saw something which took their breath away: every branch of the tall trees in the grove had gold bells hanging from it.

The Queen's guests made a poor return for the hospitality shown them: they took away all the gold bells and the gold coverings of the statues, and they stole a ton and a quarter of gold from the tombs of former princes. The expedition lasted about nine months, and the booty was appropriately rich. Heredia brought back about two tons of gold in works of art which were quickly melted down.

This area of the isthmus, particularly what are today Colombia and Costa Rica, provided the most famous gold objects from the Indian civilizations. They were either made of solid gold or gold plated. The plating sometimes consisted of a thick layer on a basis of copper; at other times it was thin as gossamer, a wire netting applied by a special process, a sort of filigree cast. This gilding was so delicate and artistic that it is still marvelled at today.

Evidently the art of working gold was already flourishing here in the first centuries A.D. and was kept up right to the time of the Spanish conquest. The Chibcha were the élite among goldsmiths, and what has come down to us of their art shows outstanding talent—jewellery, gold animals, eagles, jaguars, alligators, frogs, human figures with animal heads. Female figures in gold were very frequent, and the outlines of their arms and legs, lips and eyes, were traced in fine gold wire. The Chibcha were working gold when their primitive neighbours had scarcely started on any sort of craft. This art seems to have matured suddenly with its workmanship and shaping immediately perfect.

It was practised also by one of the neighbouring tribes, the Manabis, on the coast of northern Ecuador, who made gossamer gold objects consisting of little grains, no bigger than half a pinhead, joined into ornaments. You have to look at them through a magnifying-glass to appreciate the craftmanship. They are magnificently worked, often soldered together from barely visible small parts, sometimes hollowed out and pierced as well. The Manabis must evidently have known and practised the highly complex technique of 'granulation', which was current in our own ancient civilizations. A little gold lion, only five-eighths of an inch high, was discovered at Knossos. It is made of two hollows soldered together, and its mane consists of many tiny gold balls of exactly equal size, fixed to their base. A gold duck, about one and a quarter inches high, also from Crete, shows this granulation at the wings and tail feathers. From ancient Pylos there is a toad one inch high, its warts of granulated gold, and an owl with wings indicated by means of these tiny gold balls. We know of similar gold objects from Troy, such as granulated gold purses and ear-rings, and also from the Etruscans.

Probably the Sumerians originated this very special way of working gold. It is not only a question of fixing the little gold balls to their base, though making these balls is an art in itself. If they were soldered side by side on to a gold plate, they would quickly melt in the heat, flatten out, and lose their ball shape. But if they are first heated in coal dust, their outer layers absorb carbon, melt more easily—and will do so at a temperature lower than the melting point of pure gold. If the balls are now put on to their base side by side, they will stick to it and to one another at a low heat—too low to alter their shape—just because their surface melts so easily.

The technique is so ingenious that the scholars are convinced it cannot have been invented in two places. But after all, the peoples of the Old World were near one another geographically and had close cultural relations, taking over a great many things from one another, so there is nothing very surprising about one people passing on the practice of granulation. It *is* surprising that the practice was known and applied in the New World at such an early date—but certainly the Manabis of the Chavin empire were masters of this art.

Gold death-masks, which have been found in American-Indian tombs, were another thing current in our ancient civilizations. The remains of a princess who was buried around A.D. 220 were found in a marble sarcophagus in the Crimea; she wore a tiara and sceptre and also a gold mask. Two such masks were found in a tomb at Trebenishte also in the Crimea, and a date of A.D. 53 has been established for them. Similar masks used to cover the faces of the Egyptian pharaohs in their graves, and Schliemann retrieved gold death-masks from the tombs of Mycenae.

Central figure in the Gateway of the Sun with the jaguar god

Fabulous winged creature from the Gateway's frieze

Chimu clay vessels; *right:* syrinx player. The instrument is just like those of the Old World

In the temple city of Chavin gold had been known for a long time. A gold crown, rings, ear-rings, and nose ornaments, little works of art discovered there, bear witness to the excellence of its goldsmiths. From Chavin the gold came to Tiahuanaco, where gold nails were used as ornaments for the walls of the city's palaces; the city had a mass of gold.

Among the younger South American civilizations the Chimu had vast treasures of gold. The chroniclers wrote of the Great Chimu receiving tribute from the countries he had conquered—precious jewellery, stones, emeralds and 'chaquiras' (dresses sewn all over with jewellery and sparkling with precious stones and metals). He employed 6,000 Indians, so the chroniclers say, to extract gold and silver, copper and precious stones from the mountains. His capital, Chan Chan, and his temples were magnificently adorned with what they brought him. He was immensely rich, and these riches increased from generation to generation as the rulers' power grew.

Some of the Chimu goldsmiths' products were recovered during the excavations: gold gems, big and small ornaments, testifying to the masters' great feeling for shape. Most of the finds, little miracles of gold, are kept today in the New York Museum of Natural History. The gold and silver plating is so extraordinarily fine and even, and sometimes so very thin, that it is hard to see how it could have been produced without a process akin to electrolysis.

The first Chimu must already have had a very high standard of working metal, as is proved by the ornaments, tools, axes and knives of theirs that have come down to us. They already knew how to make fine gold, silver and copper wires; they produced filigree rings, tiaras, bangles, sleeves, brooches, breast-plates, and silver headgear in the shape of a half-moon.

When the Incas incorporated earlier empires into their own, they also adopted this magnificent technique and its patterns. But all the Central American empires were far behind South America in their knowledge of metal. The gold objects found in Mexico are over a thousand years later than the early South American ones, and the Maya, for instance, never used gold throughout the time of their empires.

At Cajamarca, when the Spaniards for the first time faced Atahualpa, the Inca of Peru, he wore a tiara of feathers, silver and gold, studded with diamonds, turquoises, rubies and emeralds; and a necklace made from emeralds as big as pigeon's eggs, with huge topazes dangling from it, the largest the Spaniards had ever seen. When they had taken him prisoner, he offered to buy back his freedom, promising to fill the room he and his conquerors were in with gold as high as his arms could reach. 'Standing on tiptoe,' say the chronicles, 'he stretched out his hand against the wall. Everyone stared in amazement.' For many of those present it must have seemed an empty boast from a man trying everything to secure his release.

But Pizarro thought differently, and accepted the fantastic offer. He drew a red line along the wall at the level shown by the Inca, and had a notary record in writing the terms of the offer. It has been worked out that 3,500 cubic feet of gold were needed to fill the room to the agreed height; the space was about the proportions of a fairly large modern living-room, twenty feet square and a little under nine feet high.

Long columns of carriers now came down from the mountains, and day by day gold poured into Cajamarca: ornaments and utensils, some weighing nearly thirty pounds. Loads of gold were brought so heavy that one man could only just carry them. One precious thing after another arrived to fill the room: goblets, water-jugs, vases of all shapes and sizes, salvers, ornaments and utensils from the imperial palaces, gold tiles which had decorated public buildings, and animals and plants sculptured in gold. The most beautiful of these were the representations of maize, its gold ears framed by broad silver leaves, with a rich fringe of silver wires hanging down from them. There was also a fountain throwing up a jet of sparkling gold, with birds and animals made of gold playing round its edge.

The conquerors kept some of these objects to send to the Spanish court, but most of them were melted down into lumps of gold by the very Indian goldsmiths who had created these masterpieces. Gold to the value of three and a half million pounds sterling was divided among the victorious soldiers, while Pizarro himself took 57,000 gold ducados, apart from the gold Inca throne, which alone was worth 25,000 ducados.

We have heard how the Spaniards broke their promise. For one thing they feared that if they released Atahualpa the whole country would take up arms against their small band within a few days. For another, they now saw a stream of gold surpassing all their dreams, and guessed there must be much more of it still in this country, perhaps hidden away beyond the mountains. So they condemned the last Inca to death and had him strangled like a common criminal: now the road to the gold was free.

'In a cave near Cuzco', Garcilaso wrote, 'they found a number of vases of pure gold, richly embossed with the figures of serpents, locusts and other animals. Among their booty were also four golden llamas and ten or twelve statues of women, some of gold, others of silver, which merely to see was a great satisfaction. In one city they found ten bars of solid silver, each twenty feet long, one foot wide and two inches thick. These too were not only admired by the Spaniards, but taken along.'

The booty at Cuzco is said to have exceeded Cajamarca's, and from records kept has been estimated at well over a ton of gold, with a value the equivalent of over two and a half million pounds. Some things, of course, were taken with no record kept, and the Spaniards missed others—like the great gold sun disc from Cuzco's Temple of the Sun, discovered forty years later at Wilcabamba where it had been hidden.

At Cajamarca the Spaniards had gradually got used to seeing this mass of treasure. But on first reaching Cuzco they came upon a fantastic sight which made even the coolest spirits gasp. A terraced garden went down from the Temple of the Sun, a garden which had a lawn peopled with lizards, birds and other creatures, and also statues of men. Everything was in gold: the statues, the creatures, even the trees and shrubs and the grass of the lawn; and there were fountains spurting jets of gold. The Spaniards were delighted to stroll in this garden, plucking a flower here and there, tearing up a plant, breaking off a branch—till a good deal of the golden garden had disappeared. The garden must have been unique in the whole world, but not a single piece of it has been found, nor the smallest part of the golden frieze surrounding the Temple of the Sun, nor any of the hundreds of golden figures which stood in the niches of the inner courts. The Indians managed to save quite a lot of the garden and hide it away, but where they hid it is not known.

They were quick to recognize that the returning White Gods were nothing but robbers, and they went by night up to their mountains, into their woods and to their lakes, to find permanent hiding-places for the country's treasures. So the Spaniards' loot was only a small part of the immense hoard: between 1533 and 1600, according to recent estimates, they took about twenty-two tons of gold out of Peru—counting only the official transports.

Perhaps the most precious single piece among the things the Indians hid was the gold chain of the Inca Huayna Capac, which a procession of his nobles used to carry to the temple square at Cuzco when an heir to the throne was born. This was a chain made from links the size of a man's fist, all of sheer gold. It was 700 feet long, tradition said, and was so heavy that ten men were needed to carry it. About a ton of gold went into its making, and 250 carriers had brought this from the Caramanca mountains. There is a deep circular lake in Peru near a place called Urcos, and according to the chronicles the chain must still be hidden in there. The Spaniards heard that report, and forty of them with 200 Indians dug a canal to drain off the water. But the lake was too deep for any canal to take all its water, so they finished still a long way from the lake-bed. The Inca's chain, with its fantastic value, has never been retrieved.

Part of Atahualpa's treasure never reached Cajamarca. Seven thousand men were taking gold to ransom their Inca, each carrying a load weighing about eighty pounds, when they heard the news of Pizarro's treachery. They went into the Andes mountains, where they left the treasure in well-hidden and inaccessible places; and from the chronicler's descriptions it must have been worth the equivalent of about thirty-five million pounds sterling. The Indians also managed to save the twelve large statues of the Inca rulers, made of solid gold, which had been erected near Cuzco.

For all the enormous riches the gold treasures of their empire represented, the Incas never reached the same artistic heights in gold-working as had the Chimu. But the Inca tribes of Esmeraldas did know alloys, for instance of gold, silver and platinum. Platinum was mined around the Gulf of Guayaquil. The alloy had the 'colour of the silver moon'; it consisted of seventy parts of gold, eighteen of silver, and twelve of platinum. This alloy is the 'white gold' mentioned by a document on the division of the booty drawn up after Cuzco was taken. The document lists a 'plate of white gold which could not be weighed at all'. It was kept in the Temple of the Moon; its length was twenty-six feet, and it weighed over a ton. The Spaniards did not have a scale large enough for this huge piece of precious metal, and could only work out its weight approximately when it was melted down.

Very little of the Aztec hoard either has come to light in later years. A few days after the Spaniards had come to Tenochtitlán to stay as guests in the great palace of the Emperor's father, they asked per-mission—which was granted—to convert a hall of the palace into a chapel. During the preparations some of them discovered an odd stain on one of the walls, which looked as if a door had recently been plastered over. Although guests in the palace, they had no scruples about knocking down the plaster and forcing their way in.

Then 'they beheld a large hall filled with rich and beautiful stuffs, articles of curious workmanship of various kinds, gold and silver in bars and in the ore, and many jewels of value'. Bernal Diaz, one of those who saw it, said: 'I was a young man, and it seemed to me as if all the riches in the world were in that room.' This was Montezuma's hoard, and Diaz's amazement was justified, for the value in gold alone has been estimated at the equivalent of a million and a half pounds. The Spaniards managed to take along only a fifth of this, as much as they could carry in the *noche triste*, the night when they had to flee from Tenochtitlán. Cortés was under obligation to deliver this part of the booty to the Spanish court to secure royal protection against his enemies. But even that never reached Spain. French privateers captured the ship which carried it, and eventually the King of France came into possession of what was left of the Aztec hoard. Apart from this hoard, the Spaniards did not find much gold later on when they conquered the capital. The Indians had stowed it in safe hiding-places—where most of it has remained hidden.

Montezuma presented his conqueror with many gifts, however. These included two 'wheels' about seven feet in diameter, one of gold, worth 20,000 ducados, representing the sun, and the other of silver, representing the moon. The Spaniards also received gold necklaces studded with hundreds of emeralds and garnets, gold shields, a gold mace, fishes, swans, twenty ducks, mussels, and a crocodile, all cast in gold; turquoise sceptres, turquoise and gold ear-rings.

In 1931 the Mexican archaeologist Alfonso Caso started on a new investigation of the Monte Alban tombs. Digging is still going on there, and over a hundred tombs have so far been discovered, either on the slopes of the mountain or as crypts under the buildings. Caso himself found something almost unique in the history of archaeology in both hemispheres. When he opened the tomb now referred to as 'Tomb 7', besides the usual funeral offerings he saw the most amazing treasure of gold and precious stones ever discovered by excavators in America.

From the artistic point of view as well, this find is the most valuable so far known from all Indian civilizations: necklaces made up of twenty rows, consisting of 854 chased gold links, ear-rings and tiaras, plaited gold rings, bangles and brooches, a lady's bag made of gilt leaves, the finest jewellery made of jade, turquoises, obsidian, pearls, corals and amber—scarcely surpassed by any jewellery produced in modern times. All this gives some idea of the wonderful works of art that perished in the conquerors' melting-pots.

What we know of metal-working in the ancient Chavin empire comprises the entire scale of metal knowledge in the Old World.

Obviously copper, gold and silver, the pure metals, will turn up first in all civilizations, because they are easier to produce than alloys: you have only to melt down the ore. Pure copper was often used in all the Indian civilizations. Copper tools, arms, jewellery, axes, breast-plates, clubs and knives have been discovered. The copper axes are either hefty weapons, real 'battle-axes', or they were worn for decorative purposes. Copper breast-plates have been found in the whole area from Peru to Argentina. The oldest copper find in the New World was made on the Peruvian coast and can be dated back to about 700 B.C.; the technique of core-casting was also known there at this time.

In the century before that the Chavin people made gold jewellery for the first time: in the mountains of Guiana or at the end of the mountain ridge near the upper course of the Orinoco. From this remote spot gold started its route through all the other civilizations of the New World, right down to Chile. The alloy which the Spaniards called 'gold of the Andes' was also developed in this area, an alloy of copper and gold with a slightly oxidized gleaming surface that can be polished. Here too the most ancient finds of 'Inca gold' were made: an alloy of gold and silver.

24. Containers in animal form from Chavin de Huantar (*left*) and from China (*right*)

Goldsmiths from the area of modern Colombia introduced gold and silver plating, soldering and welding. They were familiar with embossing, hammering, core-casting, wire-drawing, chasing, damascening, colouring of metals, and even granulation. Such complicated techniques must obviously have been introduced from abroad.

Some motifs of the Chavin civilization and the civilization which followed (known as 'Salinar') are the same as those used by the middle and later Chou style in China about 700 B.C.; and Professor Heine-Geldern assumes that they reached the New World around 500 B.C. from the northern Chinese empires of Wu and Yüeh. Later, between 400 B.C. and A.D. 100, men from the Chinese Dongson civilization reached the New World and introduced the techniques of working metal mentioned above.

But the men from South-East Asia are not mentioned in any Indian legend or chronicle, and when they came to America they must have found higher civilizations already in existence. For the first immigrants must have come to a primitive people, or the natives would have regarded them as equals instead of worshipping them as gods—and then the legend of the White Gods would never have arisen.

16

The First Men in America

TAKE a map of South and Central America and paint in the high civilizations of the Andes and of Central America and Yucatan: there will be a large wedge between them without any colour at all. This is the area which includes the present Brazilian provinces of Amazonas and Para, the three Guianas, Venezuela, and the highlands of Ecuador and Colombia—altogether about the size of Europe. Here the Spaniards found no gold or precious stones but only savage Indian tribes who shot poisoned arrows and were cannibals. In 1499, when the first Spaniards came to the Orinoco, the great river of Venezuela, they found it inhabited only by Arawaks and Caribis, at a primitive stage of civilization: mile-long dams built against flooding; simple, artless rock-paintings; clay vessels without artistic shape, decorated with simple geometrical and spiral patterns; amulets from mussel-shells and stones, mostly in the shape of a frog.

Because it seemed to have been so little explored, archaeologists have recently shown a new interest in this area. Much digging has gone on throughout the northern tip of the continent, as far south as the river Amazon, and here the spade has reached layers so deep that there is not the slightest trace of man to be found. But important discoveries were made nevertheless: for instance, that America was first settled only about 20000 to 15000 B.C.; before that it was inhabited by herds of huge animals. The first men to appear were hordes of short-headed beardless mongol types with protruding cheek-bones and straight black hair. They carried stone axes, clubs, and primitive hunting gear. They had migrated from Asia by the Bering Strait and moved down into America from north to south. Their migration towards the south lasted thousands of years. On their way they slept in caves; and remains and tracks have been found in such caves, often with the bones of the giant animals they had slain, in modern Nevada, Ecuador and Argentina.

This mass migration from Asia continued in constant new waves and so did the migration southwards from North America. It reached the narrow strip of Central America and flowed on to South America. It did not stop till about 3000 B.C.; by that time the whole of America was inhabited.

Immigrants from South Asia, Australia and Polynesia also reached America, crossing the Pacific: remains from this immigration have been found in Brazil, Ecuador, and near the Magellan Strait. Many archaeologists today believe that peoples from the Pacific area may

25. Rock carvings from the valley of the Rio Negro, Amazon area

have come direct into South America, crossing by way of Hawaii, Paumotu, the Marshall Islands and Easter Island. This belief is supported particularly by evidence of striking similarities in language on both sides of the Pacific. Moreover, it is the oldest Peruvian language which show very strong leanings towards the language of Polynesia, so the migration must have taken place in very early times: there can be no question of these immigrants having transmitted a higher civilization.

The continually growing pressure of new immigrants drove the native tribes into the virgin forests of Guiana and the Amazon, or pushed them from the Peruvian coast on to the Cordilleras. In these regions they lived in huts of leaves, hunted game, and gathered what they needed for food. When they had learnt to build canoes, they went up the big river to the mountains. These tribes were from the people of the Arawaks. Their descendants living today still roam through the vast woods of the Amazon, hunt with poisoned arrows, and catch their fish with poisoned lianas.

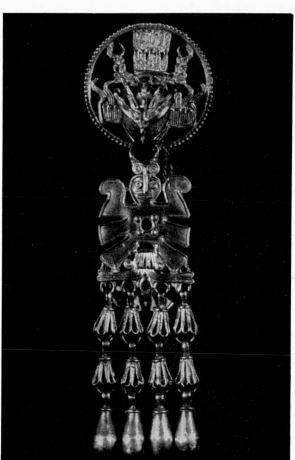

Lizard in the Quimbaya style, Columbia

The Indians worked gold with great skill

Gold ornaments from Monte Alban

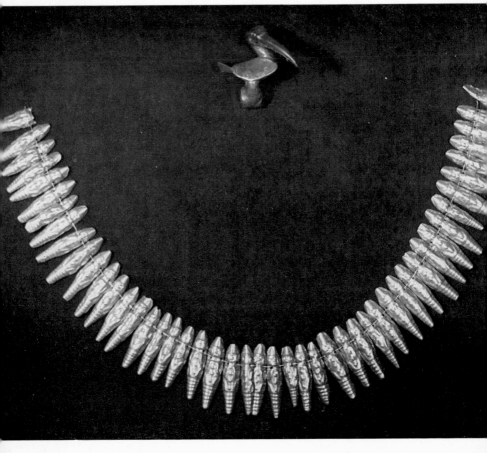

Gold ornament showing small alligators from the Colima civilization

Chronological table of the Indian empires of South and Central America.

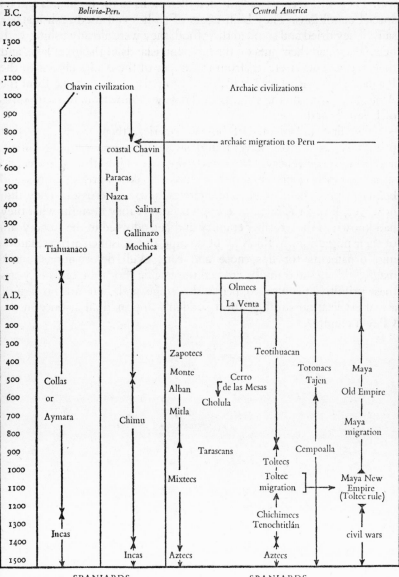

One of the tribes, the Urus or Kotsun, reached the high plateau on Lake Titicaca and found a new home on the lake with its abundance of fish. They settled there and adapted their skills to the highlands and its special conditions. They built boats of rushes and used rush-mats as sails. They dried and smoked their food, they were already fishing with nets. They had their huts on the bays and islands of the great lake, and their settlements stretched from the slopes of the Andes almost to the Pacific. Their rush boats, which archaeologists believe came from the Amazon region, are the same as the boats we know from the sculptures of Easter Island.

The first inhabitants of South America, then, were altogether primitive. Excavators have found stone weapons, scraping-knives, and primitive jewellery. Other traces are carved into the big rocks and stones: clumsy representations of birds, snakes, turtles, lizards and beasts of prey, hands and heads, circles, suns and crosses. They did, however, bring their stone age 'civilization': they brought what they had known in their former country and had adopted in the 1,000 years of their migration. In this way blow-pipe and poisoned arrows, tatooing, ornaments for lips, nose and ears, skull deformations, mask magic, old rites and myths crossed the Pacific. For thousands of years these primitive peoples stopped at that stage, and there was no sign of a real civilization starting; till it suddenly appeared all at once in the Chavin empire.

PART FOUR

Towards a Solution

17

Civilization Transfers to the New World

F WE compare the ancient Indian empires as they succeeded one
another, we meet one of the strangest parallels in world history: the
New World had two centres of high civilization—one in Central
America and one in Peru. They are thousands of miles distant, yet
many features of their history are very similar.

In both areas all higher civilization began in one centre: with the
Olmecs in Central America, with Chavin in South America. In the
early days of each, a mighty priest-city arose: Teotihuacan in Central
America, Tiahuanaco in South America; both so gigantic that legend
said only giants could have built them. Both were destroyed by savage
warrior tribes bursting in like a hurricane.

In both areas there were then petty kingdoms, civil wars, temporary
conquests and defeats, to be followed by unity under two big empires,
the Aztecs and the Incas. In both the legend survived of the White
God who promised one day to return; and in both there was the same
paralysing terror when the white men really landed. In both areas the
ancient civilizations collapsed in tragic destruction.

All the Indian civilizations, not only the two youngest, came to a
violent end, and presumably for much the same basic reason. As in
ancient Egypt, the building of the mighty temples and pyramids must
have been dictated by an amazing religious fanaticism. It seems as if
the old Indian kings and priests, in their ever more inordinate ob-
jectives, drove their subjects harder and harder, until one day the
subjects rose against them.

In both areas the first high civilization came into existence very
abruptly. In South America a primitive age had lasted for 10,000 or
20,000 years, and all at once the Chavin civilization started. In Mexico
the Olmecs sprang up just as suddenly, having migrated to Mexico

probably from South America. All the tribes to which they passed on their high civilization had also developed from complete primitiveness in a few decades. The Olmecs civilized the whole of Mexico and Yucatan in the period of mass migrations.

These migrations were connected with trade, which carried one people's achievements to its neighbours; and with the centuries almost every feature which had developed in South America made its way into Central America. So many difficult inventions could not have been made twice in the New World; and the same applies to the cosmological concepts, the calendar system, etc. All these, however, also have Old World equivalents, and could not have started independently in the New World. As Professor Heine-Geldern wrote (in 1955): 'However much may still be hypothetical in our present knowledge, we can state as established fact that the high civilizations of America must have developed in close contact with those of the Old World.'

The earliest Asian influence came from the Chou civilization of north China, starting about 700 B.C. and continuing till the second half of the fourth century B.C. It was exerted above all on the Chavin civilization and its successor, the Salinar civilization, on the Peruvian coast. The men from China probably brought knowledge of gold and its working, weaving and the weaving techniques of ikat and batik, the syrinx, and perhaps the construction of Lake Titicaca's balsa boats.

Directly afterwards another Chinese civilization, that of Dongson, Tongking and Annam, sent over a second wave, which left behind such strong influences that it looks as if a colony was deliberately planted. The influences began in the fourth century B.C. and ended about A.D. 100, affecting chiefly the coastal plain of Peru, Colombia, Panama, Costa Rica and Honduras, but not Mexico and the country of the Maya. Metal-working techniques can be traced for the first time about then on the Peruvian coast, and they may have been introduced by men from the Dongson civilization.

After that civilization perished, in the first century A.D., a new wave of people began crossing the Pacific, coming from the Hindu-Buddhist civilizations of Indo-China and Indonesia. Their voyages must have lasted till about A.D. 1200, the end of the Khmer civilization, and they introduced chiefly their native religious concepts, administrative arrangements, building styles, and ornaments.

So the transfers of civilization start about 700 B.C. in the oldest Indian civilization, that of Chavin, in South America. They can be traced through all South American civilizations, but become particularly clear in the Central American civilizations at the beginning of our era, where they do not stop until A.D. 1200.

A few years ago Heine-Geldern established that many of the

ccomplishments of the Far East were brought to China about 700 B.C.
·y a migration of people from the Caucasus area which he called 'the
'ontic migration'. On reaching China this split into three streams.
_he largest stream went to Yunnan and north-eastern Indo-China,
·roducing the Dongson civilization, which later extended from
ndonesia to New Guinea. Judging from the features brought to China
t that time, the people involved in this migration were Illyrians,

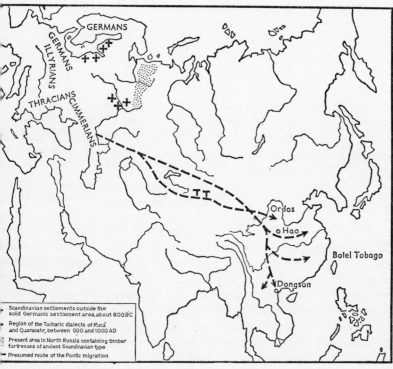

The Pontic Migration (taken from Heine-Geldern)

'hracians, Cimmerians, Caucasian tribes, Germanic tribes, and peoples
·om the eastern Mediterranean area. Thus the ikat weaving technique
f East Asia is an exact copy of the Greek geometrical style.

But the Dongson civilization later had contacts with America,
nd that is why exactly the same artifacts can be found in three different
arts of the world, in the Caucasus and with the Phoenicians, in East
.sia, and in parts of America. In fact all the features of civilization from
ast Asia which were taken over to America actually come from the
vilizations of the Caucasus and the Mediterranean, from the Danube
ountries and south Russia.

It is clear, however, on comparing the tables on pages 197–199 that many of the features must have come direct from the Mediterranean area to America, because they were not known so early in the Far East. We can safely say that the original White God of the Indians came from Europe, not East Asia. He even brought Cretan script to America which cannot possibly have come via East Asia—for the Cretan empire had been destroyed 700 years before the first Chinese reached America.

26. *Left:* Belt-clasp in bronze from the Caucasus. *Right:* Silver-plated copper ornament from Trujillo, Peru (taken from Heine-Geldern)

The White God from Crete was also the first to discover America. This must have been a thousand years before the first contact with East Asia. For when he came, the pyramids, obelisks and mummification must still have existed in his own country, or he wouldn't ever have brought them into the New World. Nobody from our modern Western civilizations would bring long-forgotten relics of the Middle Ages to a different primitive people. Moreover, the primitive Indians would scarcely have taken a Chinaman for a white man with a beard if he had been the first to come to them. Even today the difference between an American Indian and an Asiatic is not so great: both belong to the Asiatic races, which have only a small growth of beard.

THE OLDEST TRANSFER OF CIVILIZATION FROM THE WU AND YÜEH KINGDOMS OF NORTH CHINA TO THE NEW WORLD

Took place about	Traceable in New World	Men from	What they brought with them
700 B.C.	Chavin	Chinese Chou civilization 700 B.C.	Weaving, gold, Chinese motifs, gold-working
500 B.C.	Salinar Peru coast	Late Chou civilization	Motifs like interlocked snake-dragons with sickle-shaped wings
500–400 B.C.	Gallinazo Peru	Chou civilization	Gold
500 B.C.	Mochica or Proto-Chimu Peru coast	Chou civiliza-tion stopping 333 B.C.	Motifs, gold-working

THE TRANSFER OF CIVILIZATION FROM THE DONGSON CIVILIZATION OF NORTH CHINA

400 B.C.	Kingdoms of Peru coast	Dongson	Knowledge of copper, core-casting, granula-tion, gold and copper alloy, metal-dyeing
till A.D. 100	Tiahuanaco	Dongson	Knowledge of bronze, bronze patterns?

THE LATER RELATIONS BETWEEN EAST ASIA AND THE AMERICAN INDIANS

A.D. 100–200	Old Mayan empire Yucatan	Colonial civilizations from Indo-China and Indonesia, esp. Amarâvati	Stylized lotus flowers, makara sea-monsters, world directions, world ages, administrative arrangements, fans, litters

Took place about	Traceable in New World	Men from	What they brought with them
A.D. 800–1100	New Mayan empire (Puuc style)	Cambodia, Indo-China, Khmer civilization	Half-pillars as door frames and to decorate house-fronts
till A.D. 1200	Chichen Itza	Khmer civilization till its collapse a little after A.D. 1200	

TRANSFER OF CIVILIZATIONS FROM THE OLD WORLD
TO SOUTH AMERICA

700 B.C.	Chavin	Mediterranean	Mummification (?), granulation, damascening, alloys, core-casting (?), gold (?), gorgons from Syracuse, snake-worship.
500–400 B.C.	Salinar and Gallinazo civilizations Mochica or Proto-Chimu	Mediterranean	Crossing of cotton, batik and ikat techniques, weaving, crimson dye, alum-bath, obol for Charon, dance of the dead, pyramids, dog-headed god, fish-manuring, copper (?), mummies, also of animals, sun-dried bricks, syrinx
300–100 B.C.	Tiahuanaco	Mediterranean, esp. Crete	Bronze, copper rivets for building, pyramid as tomb, stelae, aqueducts, drainage systems, throne-room below ground, winged creatures, colossal buildings, obelisks, building technique, spoon, plate, cup, 'balsa' boats
End of first century B.C. till A.D. 1400	Chimu	Mediterranean	Decimal system, head-shaped jugs, house urns, double jugs, balance, flute

Took place about	Traceable in New World	Men from	What they brought with them

Took place about	Traceable in New World	Men from	What they brought with them
100 B.C. to about A.D. 800	Olmec civilization	Crete	Jade mania, ceremonial axes, mortar, stucco, asphalt, mosaics, pyramids, stelae, script, jaguar mania, lion (masks), plumed crown, sarcophagus, stone yoke
B.C. to about A.D. 800	Archaic period		
Beginning of our era to about A.D. 800	Teotihuacan	Crete	Mythical butterfly
Beginning of our era	Old Maya	Crete	Characters, old calendars, tomb under pyramids
	Totonacs	Egypt	stone yoke in ankh form
	Zapotecs	Egypt	statue of the 'Egyptian', ball-courts, colonnades
	Toltecs and Aztecs	Mediterranean	'confession', 'sacred bread', legend of the Flood

18

The White God, the Cretans and the Phoenicians

EVEN the most ingenious artist cannot paint or sculpt people of another race he has never seen. But there were stone statues from Olmec times in Mexico which showed a particularly non-Indian type so convincingly that the first Europeans to see them thought they were looking at people from countries outside America. The type is plump, often fat, with broad shoulders, short arms and legs, with a round head, high forehead, broad, coarse neck, flat nose and slit eyes. Another type appears farther north: taller and slimmer, with narrow hook-nose and often a goatee beard. And a Mayan vase from north Guatemala shows both types together.

A mural at Chichen Itza of about the tenth or eleventh century shows men of these two races in a battle at sea: a dark-skinned race fighting with a light-skinned and obviously fair-haired race. The whites are fleeing, defeated, and even end on the sacrificial stone. The seated old priest, taken to be the White God, appears on a Mayan relief from Chichen Itza, and there are a whole series of other representations there of the white man with a beard who has the characteristic features of the Caucasian race.

This is still clearer at Tiahuanaco, where some masks, a few of them with a beard and a turban, were once hanging on the walls of the old audience chamber. An old temple which belonged to the Tiahuanaco empire housed the stone head of a man, with strikingly European features, who probably represents one of the White Gods.

Statues of white men have been found also from the empire of the Chibchas. The type is quite un-Indian, with no sign anywhere of the hook-nose of the Maya and the Aztecs or the mongol eyes. These men wear their hair long, they have well-formed noses—straight or curving slightly inwards, narrow nostrils, big full eyes. They are the same type as depicted by the Olmecs, even with helmet and ear-flaps.

In a fresco at Chichen Itza the Indians portrayed a negro. They must have seen one with their own eyes, or it would never have occurred to them that there were men with black skins. But this fresco has a definite negro's head with all the marks of the black race. He would scarcely have come to the Indians from East Asia, for there were no negroes there. Perhaps he crossed the Atlantic with the White Gods.

All the Indian civilizations, Chavin and Tiahuanaco, the Olmecs and the Maya, left statues of their White Gods—but these, of course, are many centuries apart. The Maya, in fact, regarded the Toltec Quetzalcoatl as a foreign conqueror and oppressor. In old Mayan chronicles J. E. S. Thompson found a lament from Chichen Itza: 'I was a boy in Chichen Itza when the wicked man came, leader of an

27. Negro head from Chichen Itza

army, to take possession of the land. Woe! Heresy was given favour at Chichen Itza. . . . His devilry will be brought to an end.' (The heresy was the Toltec religion.) In another place the lament says: 'Their hearts are steeped in sin, they are dead in lusts of the flesh. . . . They are dissolute libertines by day and night, the scoundrels of the world. . . .'

Archaeological finds have shown that when the Olmecs migrated to Mexico they brought the Maya all high civilization. Probably one of them became the White God whom the Maya called Kukulcan. The White God Quetzalcoatl must also have been an Olmec, and the Olmecs are the 'coastal people' referred to in the legend that after his return from Tollan he went to the coastal people and there wore the plumed crown.

The White God of Tiahuanaco must have been older than Kukulcan; perhaps he was Viracocha. Assuming he came to Tiahuanaco about 300 B.C., while Kukulcan came to the Maya about the beginning of our era and Quetzalcoatl to the Toltecs about A.D. 900., this is a span of 1,200 years. In that span, as their statues show, the White Gods continued to have the characteristics of the Caucasian race; so one can speak of a dynasty of White Gods which ruled in the New World for over a thousand years. What happened when these rulers died?

Clearly the White God was immortal, or he would not be a god. So when he died, the priests secretly laid him in a magnificent sarcophagus under pyramids, and told the people he had sailed across the sea but would one day return again, for so he had promised. We come across such stories continually in the chronicles, as in the saga of King Naymlap. When he died, the priests concealed his death from the people, proclaiming that he had gone to Heaven after taking his leave of them and naming a successor. His bones were secretly buried in a grave under the palace he had inhabited during his life. If this was the procedure with mere kings, how much more must a White God's death be concealed from his people! Eagerly the people took up the story of their benefactor's promise to return; they believed it with all their heart and longed for his second coming.

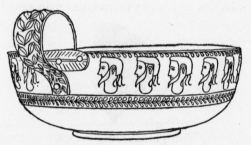

28. Bearded men on a gold beaker from the
Cretan-Minoan civilization

In the New World there is only one case where we know who is buried in one of these graves. The chronicles relate that Quetzalcoatl, the white man with a beard, visited his father's grave. It was underneath a small pyramid, which turned into a hill with the centuries. Archaeologists discovered this sacred hill in 1910.

All the Indian sagas describe their White God as being bearded, and in all their civilizations the statues which can be taken to represent him show faces with a beard. If the first White God was Cretan, as has been suggested in this book, did the Cretans have beards?

A gold chalice has been discovered in the lower city of Mycenae with twenty-one male faces on it, all of them bearded. Evans found a priest's head with a beard on a soapstone seal at Knossos. The gold masks of the kings of Mycenae all show a strong growth of beard. A relief found in the grave of an Egyptian high priest and royal treasurer shows a Pharaoh receiving foreign ambassadors, among them the Prince of Kefti (Egyptian for Crete), who has a long beard; this relief dates from the fifteenth century B.C., a time when the Cretans might have made their first voyage to America. So the tradition that the White God was bearded fits in well enough with the theory that he was a Cretan.

When the Trojan war was raging outside the walls of Troy, from 1194 to 1184 B.C., the civilization of Crete was already 2,000 years old. Its buildings surpassed any other buildings in the world at that time. Homer in 800 B.C. still described the magnificent court of King Minos. Herodotus mentions it in the middle of the fifth century B.C., and a little later Thucydides refers to Crete's mighty fleet. Aristotle in the next century states that King Minos's sea power prevailed all over the Aegean; and the Greek legends are full of Cretan stories and myths.

Above all, they are about the Cretan monster, the Minotaur, half man, half bull, living in the labyrinth at Knossos, who demanded human victims; till he was at last overcome by Theseus, King of Athens, with the help of Ariadne, daughter of the Cretan king. The word labyrinth comes from 'labrys', Crete's sacred double axe, symbol of the gods which the Greeks took over: Rhea, the Cretan mother goddess, is often represented on Greek statues with her son, both with the symbolic double axe. A pair of horns were also a Cretan religious symbol, and these mighty bull's horns in stone stood in front of temples and palaces.

The 'early Minoan' period of Crete lasted from 3400 to 2100 B.C. Bronze was already known; the princes of Knossos built the cities of Phaistos and Malli and their palaces, with temples, stairways, parapets, passages, frescoed walls, and with a water supply. The old glyphs were starting to turn into the linear script.

In the 'middle Minoan period', from 2100 to 1580 B.C., all the buildings were destroyed in a catastrophe. About 1600 the mighty palaces of Knossos, Phaistos and Hagia Triada were rebuilt out of the ruins. It was the golden age, which lasted till about 1400 B.C. Then Crete was suddenly wiped out, and now for good. From this ancient civilization the ruins of the palace of Knossos have survived, the first gigantic palace buildings of the Old World. The palace was right on the sea, the Mediterranean washed the flights of steps outside it. It contained a maze of passages and rooms, with water supply, drains and baths; and it also had an audience chamber in a sunken room with a stone throne.

The world of Crete was brought to life again with the discovery of the wall-paintings, showing vivid scenes from nearly 3,000 years ago. The people there delighted in jade, gold ornament and bronze; their craftsman were true artists. They loved depicting movement, preserving the moment—for instance when a raging bull crashes and is caught in the net. Again and again there are representations of the sacred axes and pairs of horns, winged creatures, and also snakes.

All this, of course, is to be found in the oldest high Indian civilizations as well, the Colombian and those of Chavin and Tiahuanaco.
Cretans and Indians must some time have come into contact with one
another. Whether this contact occurred once or more often, we do not
yet know for sure; but there is much to suggest that the Cretan
voyages across the Atlantic went on for a whole era, and then suddenly
stopped.

If Cretans crossed the Atlantic they must have had seaworthy
ships. It is clear they did have, and so did other ancient civilizations
of the Mediterranean area. Moreover, the period of Crete's naval
supremacy is about the time when the White God crossed the Atlantic.
In 3000 B.C. Egyptians ships reached Somaliland. In 2400 B.C.
they sailed round Africa and discovered a country of gold they called
Punt—we do not know where this was. Extensive maritime trade by
the Babylonians is recorded about 2300 B.C. Overseas trade is reported
between Egyptians and Phoenicians about 2000 B.C. In 1700 B.C.
Crete's naval supremacy began, with voyages to Egypt, Syria, Mesopotamia and the western Mediterranean. In 1500 B.C. Hatchepsut, the
woman Pharaoh, equipped an expedition to Punt, which sailed round
Africa. In 1365 B.C. the Phoenicians were reported to be making long
voyages. In 1300 B.C. the Greek fleet appeared in the Mediterranean.
In 1250 B.C. the Egyptians discovered what were probably the Canary
Isles; they sailed round Africa and carried on an extensive trade.

For a long time the ancient peoples were not credited with such
maritime experience and ability. Long voyages only became common
in the second century A.D. during the Roman empire, when ships
sailed regularly to and from Hindustan and Indo-China by way of the
Bay of Bengal. Arab sailors reached the Malayan islands and probably
China.

Ancient literature contains many reports of great voyages and
expeditions; some of these might be connected with America. Plato,
for instance, mentions a large island beyond the Pillars of Hercules
(Gibraltar), with a great sea behind it—so the island could be South
America. Theopompus describes a big continent which was supposed
to lie behind the islands of the Atlantic and which was called Meropis;
he said it was ruled by Merope, a daughter of Atlas, King of Libya.

In A.D. 45 Diodorus, the Greek historian in Rome, wrote of a great
country far away from Libya, many days' voyage in the Atlantic, with
navigable rivers and big houses, much forest and abundance of fruits
which were ripe the whole year round. The Phoenicians had discovered the country, he said, when a storm drove them far out into
the ocean. Since this description does not fit any of the Atlantic islands,

it sounds as if it must refer to South America. The Greek author Plutarch (about A.D. 100) also knew the continent ruled over by Merope; according to him, Hercules had visited it and introduced the Greek language there.

If the sailors of those times made such a wonderful discovery, one can understand their trying at all costs to keep it secret so as to avoid competition. The Phoenicians, at any rate, who sailed far beyond the Pillars of Hercules, must have had something to hide in the Atlantic,

29. *Left:* Stele of the Sun-god at Mocachi, Lake Titicaca.
Right: Stele of the Sun-god of the Althiburos at Aiin Barchouch (Phoenician)

because for a long time they barred Greek ships from going through the narrow strait and out of the Mediterranean. According to Aristotle, the Senate of Carthage decreed that, on pain of death for disobedience, no ship should sail to the great unknown island in the Atlantic.

In one of the big libraries of São Paulo, Brazil, there is one of the strangest books ever produced, and, although only forty years old, one of the rarest too. Only a few copies are left, because most of the people who acquired a copy soon threw it away, thinking its author's claims completely incredible. The author was a former rubber-tapper, a man called Bernardo da Silva Ramos, and his book is in Portuguese, yet even a Portuguese scholar cannot read it like any ordinary book.

It contains drawings of animals and shards, without any explanation. There are 1,500 illustrations, drawings and photographs, unnumbered and in no order. The text also refers to illustrations which are not there. Nevertheless, it is an extremely interesting book. Its subject is the rock-carvings in the Amazon area. Stones and boulders are photographed and then drawn; inscriptions and letters, animals and demons, catlike creatures, figures of gods and mythical monsters: all these appear in the illustrations.

They are all covered over with the letters of the Phoenician alphabet; for Ramos 'read' these drawings as we read a book. The outline of a bird, for instance, he broke up into Phoenician letters; the beak became one letter, each feather and talon another. In this way he arrived at whole texts, which are to be found in his book first in Phoenician and then in Portuguese translation. All the texts seemed to show, surprisingly enough, that the savage Indians of the Amazon spent a great deal of their time calling on the god Zeus, who is continually turning up in these 'readings'.

Ramos had been roaming the jungle for many years, a simple man without any higher education. He took his narrow paths into the wilderness, to the rubber-trees. He made an incision in their bark and hung little containers under them to catch the drops. He did his round of the trees every day, then returned to his poor hut of palm trunks, with a roof of banana leaves, smoked the rubber over an open fire, and went off every Sunday to sell his 'produce'. He scrimped and saved till he could afford to become a rubber-buyer, and as such he made a considerable fortune—one of the few rubber-tappers who had survived the 'Green Hell'.

Now that he was well off, he could realize his old plan of becoming an archaeologist. In the jungle he had kept coming upon rock-scrawls and big stones which no one before him had seen—stones with strange symbols on them. Now he roamed the jungle again, no longer in search of rubber. He photographed and drew what he could find of the remains of ancient civilizations. Even when he was an old man, he would often stay in the jungle all day up to his waist in mud, to find the symbols on the stones, which were hidden by the water. He compared the letters on his photographs and drawings with the inscriptions on old coins of the European world, and thought he saw connections. Then the learned Manáos Rabbi declared one day that these symbols were Phoenician inscriptions; and old Ramos was now convinced it was the Phoenicians who had once carved these symbols into the rocks. He became fascinated, obsessed by this idea, sacrificed all his fortune to it, and wrote his curious book on it.

Long before him, from 1850 to 1910, Brazilian travellers and explorers in the Amazon region and other parts of Brazil had found old inscriptions on rock-faces and stones. Today there is a whole library full of their reports; and they too were firmly convinced that the inscriptions were Phoenician texts. They were sure that King Solomon (975–935 B.C.) had once come to the Amazon with his ships; that the gold countries of Ophir, Tarshish and Parvaim were not to be looked

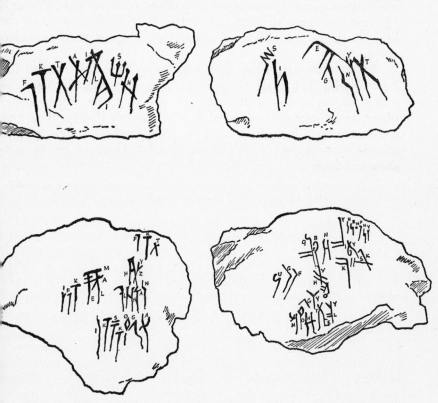

30. Stone inscriptions from the Amazon regions (letters added by Ramos)

for in the Old World at all, but here in the Amazon region on the Rio Solimoes, 'Solomon's river'. They were misled not only by the inscriptions but by the frequency of completely Semitic names for rivers, mountains and hills; for people, animals and plants.

Many of their examples were quite unconvincing, though the similarity or identity of the words in some cases is certainly striking, especially the word 'tepe' for mountain. 'Tepe' meant mountain in the Old World too; the word is known from the hill of Kul-Tepe near Troy. Then there were two monoliths in the Amazon region which the Indians worshipped as gods and called Keri and Kamiso. But Keri was a goddess of Carthage, and Kamisi or Kamos was a god of the Mabites. Moreover, as the French archaeologist Homet has discovered, the Indians on the Amazon call their water containers Cara Mequere; and the ancient Cretans had four-master barques with big water-tubs on board, which bore exactly the same name.

However, the scholars laughed at Ramos for believing that the inscriptions were Phoenician. So they disregarded the finds, although the drawings made showed clearly that there was a script from the Old World carved into these stones—even if not the Phoenician script.

About 1500 B.C., when the Cretans may have first reached the New World, they could not possibly have gone right through the vast continent of South America. But they may have landed at the places where later discoverers of America landed. Perhaps their first settlements were here, in what is now impenetrable jungle, on the mighty rivers of the Orinoco or the Amazon. There are no traces to show us where.

19

I Found the White God's Traces

WHEN the *Conquistadores* had looted all the gold they could find, they looked for still more. They had heard from the Indians the legend of a land of gold, its capital 'Dorado'.

In his *Historia General de los Indios* Francisco Lopez describes the unknown capital, which he called Manoa; it was supposed to be somewhere north-west of the river Amazon, in the mountains of Parima.

'Manoa', he says, 'is on an island in a big salt lake. Its walls and its roofs are of gold and are reflected in a gold-paved lake. All the palace cutlery, for the tables and the kitchen, was of pure gold and silver; copper and silver were used even for the most unimportant things. In the middle of the island there was a temple dedicated to the sun. Round this temple there were statues of gold, representing giants. On the island there were trees too of gold and silver. The statue of a prince was completely covered in gold-dust.'

Fernando Denis also mentioned this capital in his *History of Guiana*, and Hernando de Ribeira left a testament on 3rd March, 1545, in which he wrote: 'El Dorado is on an island in a big lake, and on it there is a temple of the sun.' Another of the gold-seekers of those days described exactly how he had reached one of the cities in the Amazon jungle, and this document was found forty years ago by Colonel Fawcett, the British explorer. He took it very seriously, and in 1925 set off for the jungle. He never returned. Despite frequent expeditions in search of him—one of them (a few years ago) included his son—no trace of him has ever been discovered.

Before his disappearance Fawcett did find the remains of an old city in the jungle.

'The existence of the old cities', he wrote, 'I do not for a moment doubt. How could I? I myself have seen a portion of one—and that is the reason why I observed it was imperative for me to go again. The remains seemed to be those of an outpost of one of the larger cities, which I am convinced is to be found together with others, if a properly organized search is carried out. Unfortunately, I cannot induce scientific men to accept even the supposition that there are traces of an old civilization in Brazil. . . . One thing is certain: between the outer world and the secrets of ancient South America a veil has descended, and the explorer who seeks to penetrate this veil must be prepared to face hardships and dangers that will tax his endurance to the uttermost. The chances are that he will not get through, but if he should—if he is lucky enough to run the gauntlet of savages and come out alive—he will be in a position to further immeasurably our historical knowledge.'

So far none of the white explorers has succeeded in penetrating that veil.

The first traveller to the Amazon we know of was the Inca captain Apo Camac, nicknamed Otorongo ('Tiger'). The sixth Inca ordered him to go into the jungle to fetch parrots and wild animals for the Inca's gardens. Otorongo mustered a force of 10,000 men and set off on the expedition. He descended into the lowlands on the banks of the river Paucatambo, and soon began to regret having ventured on such a hazardous undertaking. But in spite of losses he marched into the vast forests. Many months later the meagre remnant of the proud army reached a clearing and found men from the tribe of the Chaucas, who took them in and saved their lives. But when the return journey was about to start, Otorongo told his men to leave without him. One of the tribe's girls had found favour with him, and he preferred to say goodbye to his rank and the palace at Cuzco.

In 1539 Gonzalo Ximenes went into the jungle with 300 Spaniards and 500 Indians to seek the old city of gold. He returned with fifteen men. Antonio de Berrio fought his way on for a year with 1,000 soldiers and 700 horses; he returned with fifty men. In 1784 Bodadilla set off with 400 men, and came back with twenty-five. All modern expeditions have failed too. Schomburgk (1840), Koch-Grünberg (1908), even Hamilton Rice (1925), with his sea-planes, motor-boats, wireless stations and machine-guns, seventy bearers and oarsmen—all had to give up. Rice was forced to turn back about forty miles before reaching the Sierra Parima.

The Indians of the jungle must know these old cities. The chief of the Maku described one of them to Homet, who returned from the Amazon three years ago (equally unsuccessful):

'Opposite the rocks on the right of the river bank there is a sort of village. The houses were once of stone, but now they are completely in ruins. These houses are built in long rows and separated by wide, regular streets. If you leave this village and go straight on in the direction in which the sun goes down every day, after two days you come to a high wall in the mountains. You can't get through, but you must look for a stone gate under a big arch, which leads into the ground. Then you come to a big city of stones, but they have all fallen to the ground. The city was built in straight rows. You can follow these rows, but watch out for your steps, for where there were once dwellings, there are only big stone slabs, and many of them are split by strong tree-roots which have grown up between them. And quite near you will find a great mass of water, and in that there is much of those yellow stones and that powder you whites seek with such greed.'

In 1743 Francisco Raposo set out from what is today the Brazilian state of Minas Geraes, making for the Rio Xingu, to look for the lost gold-mines of Muribeca. On his way he came to a plain enclosed by high rocks. Following a deer, he reached the top in three hours and saw a town beneath him. When he went down, he came to a huge gate with three arches made from massive stones. Characters were carved on the second arch. He found a road with stone houses on both sides. Everything was overgrown with plants. The entrances were adorned with pillars bearing demon-like animal figures. There was a big square which had a statue of a man with one arm pointing north.

On the gate of a palace Raposo found the remains of sculptures and the statue of a man, with characters carved into the stone underneath. He copied them, and it was later established that they were archaic Greek letters. Near the city he also found a big temple, and in it a small gold piece showing a kneeling man on one side, and a bow, a crown and a musical instrument on the other. When he left this mysterious jungle city, two Indians met him—and fled when they saw him. Both had white complexions.

Colonel Fawcett also met white Indians on the Amazon, 'people with red hair and blue eyes like a gringo', and he expressly says: 'They are not albinos.' In 1906-7 he had heard a strange story from the manager of a French rubber colony:

'There are white Indians on the [river] Acre. My brother went up . . . in a launch, and one day, well up river, was told that white Indians were near. He didn't believe it and scoffed at the men who told him, but nevertheless went out in a canoe and found unmistakable signs of Indians. The next thing he knew, he and his men were being attacked by big, well-built, handsome savages, pure white with red hair and blue eyes. They fought like devils too. . . . Many people say these white Indians don't exist, and, when it's proved they do, that they

o*

are half-breeds, mixtures of Spanish and Indians. That's what people say who never saw them, but those who have seen them think differently.'

There are white Indians even today, living in the forests of Venezuela—the Motilon. In 1926 Harris made a study of the Indians of San Blas and wrote that their hair was a colour between flax and straw and their complexion almost white. More recently Homet has described meeting some Indians from the tribe of the Waika in the Amazon jungle, whose hair was chestnut brown. 'The so-called white race', he remarked, 'has even in outer appearance many representatives among the Indians along the Amazon.'

The Amazon region has not always been a 'Green Hell' hostile to man. The great river's isolation is historically quite a recent phenomenon, and the chroniclers could still report its banks as being thickly populated. There were then hundreds of villages, and one account said: 'There are so many Indians living there that you cannot drop a pin without its falling on an Indian.' The great death set in only a few years after the *conquista*. Not being immunized against the Old World's 'civilization diseases', the Indians succumbed to the most harmless infections. Tuberculosis consumed whole tribes. A hundred years later only a few wretched settlements were left on the river's banks.

Traces of the former thriving civilization have been found on the edge of the jungle, such as the gigantic buildings of Viscosa—but these have since then been knocked down and cleared away as building material for a railway. The traveller Brandão saw them, however, as late as 1911. They had walls nineteen feet high and twenty-five feet long; the massive blocks of stone were put together almost without joins.

Similar ruins were found in other places too. At Monte Alto, on the river Verde Grande, Sampaio came on stone walls over half a mile long and about five feet high; and Nimuendaju discovered ruins in the north of the Amazon region and on the Brazilian coast. More remains of a vanished past may come to light any day, retrieved from this greatest jungle on earth. But it is impossible to look for them systematically, because the forest is so dense that you can pass by even large buildings at three yards without noticing them. It is dark there even in bright sunshine.

In the last ten years up to twenty expeditions have been made into the 'Green Hell': by hunters, prospectors for oil, diamonds, gold; botanists and zoologists. Five of the twenty have returned decimated, ravaged by mosquito bites, sick and exhausted. The rest did not return, and nothing has ever been heard of them since. They must have succumbed to starvation, the snakes and jaguars, the Indians' poisoned arrows, or have become a prey for the cannibals.

As the Chinese built their first empires on the great rivers of Yangtze Kiang and Hwang Ho, the Indians on the Indus and the Ganges, the Sumerians on the Euphrates and the Tigris, the Egyptians on the Nile, so the virgin forest hides the ruins of an ancient civilization around the greatest of all rivers, the Amazon.

Six hundred miles from the coast, in the middle of the Amazon jungle, lies the old rubber town of Manáos, where Ramos, the former rubber-picker, lived; and here is the museum with all the things he collected from the jungle. But what I was looking for was not there: there was not a single stone with an inscription, though he had described and drawn hundreds in his book. No one since had seen these stones, and I had to see them—the very first traces of the White God in America.

Every day I went to the Manáos market early in the morning. The broad arm of the great river, flowing lazily eastwards, lay in thick mist. Strange Indian canoes turned up and moored at the quay, crammed with fish and fruit you hardly ever see in Europe. I went from boat to boat, from Indian to Indian, and asked every newcomer whether while roaming through the jungle he had ever seen those strange stones with carvings and scrawls. They all shook their heads. None of them had even heard of such stones. I began seriously to wonder whether Ramos had invented them.

One day, when I was near to giving up, two Indians arrived in a long, sturdy canoe, its bottom full of round wicker baskets, looking like giant eggs, in all sizes. The baskets made me curious, and I went and stood by the Indians who would be helping unload them. Then the rowers came on to the bridge, two hefty-looking savages. They opened the lids of the baskets, and I saw that these contained *achote*, pea-sized fruits of a brilliant red, which are used in Holland to colour cheese; strongly diluted they produce a beautiful yellow colour. In such masses as these two were offering them, they are found only in the heart of the jungle—these must be boys who had been all over the jungle.

When I asked about Ramos's stones, they nodded. Yes, they had once seen such stones. 'Stones of the White God,' one of them said. I would have to row up river for four days, turn off into a big tributary, and follow this for two days; then it would be simplest to hack out a path, so as to shorten our way. They offered to take me there.

We came to terms. The canoe was loaded with everything needed for such an expedition, and very early next morning, while there was still thick mist over the harbour, we rowed off up river, through a jumble of islands, keeping near the bank. The other side was out of sight, so wide is the river at this point.

In the evening we put in at a quiet creek, which was covered with a carpet of the big plants called royal water-lilies. We sat by the fire in the moonlight. Parrots squawked in their roosting tree, and sometimes a night bird flitted past, silent as a shadow. We were quite alone. There were none of the mean fishermen's huts you see on the riverbank while you are still near Manáos. The jungle's giant trees spread their mighty branches, thick as a roof, over our encampment.

One of my guides came from the region of the Apurimac, the river which makes a frontier with Bolivia, 3,000 miles farther into the jungle. He had once come down the Amazon and then stayed in the rubber town. They both addressed me as Viracocha, and while the one from the Apurimac pushed the branches deeper into the fire, he began to talk of the great White God, the ancient god of his country.

He told how once upon a time a white man with a beard had come to his people from the east, when they were still without any civilization, and brought them all knowledge, all higher skills; how he had then become the god of the Aymara people, the white, the bright, the shining god; how he had one day gone away and how he had promised some time to return. For six evenings I sat by our camp fire and heard the deeds of the great White God, Kon Tiki Illac Viracocha. On the seventh day we tied up the canoe in another creek and started on our march.

The river lay beneath us. The sun blazed down, though under our jungle roof we could not even see it: here there was green twilight. The air was humid and sultry as in a hot-house. Midges and mosquitoes fell upon us, getting into mouth, nose and ears. Thorns tore my shirt, face and arms; the defenceless skin swelled up under their stings and pricks. We had tied kerchiefs under our sun-helmets, so as at least to protect our necks.

We had to cut our path yard by yard through bush and bamboos. In front of us the green wall seemed almost impenetrable. Day after day we fought onwards in the direction of the stones I was looking for, so the Indians insisted. I doubted whether I should find Ramos' stones; more likely they were taking me to stones with primitive scrawls you find thousands of these left from prehistoric mass migrations.

We came to the last lap and found a narrow path which Ramos had used. After another two hours we reached the bank of a broad river-bed, and there lay the stones I was seeking—in dozens. They were in the water, most of them under the water.

I forgot all the hardships I had been through; I forgot hunger and thirst. For hours I stood up to my belly in the mud of the bank and

scrutinized the symbols on the stones, line for line, page for page—
a great stone picture-book which lay open in front of me.

Quite a number had their whole surface covered with a jumble of
lines and patterns, without any figures being shown; but most of the
carvings were sketches of fishes, birds, jaguars. Some had the creatures'
heads on the edge, but otherwise no figures. On one of the pictures
there was such a tangle of fishes that their bodies and heads made a
complete ornamental pattern. Other stones showed several boats and
ships, boats with a keel, which were not known to the Indians of the
Amazon. Among others the head of an ox with horns turned up:
most surprising, because there were no cattle anywhere in America
before the Spaniards came.

Sometimes there was nothing ornamental at all, the carvings were
only of creatures, singly and in groups, shown with a realism very
rare among rock-carvings: birds in flight and landing; there was even
a rhinoceros, and rhinos never lived in the Amazon regions. The
artists were clearly striving to give a realistic picture in a few lines,
with the limited means at their disposal, and to fill the surface with
animal life. But there were men represented too, and godheads with
haloes; sometimes with a helmet of horns, similar to those known from
Mycenae and Crete, from Egyptian stelae and reliefs.

Realism is a quality found in the pottery of the Chibcha civilization. Here too there were masters at work, reproducing a monkey, a
bird or any other creature with an amazing life-likeness. The representations on the stones were also like the animals in motion on
Cretan vases and murals, lions, bulls, boars, deer, gryphons, charging
or in flight. And there were wild ducks rising into the air, represented
in a similar way as on a painted floor at El Amarna from the eighteenth
Egyptian dynasty.

There can be only one explanation of these carvings. Men from
the Old World must have once been here, on the waterway which
once led to the White God's kingdom. Ramos was not carried away
by the sight of these stones: the carvings really look as he reproduced
them in his book; and the stones are still there today. When I found
them, they were under water, so I could not photograph them. For
the river subsides only every ten years, and then the great stone picture-
book rises out of the water. But these were only a few of the carvings
which Ramos discovered and described. There are other more important stones in the same area, which contain characters.

I set out again with my two guides, and found four stones with
characters. I was trembling with excitement when I came on the first
and cut away the undergrowth hiding it. The characters were those

which Ramos and his predecessors had taken to be Phoenician inscriptions. But they were typical of the Cretan script and the Cretan double axe.

We cannot read them, but all the same they tell us that the legends of the old settlements overgrown by the jungle were by no means as baseless as people said. Expeditions will go there in the future, and one day they will find the ancient city which the White God built, the first city in America. The spade will make it rise again, and an epoch 3,500 years old will be brought to new life. Science will thereby solve one of the greatest riddles of human history: the riddle of where the American-Indian civilizations came from and their connections with our own world.

When the first stones were collected and piled on one another to build this city, the history of America began. There is much to suggest that the time was about 3,500 years ago; that a man from the Old World discovered the new continent then and experienced a surprising 'sea-change'. From a simple sailor, he was transformed into an immortal god, the White God of the Indians.

31. Rock inscriptions from Pedras, Rio
Utama, Amazonas (from Ramos)

A Selective Bibliography of Works in English

THE DISCOVERY AND CONQUEST OF THE NEW WORLD

Maurice Collis: *Cortés and Montezuma*, London 1954
Weise: *History and Discovery of America to the Year 1525*, New York 1884
W. H. Prescott: *History of the Conquest of Mexico*, 1844; *History of the Conquest of Peru*, 1847

MYTHS AND POETRY

E. R. Emerson: *Indian Myths*, Boston 1884
D. G. Brinton: *Ancient Nahuatl Poetry*
E. J. Payne: *History of the New World*, Oxford 1892

POST-SPANISH WRITINGS

Codex Mendoza: James Cooper Clark, London 1938

EXPLORERS DISCOVER THE NEW WORLD

1841: Stephens: *Incidents of Travel in Central America, Chiapas and Yucatan*, New York
1843: Stephens: *Incidents of Travel in Yucatan*
1853: Herndon: *Exploration of the valley of the Amazon*, Washington
    Wallace: *Narrative travels on the Amazon and Rio Negro*, London
1854: R. N. Prevost: *Report on the Isthmus of Darien*, London
1856: T. Ewbanks: *Life in Brazil*, London
1859: Markham: *Expedition into the valley of the Amazon*, Hakl. Soc., London
1860: William Bollaert: *Antiquarian, ethnological and other researches in New Granada, Peru and Chile*, London
1861: H. W. Bates: *The naturalists in the river Amazon*, Everyman Library, London
1877: E. A. Squier: *Incidents of travel and exploration in the Land of the Incas*, London 1877
    Orton: *The Andes and the Amazon*, London
1879: Mathew: *Up Amazon and Madeira*, London

218   BIBLIOGRAPHY

1889: A. P. Maudslay: *Biologii Centralii Americana*, London 1889–1902,
      I—IV Guide to the Maudslay collection: Brit. Museum, London
      1938
1910: C. Markham: *The Incas of Peru*, London
1912: T. A. Joyce: *South American archaeology*, London–New York
1920: F. Stahl: *In the land of the Incas*, Mountain View, Calif.
1931: P. A. Means: *Ancient civilizations of the Andes*, New York

THE RESULTS OF EXCAVATIONS

W. C. Bennett: *Ancient arts of the Americas*
Desiré Charnay: *The ancient cities of the new world*, London 1887
P. A. Means: *The Spanish Main*, New York 1935
Verril: *Old civilizations of the new world*, New York 1943
W. H. Holmes: *Arch. Studies among the ancient Cities of Mexico*, 1895–7

THE AZTEC EMPIRE

G. C. Vaillant: *Aztecs of Mexico*, New York 1941; *Early cultures of the
      valley of Mexico*, 1935; Vaillant: *The History of the valley of Mexico*, New
      York 1936
E. Kingsborough: *Antiquities of Mexico*, London 1831–48
J. E. Compiler: *Design motifs of ancient Mexico*, New York 1953
C. A. Burland: *Art and life in ancient Mexico*, Oxford 1948
M. H. Saville: *Goldsmith's art in ancient Mexico*, 1920

THE INCA EMPIRE

H. Bingham: *Lost city of the Incas*, London 1951, New York 1948
Fergusson: *Handbook of architecture II*, 775, London 1865–7
W. C. Bennett–J. B. Bird: *Andean culture history*, New York 1949
J. H. Howland–Rowe: *Inca culture at the time of Spanish Conquest*,
      Washington 1946
A. L. Kroeber: *Peruvian archaeology*, New York 1954
H. P. Means: *The Spanish Main*, New York
S. Hagar: *Cuzco the celestial City*, New York 1902

THE MAYA EMPIRE

H. J. Spinden: *Maya art and civilization*, Indian Hills, Col. 1957
J. E. S. Thompson: *The rise and fall of Maya civilization*, London 1956
Sylvanus G. Morley: *The ancient Mayas*, London 1946
H. J. Spinden: *Ancient civilizations of Mexico and Central America*
Smith–Beyer–Thompson: *Contribution to American archaeology*, Carnegie
      1937
J. E. S. Thompson: *Civilization of the Mayas*, 1927; *People of the serpent*, 1932
Chilam Balam: *The book of Chilam Balam of Chumayel*, 1933
T. Gann–J. E. S. Thompson: *History of the Mayas*, New York 1931
L. G. Hay: *The Mayas and their Neighbours*, New York 1940

Tatjana Proskouriakoff: *An album of Maya architecture*, Carnegie Inst. Publ. No. 558, Washington

K. Ruppert: *The Caracol of Chichen Itza*, Carnegie No. 454, Washington 1935

E. H. Morris–J. Charlot–A. A. Morris: *The temple of the warriors at Chichen Itza*, Washington 1931

F. Catherwood: *Views of ancient monuments in Central America*, London 1844

INDIAN CALENDARS AND WRITING

S. G. Morley: *The correlation of Maya and Christian Chronology*, 1910

J. E. S. Thompson: *A correlation of the Mayan and Christian Calendar*, Chicago 1927

G. C. Vaillant: *Chronology and stratography in the Mayan area*, New York 1935

H. J. Spinden: *The reduction of Maya dates*, 1926; *Maya dates and what they reveal*, 1930

S. G. Morley: *An introduction to the study of the Maya hieroglyphs*, Washington 1915

CULTURAL RELATIONS BETWEEN SOUTH AMERICA AND SOUTHERN ASIA

R. Heine–Geldern–G. Ekholm: *Significant parallels in the symbolic art of Southern Asia and Middle America*, 29 Americ. Congress, New York 1949, Chicago 1951

E. B. Taylor: *An American lot game as evidence of Asiatic intercourse before the time of Columbus*, 1896

I. B. Hutchinson–R. A. Silow–S. G. Stephen: *The evolution of Gossypium*, London 1947

G. F. Ekholm: *A possible Focus of Asiatic influence in the late Classic Cultures of Mexico*, Mem. Soc. Amer. Arch. 9, 1953

THE TOLTEC EMPIRE

K. S. Lothrop: *Tulum*, Washington 1924

E. H. Thompson: *The high priest grave at Chichen Itza*, 1938

S. K. Lothrop: *Metal from the Cenote of sacrifice, Chichen Itza*, 1952

K. Ruppert: *The Caracol of Chichen Itza*

E. H. Morris–J. Charlot–A. A. Morris: *The temple of the warriors at Chichen Itza*, Washington 1931

ZAPOTECS AND MITLA

A. Caso: *Monte Alban, richest archaeological find in America*, Washington 1932; *Las exploraciones en Monte Alban*, 1932–5

M. H. Saville: *Explorations of Zapotecan tombs in North America*, New York
1899
E. C. Parsons: *Mitla, town of souls*, Chicago 1936

THE OLMECS

M. W. Stirling: *Expedition unearths buried masterpieces of carved jade*,
Washington 1941; *Finding jewels of jade in a Mexican swamp*, Washington
1942; *Stone monuments of south Mexico*, Washington 1943
M. H. Saville: *Votive axes from ancient Mexico*, New York 192

ANCIENT MEXICO

Zelia Nuttall: *The Island of Sacrifice*, Lancaster (Pa.) 1910
Manual Gamio: *Cultural evolution in Guatemala*, Washington 1926

THE CHIMU EMPIRE

S. Linné: *The technique of South American Ceramics*, 1925
J. B. Hutchinson–R. A. Silow–S. G. Stephens: *The evolution of Gossypium
and the differentiation of the cultivated Cotton*, London–New York 1947
W. C. Bennett: *A reappraisal of Peruvian Archaeology*, 1948

TIAHUANACO

A. Kidder: *Some early sites in the northern lake Titicaca basin*, 1943
Sol Tax-H–W. C. Bennett: *The civilizations of ancient America*

THE CHAVIN CIVILIZATION

W. C. Bennett: *Chavin stone carving*, Yale Univ. Press 1942
J. Tello: *Andean civilizations*, New York 1930
P. A. Means: *Ancient civilizations of the Andes*, New York 1931
W. C. Bennett: *Archaeological region of Columbia; Ecuador archaeology*,
London 1946
James A. Ford: *Excavations in the vicinity of Bali*, Columbia 1944
C. Osgood: *British Guiana archaeology*, 1946
E. C. Squier: *Nicaragua*, New York 1860
M. Saville: *The gold treasure of Sigsig Ecuador*, New York 1924
A. Kidder: *Archaeology of north-western Venezuela*, Yale Univ. Publ. 28–9
P. Bergsoe: *The metallurgy and technology of gold and platinum among the
pre-Columbian Indians*, Copenhagen 1937; *The gilding process and the
metallurgy of copper and lead among the pre-Columbian Indians*, 1938
W. C. Bennet: *Peruvian Gold*, 1952

THE EARLIEST CIVILIZATIONS

H. T. Wilkins: *Secret cities of South America*, 1950
Heine–Geldern: *Heyerdahl's hypothesis of Polynesian origin*, London 1950

E. Nordenskjold: *Origin of the Indian civilization in South America*, Gothenburg 1931

WESTERN CONTACTS BEFORE COLUMBUS

De Costa: *The pre-Columbian discovery of America by the Northmen*, Paris 1874

P. H. Fawcett: *Exploration Fawcett*, London 1953

THE MINOAN CIVILIZATION

J. D. S. Pendlebury: *The archaeology of Crete*, London 1939

A. J. B. Wace: *Mycenaea, an archaeological history and guide*, 1949; *The Chamber tombs of Mycenaea*, 1932

Index